D1649091

The Role of Research in Educational Improvement

.

The Role of Research in Educational Improvement

Edited by

JOHN D. BRANSFORD
DEBORAH J. STIPEK
NANCY J. VYE
LOUIS M. GOMEZ
DIANA LAM

HARVARD EDUCATION PRESS
CAMBRIDGE, MASSACHUSETTS

\# 301893255

Library of Congress Control Number 2008942553

Paperback ISBN 978-1-934742-12-9
Library Edition ISBN 978-1-934742-13-6

Published by Harvard Education Press,
an imprint of the Harvard Education Publishing Group

Harvard Education Press
8 Story Street
Cambridge, MA 02138

Cover Design: Nancy Goulet

The typefaces used in this book are ITC Stone Serif for text and
Stone Sans for display.

Contents

Preface

This book represents the culmination of years of work by a group of educational scholars and practitioners brought together by the John D. and Catherine T. MacArthur Foundation in what became the Network on Teaching and Learning. In 2000 the group was given the task of analyzing the reasons for the slow and uneven pace of education reform and examining ways in which evidence might be used more productively to promote improvements in teaching and learning.

From the beginning we recognized that meaningful reform at the classroom level required attention to the many facets of education, referred to in the introduction of this book as the "education elephant." Thus, members of the Network represented a broad array of expertise and experiences.[1]

We embarked on three sets of activities to accomplish our task. First, we designed a metastudy to examine existing efforts to improve teaching and learning through research and development. The first goal of the metastudy was to document problems encountered in the larger sociopolitical context and in districts and schools by those endeavoring to promote research and development (R&D) on a large scale. The second was to identify and articulate approaches being used in ongoing projects that showed some promise of addressing the problems found.[2] The hope was to produce knowledge that could be used to guide the creation of the institutional infrastructure and organizations that are needed to bring research and practice into closer alignment.

Second, the Network launched what we referred to as the "learning by doing" project. By implementing its own R&D work, the Network had the opportunity to study the impediments and promises of connecting research to practice prospectively and more closely than it was able to do by studying projects undertaken by others. One of the projects worked to create a multidimensional technology infrastructure designed to enhance student and teacher learning, organizational learning (e.g., at the school or district level), communication with parents and other community members, and communication with health care services and other agencies that interact with students.[3] The second "learning by doing" project put Network members in the role of helping school districts engage in large-scale, continuous, and evidence-based improvement of teaching and learning.[4]

This volume is informed by the first two activities and is the conclusion of the third—analyzing and summarizing the current state of affairs in education reform and promising approaches for improving education by increasing evidence-based practice. All of the Network members were involved, and others, including chapter authors who were not in the Network, were invited to help in this work. The expanded group met twice, in addition to engaging in many smaller conversations and exchanges of ideas in writing. It was an intellectually enriching experience for all of us who were fortunate to participate, and I believe it contributed greatly to the quality of the thinking, analysis, and recommendations made in this book.

We are grateful to the MacArthur Foundation for their support, and particularly to Paul Goran, Laurie Garduque, and Connie Yowell, Foundation officers who contributed enormously to the substantive work of the Network. We think that readers will agree that the Foundation made possible a very effective and productive process for grappling with one of the greatest challenges the country faces.

We also express our thanks to a talented group of individuals from the College of Education at the University of Washington, without whose help we would not have been able to complete this book: Hank Clark, Joan Davis, Daryl Lawton, Tiffany Lee, Kieran O'Mahony, Rachel Phillips, Kari Shutt, Susann Smith, and Katie Sweeney. Nancy Pinkerton, at Stanford University, was also an invaluable member of the team, organizing people, meetings, and finances for us throughout the process.

We dedicate this book to the memory of our friend Tom Glennan. Tom's encouragement, generosity of spirit, and wisdom contributed greatly to the work of the Network. He inspired us, as he did so many in the field of education throughout his life.

Deborah Stipek
Chair, MacArthur Foundation
Network on Teaching and Learning

Equity, Excellence, Elephants, and Evidence

John D. Bransford, Nancy J. Vye, Deborah J. Stipek,
Louis M. Gomez, and Diana Lam

Three key themes reverberate throughout this volume. An *equity and excellence* theme emphasizes that the creation of high-quality learning opportunities is a core value shared by all the authors of this volume. An *elephants* theme (as in the poem "The Blind Men and the Elephant" by John Godfrey Saxe)[1] reminds us that our educational system includes a multiplicity of subsystems that may or may not amount to a fully functioning and healthy elephant and needs to be understood holistically in order to make true progress. An *evidence* theme highlights our assumption that everyone wants to do what is best for students; that evidence of what works, and why, is necessary to be as effective as possible; and that the idea of using "evidence based practices" is more complex than it might appear at first glance and needs to be understood and explored from multiple points of view. We elaborate on each of these themes below.

EQUITY AND EXCELLENCE OF EDUCATIONAL OPPORTUNITIES

Each chapter in this volume focuses on the goal of creating equity and excellence of educational opportunities. As noted elsewhere by Bransford and colleagues, it is easy to forget how important this is for people's lives.

> Anyone who has been highly motivated to learn something new—especially something important for their lives—understands the advantages of

finding expert mentors who can help them. Gaining access to high-quality instructional expertise has been a challenge throughout much of human history. Many secrets of success (e.g., how to make glass vessels, axe heads, or scalpels; how to read, write, hunt or grow food) were provided through apprenticeships and mentorships that were often available to only a select few. . . . In today's world, vast inequities still frustrate people's opportunities to gain access to high quality instruction. Nevertheless, nations throughout the world are beginning to view increased access to learning opportunities as a moral and economic imperative that can make far-reaching differences in the quality of people's and nations' lives.[2]

Public education represents a major effort to provide all citizens with high-quality opportunities for learning. It is a relative newcomer in the history of humankind, and the sophistication of the learning goals it attempts to achieve has increased dramatically over time. For example, in America in 1860 there were many public elementary schools but only forty public high schools. Until the 1900s, most Americans' formal education ended with elementary school, which was organized around the agrarian calendar since students were needed to work in the fields. Between 1860 and 1900, the number of public high schools in American grew from forty to 6,000 thanks to a watershed ruling by the Supreme Court in the 1870s that had been preceded by a vigorous debate over who should pay for secondary school for what were called "the masses." Many argued that elementary school was sufficient for most people, and, in fact, further education could actually be harmful because it would only drive the poor to strive for unrealistic economic levels and alienate them from manual labor, which was vital to the economy of the country.

During the past century the United States and other nations have realized that a high school education is extremely important and that at least some college education—and even graduate education—is necessary in order to be successful in the twenty-first century. The overall quality of peoples' lives increasingly requires a rich national diversity of sophisticated skills, knowledge, attitudes, and technology proficiencies that allow individuals, communities, organizations, and government agencies to innovate continuously in order to adapt to our fast-changing global world.[3]

Shortcomings in Equity and Excellence

Despite the fact that the United States and other nations have done a remarkable job of creating schools, colleges, and universities for educating their citizens, the mere existence of schools does not guarantee effective educational outcomes. In the United States, for example, the number of high school dropouts is alarming.[4] Other nations often refer to dropouts as "early school leavers," and these nations have problems as well.[5]

Ms. Trish Diziko is an extraordinarily talented leader of the Technology Access Foundation in Seattle, a nonprofit organization that works with underserved youth to help them excel. In a recent email statement about the reasons and vision for her foundation, Ms. Diziko said,

> Last week I was reading an article in the Washington CEO journal.[6] In light of the fact that one of our learning labs was burglarized recently, here's what stuck out for me: Studies show that people without a high-school diploma or a general education degree are more likely than others to land in prison or on welfare. The state budget for corrections more than doubled between 1991 and 2001, outpacing all other expenditures except for health care. The average cost per prisoner is $27,170 per year. That same money could cover a year's worth of education at the University of Washington for two medical students.
>
> Articles like this make me wonder why our state, with all its resources, cannot manage to create the best education system in the nation. Would we rather build jails? Would we rather increase our welfare rolls? I would bet that we could reduce our state healthcare costs if people had a better education. What are we waiting for?[7]

UNDERSTANDING THE WHOLE ELEPHANT: THE NEED TO COORDINATE MULTIPLE POINTS OF VIEW

Problems like the one so elegantly described by Ms. Diziko focus on issues of equity and excellence and also introduce the problem of the "elephant." She asks what we can do to solve current and future educational problems, and this raises the important question of who the "we" is. Answers include the federal government, state governments, national and state school leadership and teacher organizations, school districts and school boards, individual schools, individual parents and families, foundations, the private sector, the nonprofit sector, parent-based groups such as the PTA and those who support home schooling, the educational research community, and others. Lagemann's classic article on "Contested Terrain" provides a gripping history of conflicts about who owns the schools and who should have a major say in how they work.[8]

To sociologists, the groups noted above would qualify as "loosely coupled."[9] There is no central authority that has the power to determine all of the nation's educational policies and practices. Although there *are* ways that the U.S. government can yield considerable power (e.g., consider NCLB), it is only one of many players, unlike countries like Japan (see this volume) where most important education decisions are made by the central government. As this book illustrates, the decentralized nature of American education, while a strength in some respects, makes major reform efforts extremely difficult to achieve on a broad scale.

In the first chapter, Mosher and Smith remind us that the educational powers of the federal government are strongly affected by states' rights, which are further affected by traditions of local control within states. The latter includes district control, which requires accountability to the local communities that they serve (including their school boards) and, ideally, to the needs and talents of each of the students and families in the local community. We see here a major tension: How do we as a nation achieve coherence with respect to key academic policies and learning opportunities while also acknowledging that we may need to contextualize our actions in order to be maximally responsive to each individual and local situation? In short, how do we envision the whole elephant while also respecting the vital functions and authority of each of its parts? This requires helping education stakeholders develop a clearer picture of the educational needs, priorities, and opportunities that surface when one looks at educational issues from different perspectives—including the nation, the state, the district, the school, the research community, the individual family, and the overall "learning ecosystem" of the child.[10]

ISSUES OF EVIDENCE

Different groups of stakeholders (e.g., teachers, superintendents, researchers) assign different priorities to the most important questions to be tackled in order to improve teaching and learning, and they often use different criteria to signify "success." This brings us to issues of *evidence* and how it differs for different groups of stakeholders. Some of the differences involve the priority of the questions to be asked and answered. Others involve differences in what is meant by "evidence" and how evidence is used differently by different groups of stakeholders.

Disconnects in the Priority of Questions

Illustrations of some of the disconnects in key research questions to be answered were discussed in an address delivered by Grover Whitehurst, director of the National Institute of Education Sciences, at the 2003 meeting of the American Educational Research Association (AERA).[11] Whitehurst voiced strong concerns about the mismatch between the educational research that is produced (supplied) and the kinds of research demanded by practitioners in the field.

To illustrate his point, Whitehurst discussed the 2003 AERA conference program, which listed hundreds of sessions and papers. He explained that the titles of some of the sessions and papers seemed straightforward, for example "Technology for Formative Assessment." However, Whitehurst notes that many titles seemed arcane and idiosyncratic, such as "Episodes of Theory-Building as a Transformative & Decolonizing Process: A Microethnographic Inquiry into a Deeper Awareness of Embodied Knowing." Though not a real title in the program, he claimed that it was close to some of the actual titles that appeared.

It is noteworthy that to many members of the research community, the topic mentioned by Whitehurst (embodied knowing) is extremely relevant for education. However, it makes sense only if one is already immersed in the "embodied knowing" literature and understands the potential importance of exploring this issue. We assume that Whitehurst's point was that to outsiders looking for guidance about everyday educational problems, the title will not make attendees think, "I must attend this session or read this paper immediately." Whitehurst reminded researchers that many of their talks and writings seem impenetrable to people who are not directly involved in their particular area of research.[12] In other words, the "supply side" of educational research (the parts supplied by many researchers) often fails to connect with the "demand side" of practitioners and policymakers.

Whitehurst further illustrated mismatches between the "supply side" and "demand side" for research by summarizing the results of a questionnaire that asked professionals—mainly superintendents and chief state school officers—to provide their assessments of the research literature and its value to them and their work. The responses suggested a lack of enthusiasm for most education research. For example, 77 percent of the respondents criticized research for its overly theoretical and academic orientation. They asked instead for research that is meaningful to teachers and that gives them strategies to help children learn.[13] Examples of key topics they believed should be studied include effective instructional practices in reading, math, and science; standards and assessment; education finance; and guidance on how to close the achievement gap. Whitehurst noted that in the context of the requirements of No Child Left Behind (NCLB) and increased public scrutiny, education leaders feel that they can no longer afford to make decisions based on intuition or opinion. Yet they do not believe they have access to the evidence they need to make well-informed decisions.

In fact, there is quite a lot of research on the key topics mentioned above. But it is rarely conclusive and is often not shared in forms that education leaders and other practitioners either have access to or can make sense of. These are just a few of the "disconnects" between research and practice that are discussed in this volume, among the many other parts of the education elephant that are misaligned.

What Counts as Evidence?

In addition to recognizing the need for better alignment between what educational researchers study and what practitioners need, we need to explore differences in the nature of the evidence needed for decision making by different groups of stakeholders. Everyone contributing to this book agrees that attempts to use "evidence-based practices" represent extremely important goals for education, but it has also been clear to us as we worked together that there are important differences in what people mean by "evidence" and in how they believe it should guide decisions and actions to promote student learning.

As we met to begin writing this book, questions about the kinds of research needed to support evidence-based practice were receiving a great deal of attention from the U.S. Department of Education. Despite its very negative review of the current state of education research (as evidenced in Whitehurst's comments), its strategic plan included a note of optimism about research: "We will change education to make it an evidence-based field."[14]

References to "scientifically-based" and "evidence-based" practices occurred over 100 times in the NCLB legislation, and implications of this policy are pervasive. For example, Reading First, a major program authorized by that legislation, authorized federal funding only for states and districts using "research-based" reading programs. Considerable debate has ensued about how that phrase was interpreted by the Department of Education, but its very existence underscores the view that evidence should be valued.

The desire to promote evidence-based practice also motivated the creation of the What Works Clearinghouse, established by the Department of Education in 2002 to "provide educators, policymakers, researchers, and the public with a central and trusted source of scientific evidence of what works in education."[15] Its website includes reviews produced by a technical advisory group on the effectiveness of educational interventions (programs, products, practices, and policies) deemed to have sufficient research evidence to recommend them. Not surprisingly, there are both supporters and critics of the criteria used to designate "success." Most contentious has been the Department of Education's emphasis on randomized trials. [16] The Network, along with many other critics, worried about a number of dangers with this focus, among them the lack of attention to context, including efforts to understand where interventions worked, for whom, and why, and the many educational questions that are not amendable to this kind of research.

The issue of transferring lessons learned from one setting to others is particularly important and is directly relevant to our point about needing to attend to multiple levels of the education ecology in efforts to improve education. If we run a successful randomized trial of an educational intervention and transfer it to a new setting, can we be sure that it will be successful? The answer seems to be a clear "no," unless we attend to a large set of contextual and social capital issues that have to be in place for new innovations to work.

A simple but elegant model (see Figure I.1) developed by James Jenkins is useful for thinking about sets of variables that simultaneously affect the success of particular educational actions. [17] It can be used to help educators see that the impact of using particular types of teaching and learning activities depends on the subject matter to be learned in relation to the nature of the skills, knowledge, and attitudes that learners bring to the situation, and the goals of the learning situation and the assessments used to measure that learning relative to these goals (i.e., the criterial tasks). If we imagine a circle around the whole model, it can remind us of how the classroom, school, and community climate also plays a major role in learning. [18]

One of the important points of the Jenkins model is that a teaching strategy that works within one constellation of these variables may work poorly when that overall constellation is changed. All the variables in the Jenkins model must be taken into account when analyzing such claims as "data show that teaching strategy X is better than Y."

Broader Applications of the Jenkins Framework

Needs for contextual sensitivity extend to policy research. For example, many authors throughout this book refer to the famous "class size" study in Tennessee, [19] which involved a careful use of randomized trial methodologies and yielded evidence that smaller class sizes affected the academic achievement of students in the early grades, achievement gains that seemed to persist in later grades. Nevertheless, the effects did *not* transfer when it was tried in California, and researchers began to dig deeper to understand why. Answers are provided in a number of chapters in this book.

FIGURE I.1   The Jenkins Tetrahedral Framework (adapted from the original)

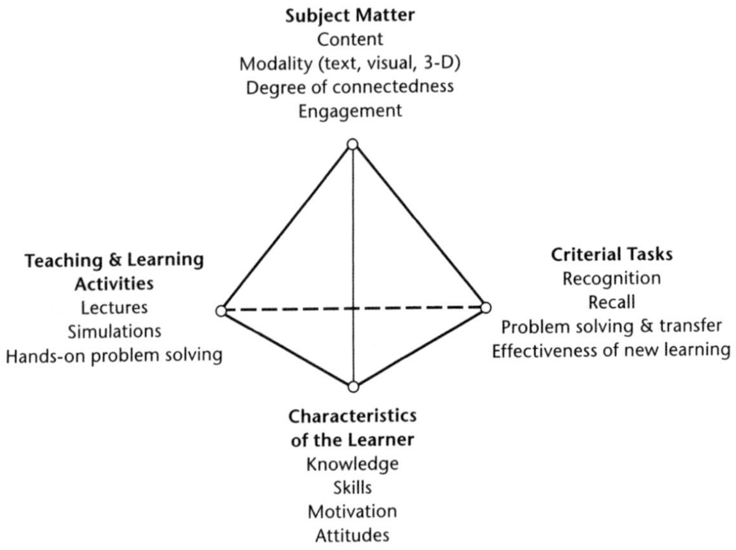

Subject Matter
Content
Modality (text, visual, 3-D)
Degree of connectedness
Engagement

Teaching & Learning Activities
Lectures
Simulations
Hands-on problem solving

Criterial Tasks
Recognition
Recall
Problem solving & transfer
Effectiveness of new learning

Characteristics of the Learner
Knowledge
Skills
Motivation
Attitudes

Source: James Jenkins, "Four Points to Remember: A Tetrahedral Model of Memory Experiments," in Laird S. Cermak and Fergus I. M. Craik, eds., *Levels of Processing and Human Memory* (Hillsdale, NJ: Erlbaum, 1978), 429–46.

Presumably, having smaller class sizes allowed the Tennessee teachers to teach differently than they would have under "typical class size" conditions. This relates to the component of the Jenkins framework, the nature of the teaching and learning activities in the classroom, which is greatly affected by classroom teachers and the schools and communities within which they work. If the teachers with smaller classes had exactly the same number and types of oral and written interactions with the students and parents as those in the larger class conditions, the findings showing advantages for small class sizes would be puzzling. This is where other methodologies, such as ethnography, become extremely important. Ethnographers know how to analyze the nature of interactions in ways that can reveal differences in the teaching and learning activities that were made possible by small class sizes.

A major contextual difference between the Tennessee and California studies was eventually discovered to be extremely important. It turns out that there was a plentiful supply of well-trained teachers in Tennessee who could help fill the extra slots needed to reduce classroom sizes in the school. This condition was not met in many areas of California, however, which resulted in a number of the newly created small classes being taught by untrained teachers.

Increasing Sophistication of Randomized Studies

The Tennessee class size study was an early pioneering effort in educational randomized trials research. Much has been learned since that time, especially about the crucial roles of contextual variables such as teacher quality, the nature of the assessments, and opportunities for professional development.[20]

Jeremy Roschelle and colleagues recently tested a technology-enhanced mathematics (SimCalc) innovation in a large-scale randomized trial in Texas. They found that SimCalc had very positive effects compared to a comparison group that received traditional mathematics instruction, but they learned a great deal more than simply "who won the horserace." A major goal was to use their results to discover the kinds of teachers, settings, and classroom practices in SimCalc that were the most effective. Furthermore, they spent a great deal of time exploring assessments that were more sophisticated than the Texas achievement tests. It turns out that if they had restricted their assessment to items like those found on the existing Texas state tests, they would have found no differences, since those items have very low cognitive demand and students do relatively well on the tests before as well as after instruction. They saw gains on items with higher cognitive demand in ways that aligned with future algebra learning trajectories.[21] In essence, Roschelle's research team explored all parts of the Jenkins model noted earlier and went beyond the model by studying teacher characteristics and behavior that helped predict the effect of the innovation on learning. As Roschelle explained,

> It's the lessons about the variability of effects, and reasons for them, that have been most valuable to us as a research team. We are seeing that teacher attitudes, background, certification-level, expectations, beliefs, etc., as well as many student and classroom characteristics, have very weak effects on student learning compared to factors closer to the acts of teaching and learning. For example, our data shows that it matters relatively less whether teachers say they have high expectations for all students than whether they engage at least some students in extended mathematical reasoning during classroom discussions. Likewise, one of our graduate students found that the "cultural match" between a teacher and a student is not a predictor of how much students learn, but that teachers who encourage more diversity in student responses to open-ended math problems have students who learn more.[22]

Roschelle and his team's comments about systematic variability of out-comes raise another issue about practitioners' need for personal judgment and expertise, even if the evidence is clear and consistent. The medical pro-fession is often touted as a model for research-practice connections that edu-cation would do well to emulate. However, many key findings suggest that high-quality medical decisionmaking is a far cry from simply looking at ran-domized trials data in order to determine the best treatment.

> Good doctors use both individual clinical expertise and the best available external evidence, and neither alone is enough. Without clinical expertise, practice risks becoming tyrannized by evidence, for even excellent external evidence may be inapplicable to or inappropriate for an individual patient. Without current best evidence, practice risks becoming rapidly out of date, to the detriment of patients.
>
> Evidence-based medicine is not "cookbook" medicine. Because it requires a bottom-up approach that integrates the best external evidence with indi-vidual clinical expertise and patient-choice, it cannot result in slavish, cookbook approaches to individual patient care. External clinical evidence can inform, but can never replace, individual clinical expertise, and it is this expertise that decides whether the external evidence applies to the individual patient at all and, if so, how it should be integrated into a clini-cal decision.[23]

Andy Hargreaves and Carrie Stone-Johnson provide in chapter 4 additional wisdom about evidence and clinical practice. They cite David Hargreaves (no relation), one of Britain's staunchest advocates for evidence-based educa-tional change along medical lines, who acknowledges that while randomized trials and new technologies form part of the basis of professional judgment, physicians make their own decisions according to other criteria as well, based on "what is known from natural science (basic laws and causes), from medi-cal sciences (e.g. the effects of drugs on organs), from tradition (inherited within the specialty), from what one was taught (early professional socializa-tion) and from personal experience (what therapeutic action one has learnt works with what kind of patient in what situation)."[24] Hargreaves and Stone-Johnson make a strong case that effective medical judgment and practice is not merely informed by technical or even intellectual evidence but also by practical, emotional, situational, ethical, and political criteria that make up other forms of evidence and affect the conditions supporting or impeding their use.

Ongoing Assessments of Progress

It is also noteworthy that physicians often regard initial diagnoses and treatments as working hypotheses that need further evidence, which includes gathering information about the patient's progress and trying different combinations and doses of treatments. Good teachers and educational leaders follow similar procedures of monitoring progress after new interventions—keeping in mind that there initially may be "implementation dips" during early attempts to learn and use new innovations.[25] In both medicine and education, the faster and better the feedback from monitoring progress, the better the prognosis overall.[26]

Varieties of Evidence

Preparing Teachers for a Changing World, a book written by a National Academy of Sciences committee, includes a discussion of the range of evidence used to guide their recommendations for preparing new teachers.

> The recommendations for teacher education discussed in this volume represent the considered judgments of a large number of experienced practitioners and scholars in the field of education. Whenever possible we refer to research studies to support our conclusions. But just as was the case in the early days of forging new medical, law, engineering and bioengineering education programs (and is still true in all these fields today), our evidence for preparing new teachers also comes from consensus among experienced researchers and practitioners.[27]

In addition to professional consensus, editors Darling-Hammond and Bransford discuss four kinds of research evidence to support their recommendations (see Figure I.2).[28]

- The first is *basic research on how people learn,* both generally and in specific areas like language, reading, or mathematics.
- The second kind of research looks at *the influences of different conditions—including specific teaching strategies—on what and how people learn.*
- The third kind of research looks at *what kinds of teacher learning opportunities are associated with teaching practices that, in turn, influence student learning.*
- The fourth kind of research examines *how teachers learn* to engage in practices that successfully support student development and learning.

Darling-Hammond and Bransford note that although each of these kinds of research comprises distinctive lines of study, they build on each other con-

FIGURE I.2   **Research Bases Supporting Teacher Education Recommendations**

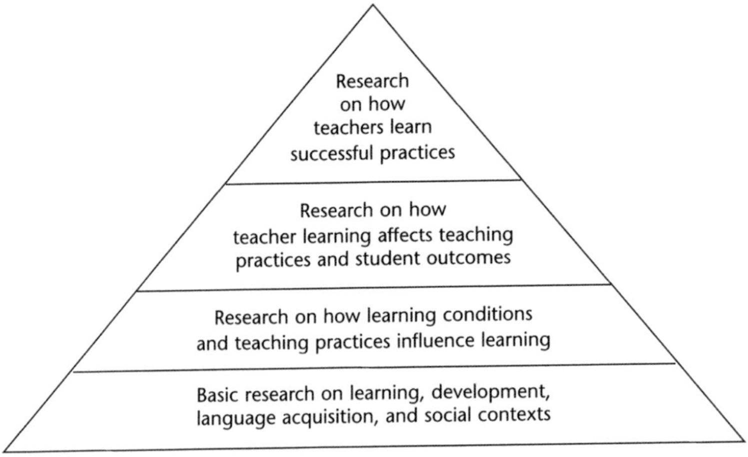

Research
on how
teachers learn
successful practices

Research on how
teacher learning affects teaching
practices and student outcomes

Research on how learning conditions
and teaching practices influence learning

Basic research on learning, development,
language acquisition, and social contexts

ceptually. Knowledge of how students learn ought to influence teaching practices, and knowledge of effective teaching practices, as well as teacher learning, should influence teacher education. The amount of these various types of evidence varies greatly. There is a smaller body of research on the relationship between teachers' learning opportunities and what they do in the classroom as well as what their students learn, and a small but growing body of research on how it is that teachers learn to engage in the kinds of practices that research suggests are most successful for students. The present volume touches on issues of evidence on teaching, to some degree (see especially those by Hargreaves and Stone-Johnson and by Schoenfeld). As a group, the chapters help provide much-needed examples of the many faces of *evidence* and how, when, why, and where it can be used.

With regard to evidence, all the authors in this volume agree that the field of education needs to (1) support a variety of approaches to research that leads to new innovations; (2) go well beyond the "horserace model" of randomized trials to also learn about variability of outcomes and necessary resources for implementation (e.g., financial, human capital, time for training, sensitivities of assessments used, etc.); and (3) realize that there is always a need for effective clinical judgment, including treating one's ideas as initial hypotheses about treatments and creating "fast feedback cycles" that monitor successes and failures (see especially Hargreaves and Stone-Johnson chapter). Discussions about the nature of evidence and how, when, why, and for whom different types are useful occur throughout this book.

Central to issues of evidence are the metrics used to assess students progress. Many authors note that existing standardized tests capture some of the skills needed for successful lives in the future; in particular, they capture the acquisition of schematized knowledge and skills. However, they typically fail to capture the degree to which people have been prepared for continuous lifelong learning, as well as abilities to solve novel problems or be inventive. This requires approaches to assessment that, instead of being sequestered, are nonsequestered and include access to tools, technology, social networks, and other kinds of resources that are available to people in and out of school settings.[29] As noted by many contributors to this volume, the best randomized trials in the world can be misleading if the assessments of learning are flawed. Issues of sequestered versus nonsequestered testing and problem-solving are likely to receive increased attention in the coming years.[30]

The authors in this book also agree that efforts to improve education must simultaneously consider many parts of the education elephant. The chapters provide countless examples of how one sector's efforts or intervention at one level of education were undermined, and in some cases had negative effects, because other sectors and levels of education were not aligned. Along with more thoughtful strategies for developing and using evidence, the book strongly endorses a more multidimensional, integrated approach to education reform.

OVERVIEW OF THE BOOK

Chapter 1: The Role of Research in Education Reform from the Perspective of Federal Policymakers and Foundation Grantmakers

The authors of this chapter, Fritz Mosher and Marshall Smith, base their writing on forty-plus years of experiences as federal policymakers and private foundation grantmakers. They note that in many countries a central educational authority could plan and direct the changes assumed necessary to achieve new goals. Although in the United States the official power of education lay with each of the states, the federal government and many foundations that have a "national perspective" have searched for ways to leverage educational successes that meet the twin goals of equity and excellence.

Mosher and Smith's chapter explores three major themes that are relevant to this increased involvement: (1) opportunities for federal policymakers and foundation grant makers to guide large-scale education reform; (2) examples of landmark research that affected educational thinking generally, including policymakers and grant makers; (3) key lessons learned that can be applied to further the goal of coherent and continuous educational progress in our rapidly changing world.

Chapter 2: Research-Based Evidence and State Policy

Authors Robert Schwartz and Susan Kardos write that fifty years ago schooling was principally the responsibility of local government. They note, however, that the past twenty-five years has seen a steadily expanding role of the states in setting education policy.

This chapter cites a major survey study in 1985 by David Cohen that describes how and where policymakers get information to inform their policymaking and how the current policy environment has changed since that survey.[31] They note that policymaking is still susceptible to the inertia of politics and ideology, yet the policy environment seems to demand evidence-based policymaking and appears to have greater capacity to use it. They end by summarizing key lessons learned from their inquiry and present recommendations to increase the likelihood that research-based evidence will inform education policymaking, and vice versa.

Chapter 3: What's the Evidence on Districts' Use of Evidence?

The authors of this chapter, Cynthia Coburn, Meredith Honig, and Mary Kay Stein, focus on school districts and note that the federal No Child Left Behind Act has significantly raised the profile and the stakes of student-achievement data as well as the importance of research-based programs. Thus, the use of evidence in district central office decisionmaking is emerging as a critical arena of educational leadership and administrative practice. Reviewing research on evidence use in school district central offices, the authors argue that administrators do use evidence in their decisionmaking but in ways that are complex and at times messy, mediated by individual and collective interpretation, and shaped in fundamental ways by organizational and political conditions. They finish by offering key lessons for encouraging uses of evidence in ways that help districts understand the social process required to change behaviors in positive ways.

Chapter 4: Evidence-Informed Change and the Practice of Teaching

Focusing on teaching, Andy Hargreaves and Corrie Stone-Johnson note that people differ in what they mean by "evidence," the kind of evidence they demand, and the role evidence plays in the context of other sources of knowledge. They organize the chapter by reviewing the role of evidence in teaching, differentiating among aspects of the practice. They argue that different aspects of teaching require different kinds of evidence.

The chapter culminates with a vision for research-informed teaching that is embedded in a set of professional learning communities. The role of professional learning communities is to stimulate and support teachers to review critically and apply judiciously the evidence of research and experience together in the service of continuous improvement of all students' learning. This chapter emphasizes the importance of promoting expertise and judgment in teachers, not just familiarity with research findings.

Chapter 5: Nonprofit Organizations and the Promotion of Evidence-Based Practice

In this chapter, Mark Smylie and Thomas Corcoran explore the roles of nonprofit organizations (often called "intermediary organizations") in working with schools and school districts. They explain that intermediary organizations are typically involved in promoting improvements in services to low-achieving populations or in advocating the use of particular strategies or programs deemed consistent with their philosophies and missions, not those based on research evidence. Nonetheless, Smylie and Corcoran contend that these kinds of organizations are increasingly paying more attention to evidence regarding the effectiveness of the practices they promote, and they discuss important characteristics and capacities of organizations that are needed to do so. They point out, however, that increased demand for evidence of effectiveness, among other dynamics that shape their behavior, may make nonprofits more conservative and risk averse.

Chapter 6: K–12 Education: The Role of For-Profit Providers

Louis Gomez and Guilbert Hentschke explore the role of for-profit businesses in education, the relationship between the products and services that schools buy from business, and schools' abilities to transform themselves into twenty-first-century learning environments. They begin by discussing the kind of instruction and schooling that the greater society is requesting of its schools and go on to discuss the goods and services needed to accomplish these ambitious goals.

They then examine reasons why private intermediaries have not provided a host of products that assist schools in transforming themselves into twenty-first-century learning environments. The authors propose that ideas from research must impact educational policy before they can shape school and district demand for goods and services; demand for goods and services is needed to convince for-profit businesses to develop tools to support desired improvement in practice.

Chapter 7: Instructional Research and the Improvement of Practice
Alan Schoenfeld notes that in spite of making great progress in terms of both theory and method over the past thirty years, educational research faces several serious cultural and institutional obstacles. He describes significant changes needed in the professional preparation of educational research-ers and proposes new models of research-and-practice partnerships. Schoe-nfeld concludes with specific recommendations for improving educational research and practice.

Chapter 8: How Craft Knowledge of Teaching is Generated and
Disseminated in Japan
Hidenori Fujita examines features of the organization of schooling and teach-ing in Japan and strategies for connecting research and practice that most likely contribute to the relatively high performance of Japanese students that is frequently found in international comparisons. He discusses three features of Japanese education that are relevant to the use of systematic evidence in the practice of education: (1) centralized decisionmaking for education poli-cies and practices; (2) the greater prestige, pay, and training of teachers; and (3) the many institutional mechanisms for practitioner and researcher inter-action. The chapter also describes differences in school management and organization and in mechanisms for the construction and dissemination of practical knowledge.

Chapter 9: Toward a Deeper Understanding of the Educational Elephant
In the final chapter, coauthors Louis Gomez, Janet Weiss, Deborah Stipek, and John Bransford revisit the three themes of the book—equity and excel-lence, the elephant, and evidence—noting that educational enterprise oper-ates as well-developed silos and has failed to develop systematic and insti-tutionalized processes that encourage communication, cooperation, and collaboration across its parts. They also point out that the book helps us see that much of the knowledge gained from research is not usable in prac-tice, even if it reaches practitioners. They caution that improving education research will require a commitment by funding agencies and a willingness to change on the part of the institutions where research is currently conducted. They discuss strategies for building shared understanding across institutional

boundaries and the design of tools and routines that have the potential to encourage the development of better evidence. They urge practitioners to pay more attention to evidence—all toward the goal of helping parts of the education elephant fit together and function as a whole in ways that promote equity and excellence for students.

The time to write this chapter was supported in part by a grant from the National Science Foundation (NSF#0354453). Any opinions, findings, and conclusions expressed in the paper are those of the authors and do not necessarily reflect the views of the National Science Foundation.

The Role of Research in Education Reform from the Perspective of Federal Policymakers and Foundation Grantmakers

Frederic A. Mosher and Marshall S. Smith

Federal policymakers and private foundation grantmakers are among the many groups whose efforts play important roles in educational progress and decisionmaking. Our historical review in this chapter is based on more than forty years of experience for each of us as federal policymakers and private foundation grantmakers.[1] During this period we observed a major sea change in expectations about the nation's schools; only in the last decade or so have schools been asked to bring all of their students to high standards of academic proficiency. Federal policymakers and foundation grantmakers have played significant roles in this shift. We explore three major themes that that are relevant to their involvement: (1) opportunities and constraints on federal policymakers and foundation grantmakers for guiding large-scale education reform; (2) examples of landmark research and its effects on educational thinking by researchers, policymakers, and grantmakers; (3) what might yield coherent and continuous educational progress in our fast-changing world.

GUIDING LARGE-SCALE EDUCATION REFORM

The federal government did not start out with much of a role in public education. The U.S. Constitution makes no explicit provision for federal responsibility for education, and the Tenth Amendment reserves to the states ("respectively, or to the people") "the powers not delegated to the United States by the Constitution, nor prohibited by it to the states." As a consequence, U.S. public school systems have been established under state constitutional authority, and in most states even state authority has been limited, with considerable deference paid to sometimes fierce traditions of local control, particularly with respect to curriculum and instruction—traditions bolstered by the fact that substantial portions of the funding for schools came from local (usually property) taxes.

The tradition of decentralization notwithstanding, the federal government has played an increasingly important role in education policy, and we argue that research has been influential in work initiated by the federal government as well as by foundations. However, much of its influence has consisted of calling attention to problems and calling into question the efficacy of attempts to solve those problems. Both of these forms of influence have, of course, provoked theories and hypotheses about current practices and possible strategies for improvement, and there have been some instances of improvement and advances in understanding, but these have not been sufficient to provide confident assurance that success for all children is achievable. In this essay we offer a hypothesis about how research and development might be managed and organized in the future to help the schools learn how to succeed, and we suggest how policymakers and funders could do better by investing more heavily and strategically in research and development.

Why Discuss Federal Policymakers and Foundations in One Chapter?

At first glance it may seem strange for us to discuss federal policymakers and foundation grantmakers in the same chapter, since they appear to live in different worlds. They do, to a large extent, but there are important similarities as well. Policymakers, whether from the executive or legislative branch, work in a political context. They have to take into consideration the full range of interests at play in an issue and whether what they are promoting furthers their or their party's electoral fortunes as well as whether or not it happens to be a good idea. They can enjoy some electoral mileage in simply promoting the perception that there is a problem and by being seen to be moving to solve it, or to be delivering goods to one's district. For any project or program beyond the immediate pork barrel, there are pressures to spread the benefit around as much and as equitably as possible and to show the benefits of initiatives before the end of the current electoral cycle.

Foundations are usually established by benefactors who hold lofty ambitions for them—to advance and diffuse knowledge or promote human welfare, and so on—and in principle they are answerable only to their boards and the discipline of the markets in which their endowments are invested, as long as they live within the restrictions placed by the tax code on exempt private foundations. However, in practice, since the Tax Reform Act of 1969, foundation leaders and boards have become more sensitive to public reactions to their programs and to appearing to be responsible and responsive to the public interest (given the fact that their resources come in part from funds that would otherwise have gone to the government in the form of taxes). In more recent times the members of foundation boards, particularly those with corporate backgrounds, often have tried to promote attention to the nonprofit equivalent of the bottom line by defining precise goals, evaluating their attainment, and seeking efficiency.

To be sure, foundations have great leeway to fund ideas, causes, and projects whether they are popular with the general public or not, as long as someone is willing to accept their money for the purposes they have chosen. They also can be content simply to do good, to contribute to worthy causes, respond to requests without applying any particular priorities or strategy, and augment the current activities of schools or other grantees rather than support change or reform. But the rhetoric of the great philanthropists tends to encourage foundations to look for ways to tackle the root causes of problems and to seek greater "leverage" than simple beneficence would offer. An early assertion of this came from John D. Rockefeller in the 1890s: "The best philanthropy is constantly in search for finalities—a search for cause, an attempt to cure the evils at their source."[2] And foundations have the advantage of being able to take the long view and persevere with a problem well beyond any particular election cycle.

As mentioned above, in the United States constitutional authority for governing and maintaining a public education system rests with the states. In very real ways, federal policymakers in both the executive and legislative branches are in the same boat as private foundations when it comes to exercising influence on public schools. Their main source of leverage on what actually happens in schools lies in their ability to provide additional funds to them on the condition that the states and districts are willing to agree to contractual or quasi-contractual conditions in return for receiving the funds.[3] Of course, there are orders of magnitude differences between the resources potentially available to the federal government and to foundations.

Also, because of constitutional leverage rooted in provisions concerning equal treatment and related provisions of civil rights legislation, the federal government does have other avenues of direct influence on aspects of public education policy and practice.

Still, when it comes to influencing the core activities of schools in terms of choices of curriculum, setting of standards, approaches to instruction and accountability, and many other central functions, both the feds and foundations have to rely on funding specific programs or policies; tying financial incentives to explicit conditions; and/or persuading educators to do the right thing through supporting research and development, synthesizing evidence and argument, and disseminating and advocating for policies and products based on such studies. Alternatively, they also can promote plausible and appealing arguments and proposals rooted in ideology, perceived interests, folk or practitioner wisdom, and "common sense."

It is true that the limits on federal influence over local instructional matters have been tested in recent years and are still very much in contention. On the one hand, for example, federal education legislation is shot through with prohibitions against construing their provisions to authorize federal officials to "mandate, direct, review, or control a state, local education agency, or school's instructional content, curriculum, and related activities" or to "endorse, approve, or sanction any curriculum designed to be used in an elementary school or secondary school," and so on (from sections of the most recent elementary and secondary education act). On the other hand, these laws require funds to be spent on curricula and practices that are based on evidence from "scientifically valid research" and lead to regulations that have, in practice, come very close to sanctioning or approving particular approaches. By conditioning funding on states' establishing content and performance standards and associating them with outcomes-based accountability provisions, the federal actions also have had the effect of increasing states' authority over these matters in areas where, in the past, they might have been more reluctant to challenge local control.[4]

EXAMPLES OF LANDMARK RESEARCH AND ITS EFFECTS ON THINKING

Our current goal is to ask how research has informed, and could inform, what the federal government and foundations do with their resources to promote education improvement. We begin with an overview of some of the landmark studies on education that have influenced how people think about educational systems, processes, and their effects and which have had an impact on both federal education policy and foundation activity.

The research and policy history that concerns us starts in the late 1950s and 1960s with the arrival in school of the post-WWII baby boom, the civil rights movement, the assassination of JFK and the succession of LBJ, the Great Society, the War on Poverty, Title I, and the Coleman Report.[5] There was widespread recognition then that children from poor and minority families were likely to remain on the low end of the economic ladder as adults and that persistent poverty and class divisions were likely to be a source of "social dynamite."[6]

Lack of success in life was seen as being correlated with a lack of educational attainment. It was assumed that better schools would provide children with better chances to succeed, and it was further assumed that the schools in which large numbers of children were failing were ineffective primarily because of inadequate and inequitable funding. Many of the key figures behind the push for federal funding for public education—John Gardner, Francis Keppel, James Conant, and others—wanted to increase the resources available to, and the standards expected of, all schools. However, they also were concerned about the gross disparities in school spending between states and regions and between schools serving affluent and poor communities within states.[7]

These civil rights and poverty concerns and beliefs influenced the Elementary and Secondary Education Act of 1965, in particular the rationale for its Title I directive that federal funds should be focused on students who were educationally deprived by being in schools that had high proportions of students from low-income families, including benefits to poor children in private and parochial schools. (The funds were to be targeted at low-performing students in such schools, whether or not they were themselves poor, and the funds were distributed to districts according to their numbers of low-income students and within districts to schools according to their poverty levels, though at least half their schools could receive some funding. In this way the funds were distributed rather widely across the country). The 1965 federal legislation produced a breakthrough against the long resistance to federal funding based on "the Three Rs" (race, religion, and reds), which included: southern concerns that funds would be used to further integration; resistance to Roman Catholics' and other religious interests' insistence that funds should go to parochial/sectarian schools as well; and the worry that federal involvement would somehow further socialist thinking.

The Coleman Report

Assumptions about the effectiveness of better and more equitably funded schools quickly came up against the results of one of the landmarks of social science research, the congressionally mandated Study of Equal Educational Opportunity (SEEO), carried out by sociologist James Coleman and his colleagues.[8] Coleman's study was a massive sample survey of American schools and students, which included measures of student achievement on standardized tests and an array of measures of school and teacher characteristics and family and demographic background for the participating students. The weak or nonexistent associations between the resource variables measured and student achievement were seen as a blow to the hopes and assumptions of the proponents of greater and more equitable school funding programs such as Title I and to the idea that school policies could be the primary source of leverage to help bring about a more equitable society (a hope further dashed by the Jencks et al. study, *Inequality*, supported by Carnegie Corporation of New York, which extended and refined the Coleman argument[9]).

Marshall Smith reanalyzed the Coleman Report data and summarized the implications of the study concerning the determinants of verbal achievement for the Harvard Faculty Seminar on the SEEO (also funded through a Carnegie Corporation grant handled by Fritz Mosher). The reanalysis took account of many of the methodological criticisms of the study but, nevertheless, came to the same conclusion as the original authors that differences in the resources available to schools serving students of differing backgrounds had much smaller effects than had been expected, and when student background was controlled for, differences in schools had very little relationship to differences in students' achievement. After documenting the limitations of the Coleman study, Smith proceeded to argue that

> in order to solve this problem [the limitations of research based on longitudinal correlational studies of the effects of existing variations in schools] we must modify substantially our present strategies of both research and schooling. Fully controlled and large-scale experiments must be funded and carried out. Until we adopt the experimental model, we will continue to founder in the swamp of uncontrolled plausible hypotheses. Furthermore the available evidence strongly suggests that our present thinking about the problems of education is inadequate. If the beliefs of the nation lead to a policy of equality of opportunity in terms of achievement outputs, we may need to think about ways to restructure radically the educational institution rather than about ways to reallocate ineffective resources.[10]

We say more about research designs as our discussion proceeds.

Some Positive Effects from the Coleman Report

The surprisingly discouraging implications of the Coleman study were not entirely dispositive. The study strongly provoked researchers, practitioners, and policymakers to search for differences in schools or teaching that *did* make a difference in student outcomes independent of students' class and family backgrounds (which included a running battle over whether, and/or how, money "matters," often framed in terms of a choice between investment in the current system versus proposals for radical structural or market-based reforms of that system).

We cannot try to cover all of the twists and turns of research sparked by the Coleman Report, but there have been a number of recent useful reviews of the evidence, and many earlier reviews and meta-analyses, that we in turn will exploit to provide a modest framework to guide thinking about what policymakers and funders have to turn to if they seek to base their education reform decisions on evidence and research-based knowledge.[11]

Additional Studies

One outcome of the Coleman Report was that it motivated a series of privately funded reports that amplified attention to twin concerns. The overall performance of American students was seen to be falling far short of what would be required to succeed in the new global economy and in a competitive world. In addition, the gap between the performance of white and advantaged students and those who were minority and disadvantaged was large, growing, and worrisome because the proportion of the student population who were minority and disadvantaged also was growing. Thus, there were increasing concerns about both "excellence" and "equity." The period was notable for the greatly increased public engagement of both business leadership and the states' governors in issues of education policy. Private professional groups such as the National Council of Teachers of Mathematics and then the federal government itself through support of private disciplinary efforts began to develop more ambitious and explicit standards for what students should know and be able to do in the core school subjects, and aspects of these standards began to be reflected in state curriculum goals and frameworks, most notably in California, under the leadership of Commissioner William Honig, but also in a number of southern states.

This continuing activity and concern was undergirded throughout by "evidence" from international comparative studies of student achievement and from the results of the National Assessment of Education Progress (NAEP), which took on special prominence as *The Nation's Report Card*, once it began reporting the percentages of various groups who were performing above and particularly below various "achievement levels" (*basic, proficient,* and *advanced*) and then reporting results on a state-by-state basis. An appetite for comparative reporting of results had been whetted by the public impact of the "wall chart" summaries of how the states were doing on such things as attendance and graduation rates and college entrance examination scores that had been adopted by the new Department of Education's first secretary, Terrell Bell.[12] The shift from a focus on basics and minimums to more ambitious expectations for American students was consolidated at the Charlottesville Education Summit convened in 1989 by President George H. W. Bush. With almost all the state governors in attendance, including Bill Clinton and Richard Riley in key roles along with significant representation of corporate leaders, the summit committed the participants to develop and agree on significant national goals for American education to be achieved by the new millennium. While we say more about these goals and the policies suggested for achieving them later on, the point here is that this period brought about a significant increase in the involvement of federal policymakers in K–12 education, and that research played a role in engendering concerns and promoting involvement.

Changes in Research Designs

Discussions of the Coleman Report also led to studies that widened substantially the kind of school "inputs" examined and generally found that *processes,* particularly those that can be seen in classrooms, predict student achievement better than broad categories of resources, which may or may not affect what transpires in the classroom. Researchers began to look at differences between receiving resources for new teaching materials versus actually using them correctly.

In their influential RAND "change agent" study, Berman and McLaughlin looked at the results of a broad range of federal funding programs designed to enable schools to adopt new practices (including "Right to Read," Title III of ESEA, vocational education, and so on) and found very weak implementation of the innovations on the ground in schools. At best, and in a small number of cases, there was a kind of mutual adaptation, in which the schools changed in the desired direction, but the innovations changed too, and they tended to go away when the external money went away.[13]

This paralleled earlier findings on the limited implementation of the major, ambitious curriculum reform efforts of the 1960s (e.g, "the new math") and the results of the large-scale federally supported experiments with alternative preschool and elementary school curriculum designs: the Headstart Planned Variation and the Follow Through Planned Variation experiments. The latter showed that some of the interventions had a positive impact but that the degree to which any of the programs was actually implemented in the schools varied quite widely, so overall average effects were diluted in comparison to the much smaller number of instances in which interventions were well implemented. This line of research demonstrated that mandating a particular curriculum or approach in no way guaranteed its actual implementation at the classroom level. In retrospect this may seem obvious, but it represents a very important lesson learned.

The RAND study, and subsequent intervention studies, began to develop evidence about the conditions under which externally developed interventions could in fact be implemented in schools. This evidence stressed such things as providing professional development focused on the particular innovation; sometimes bringing in people associated with the innovation to act as "coaches" and managers of its implementation; seeking situations in which the innovation was compatible with the interests and concerns of school personnel and encouraging their "buy-in"; engaging school and district leadership in support of the program; and, in later stages, focusing on getting the support of other stakeholders in the district or school and enlisting or developing third-party support and advocacy organizations to help ensure the survival of the innovation in the face of leadership or political changes.

The initial evidence about lack of implementation was sufficiently discouraging, however, that some proponents of school change shifted to the idea of concentrating on the development of "local capacity" to focus on a school's problems and the changes those seemed to require, and that has produced a continuing tension in the school improvement movement between emphases on external, or "top-down," sources of change and those that are "bottom up," or driven by the school professionals. The answer to these tensions can of course be "both/and" rather than "either/or," and many modern reform efforts attempt to take a more balanced approach.

Two Different Approaches to Educational Research

The Coleman Report focused attention on two different approaches to research on schools: a relatively passive approach that examines "what is" and a more interventionist approach that actively manipulates variables. Each of these is discussed below.

The Passive Approach

The first approach involves statistical and descriptive studies—cross-sectional and longitudinal examinations of associations and correlations coupled in some cases with closer observations and case studies—of existing variations in system, school, and teacher resources and practices to try to find, and explain, those that seem to be most associated with student achievement. These are what Cohen, Raudenbush, and Ball call "passive" studies.[14] These sorts of data are also used to locate problems in the performance of our schools and to track progress, or the lack of progress, in addressing them. The most prominent examples of the latter function are the National Assessment of Educational Progress (NAEP) and the influential series of international comparative studies, most notably TIMSS (originally "the Third International Math and Science Survey"). Starting with the 1983 National Commission on Excellence in Education report, *A Nation at Risk*,[15] these data have mainly fueled a continuing sense of concern and crisis.

The passive studies looked at existing variation; some began with the attempt to find schools that were statistical outliers, where their students averaged much higher performance than would be expected given the average socioeconomic background of their students, and then to ask what it was that differentiated such schools from less successful schools in the sample that were otherwise comparable. The prototypical study along these lines was undertaken by Ron Edmonds as an explicit response to Jencks's *Inequality*, and it launched the "effective schools" research movement, claiming that such schools existed and that they shared a set of predictable characteristics: strong leadership; clear and high expectations that all students could and would succeed; explicit attention to student performance and timely intervention when problems were identified; respectful attention to the surrounding community and students' families; a safe and orderly setting; and so on.[16] Mosher, who was responsible for handling the funding of Edmonds's study from Carnegie Corporation of New York (there was substantial additional support from the National Institute of Education [NIE]), can testify that Edmonds's results reflected the insights and instincts of a brilliant and charismatic practitioner more than they did convincing statistical and observational evidence, but they did launch an important line of work that continues to inform thinking and research about what it might take to organize a school so that it is effective for students who would otherwise not be expected to succeed.

A companion line of work began to look at whether it might be possible to identify teachers who are unusually effective in boosting their students' performance. Some of this involved small-scale studies of teacher practice, which indicated that teachers who were more effective were more likely to be coherent in their instruction, to maintain a fast pace, to have high expectations and clear goals for their students, to keep class time focused on content, and so on.[17] This work morphed into later statistical work that showed that teachers differed significantly in the degree to which they add value to their students' learning.[18] However, while this work showed that different teachers are reliably associated with differential achievement growth for their students, it does not (so far) provide much statistical or observational evidence on what it was about those teachers that might have caused the differential effects. Nevertheless, these findings underlie the widespread acceptance of the idea that teachers represent one of the most—if not *the* most—potentially important factors that could enable schools to reduce the correlations between student achievement and family background and improve student achievement overall.

Other results from statistical and descriptive studies have identified other school factors that influence achievement; many of them use the data bases generated by the very useful longitudinal and large-scale surveys sponsored by the National Center for Education Statistics in the U.S. Department of Education. An important set has to do with curricular exposure, both in terms of content and amount of time devoted to it, a result stressed by Harvard psychologist John B. Carroll in the 1960s. It turns out that students tend to learn what they are taught and not learn what they are not taught. Attention focused on school tracking policies and on the low expectations and content exposure characteristic of the lower tracks, which in turn tended to be disproportionately populated by students from poor and minority backgrounds. This also highlighted the fact that the variation in achievement tends to be much greater within schools than between them, on the average, raising the possibility that students in the same schools with ostensibly the same resources are getting different doses of instruction. Tracking was one culprit, and possibly a clue as to why it was hard to find consistent correlations between overall school resource levels and outcomes. The international comparative studies had the virtue of allowing researchers to look at a much wider range of practice than is found in American schools, and those studies raised additional questions about the levels of content and intellectual demand most American students are exposed to as compared to their counterparts in other, higher performing countries.

The research looking at the relationships between outcomes and the content and cognitive demands of instruction have raised ongoing and unresolved issues about the appropriateness and validity of the kinds of tests and assessments that tend to be used to measure outcomes. These measures are considered by many to be more like "status" measures in that they are influenced by the whole history of students' learning, whether from school or from other nonschool sources; so they may not be well adapted to assessing the changes resulting from specific curricula or instruction, say in a particular year or from a given intervention. If these concerns prove to be well-founded, they could call into question much of what we think we have learned from these large-scale studies.[19]

The Active Approach

An alternative to the passive approach to school research involves various kinds of interventions (often based on insights and hypotheses derived from the passive studies) designed to change practices and/or resources in order to improve outcomes. When these interventions are experimental, and evaluated and documented appropriately, Cohen, Raudenbush, and Ball call them "active" research programs.

This second approach to research ranges from small-scale laboratory or classroom studies of the teaching and learning of specific subjects; to trial curricula and pedagogical and technological approaches based on such studies; to interventions in preservice and in-service professional development for teachers, instructional leaders, and administrators; to compensatory funding and/or class size reduction; to detracking or increased expectations for students at risk; to more time on task through more flexible scheduling, afterschool programs, or summer school; to whole school or whole district designs and restructuring; to school or school district consolidation or, more recently, to breaking big schools into smaller units; to decentralization or school-based governance; to changes in the policy context, including the introduction of specific content and performance standards and/or district- or school-wide curriculum coherence and continuity; to outcomes-based accountability and incentives for schools, teachers, and students; to exposing the public system to competition through charters, vouchers, or contracting with private service providers. Some research also examines any number of attempts to deal with students' situations before they reach school through early interventions and preschool; or to improve the schools' relationships with their families or communities; or to ensure that they are healthier, better fed, and have a safe and drug-free context in which to learn; or to give them motivation and hope by tying their education to the world of work or offering scholarships or other incentives to do well. And there are many other such interventions.

The many sorts of interventions have generated their own kinds of evidence, both about what does or does not seem to affect outcomes as well as about the process of intervention itself. Rowan, Camburn, and Barnes provide an excellent review of the evidence from the history of large-scale school improvement efforts as part of their own analysis of the more recent attempts to develop and disseminate "Comprehensive School Reform" designs and programs.[20] As noted earlier, issues of implementation are being taken very seriously in all kinds of large-scale designs. There are also issues of the specificity of the implementations used.

Issues of Specificity

Issues of specificity include, for example, whether the proposed intervention or policy is focused directly on changing instruction or whether it is designed to operate at a more general level that changes the context of instruction in ways that provide leeway and/or incentives for instruction to change without focusing on or specifying the particular changes that should occur.

General contextual reforms include such things as school choice (charters, vouchers, etc.), smaller schools, class size reduction, more equitable or compensatory school funding (including Title I), school-based management and other forms of decentralization, and outcomes-based accountability schemes with incentives or sanctions for performance but without specific prescriptions for curriculum or instruction. Of course, a reform like choice may make various approaches to instruction available (matching instruction with students' needs or preferences might be what would make choice-based reform work), but the specifics of instruction are not detailed within the reform idea. Reforms that try to focus directly on changing instruction can include modifying pre- and in-service training of teachers to the extent that they deal with teaching and learning as opposed to noninstructional agendas such as discipline or conflict resolution; changing or adopting school- or districtwide curriculum, materials or exercises, or pedagogical approaches, including comprehensive or whole school reforms that focus on instruction; encouraging school leaders to be instructional leaders and/or creating new instructional leadership roles, such as "coaches"; introducing compensation and other incentives based on measures of teachers' pedagogical or other content knowledge or on acquisition of specific pedagogical skills (as opposed to basing them on their students' outcomes without regard to the teachers' particular approaches); detracking and other approaches designed to upgrade expectations and exposure to content for at-risk students; and specifying and increasing standards and aligning curricula, assessments, and professional development with those standards.

There certainly are approaches to reform that combine concerns about context with specific attention to instruction, and there are other contextual approaches to facilitating students' learning that are not specifically focused on freeing up or motivating instructional efforts—ones that concern such matters as safety, security, and order or nutrition and health or such big issues as desegregation and integration. Attention is also being paid to what happens to students before and after school in the community and in the home, and that, too, can focus on context or instruction or both. Nevertheless, we think our distinction—between reforms that try to shape instruction directly and those that are agnostic about what particular approaches to instruction are correct but assume that freeing up choices and providing incentives for success will lead schools eventually to discover and adopt effective instructional practices—captures and classifies a substantial portion of the major contending approaches to school reform.

One version of the instructional change effort focuses carefully on processes of human learning. In light of the general recognition that instruction has to improve if students' outcomes are to improve (whether or not that improvement is the specific focus of reform), it is interesting how little definitive work exists concerning the most effective ways to teach specific subjects.[21] Yet given the amount of paper and breath expended on the various pedagogical "wars," one might think that by now there would be more definitive knowledge and agreement on what to do.

There is a general understanding of how people learn based on current cognitive science which stresses that human beings in learning new things will be influenced by the prior knowledge that they bring to the situation; that learning is active, serving the purposes of the learner; that learners construct larger conceptions of areas of knowledge that help them organize the specific facts and pieces of knowledge in a domain; that experts have conceptual structures or schemes of this sort that give them much more powerful and flexible control over knowledge in a domain and the ability to apply it in new situations, compared to novices, though it also is true that these conceptual schemes cannot operate in a vacuum but are built on knowledge of facts and well-practiced skills.[22] In addition, sociocultural approaches have described the ways in which individual human knowledge is fundamentally a social product derived from the interactions, tools, artifacts, and affordances provided by one's family, peers, and cultural milieu. These general insights make it clear that it should be important for instruction to go beyond simple didactic drilling on specific facts and call attention to higher-level ways of organizing and understanding those facts. It should provide active opportunities to use knowledge in meaningful activities and to have the experience of making sense of new information in the light of prior experience and current active engagement. That said, however, there is much less rigorous help available on how the balance between didactic and active learning should be struck, and how it might vary, for particular students and particular subjects at particular stages of learning. Nevertheless, research that connects principles of learning and instruction to particular ages and areas of content has received more attention in recent years.

In the area of reading, massive effort has led to the identification of an individual difference in the tendency to attend to the fundamental phonemic distinctions in human language that makes it much harder for some pupils to learn to decode alphabetic languages fluently than for others who are more phonologically aware. And there is evidence that instructional interventions designed to call pupils' explicit attention to these distinctions and to encourage practice on associating them with letters and words can help pupils who have trouble making phonemic distinctions.[23] But there is still a lot to learn about just what kinds of and ordering of practice of this sort will prove to be most effective for pupils of varying characteristics (and about which characteristics should be attended to in order to support such diagnostic matching), and there is even more to be learned about how to balance these efforts with pedagogical approaches designed to help students acquire vocabulary and focus on the meaning of what they are able to read and comprehend and to use text material in various genres and registers for various purposes.

In early mathematics learning, there is good work on ways to help children comprehend and learn numbers, counting, and early arithmetic that has been fairly rigorously tested.[24] There are thousands of other studies of pedagogical approaches, tools, and materials, many of them showing great promise and good local effects, and there are quite compelling rationales for why these approaches should work. Additional progress includes the National Academy of Science books *How Students Learn*, which focuses on connections between new theories of learning and the teaching of history, mathematics, science, and social studies, and *Taking Science to School*, which is an analysis of effective science instruction.[25] There is also a host of additional content-specific studies that are helping us learn to improve what, when, and how to teach.[26]

It is important to recognize that much of this work connecting instruction with particular learning outcomes has emerged from hypotheses derived from descriptive and correlational studies. Other work is based in rigorous experimental designs, although these have often been conducted in laboratories and relatively small-scale studies in schools. Only a small portion of this work has involved the development and testing of materials and approaches in experimentally controlled situations across a wide enough range of circumstances, teachers, and students to be able confidently to say where, when, and with whom to use them.[27] We are still too close for comfort to where Marshall Smith predicted we would be absent such work—in a "swamp of uncontrolled plausible hypotheses." Still, rigorous experimental and empirical work focused on learning in specific content areas (math, science, reading, history, engineering, etc.) is gaining in frequency. And work connecting learning in school with learning outside of school is on the rise as well.[28]

SOME KEY LESSONS AND CONJECTURES FOR THE FUTURE

We hope that the preceding discussion illustrates some ways that, over the past forty years, the field of education and the current authors have learned important lessons about schools and what makes them effective. At this point in time, our experiences do *not* prompt us to suggest that experiments using randomized assignment to treatments will necessarily save the field of education research, although if guided by theory, and if conducted with an eye toward context and variability and the development of clinical judgment, they can be helpful. (See the introduction to this volume.) One issue that we believe to be important for the future is the degree to which effective instruction needs to be adapted to each child rather than scripted. As we elaborate below, a focus on adaptive instruction makes it much harder to do randomized trials because one needs to look at the actually implemented performances and not simply a scripted version that is the same for each school or classroom or child. Nevertheless, our experiences suggest that more is needed to truly enhance learning and instruction—a concept we call *adaptive instruction*.[29] At this point it remains an informed conjecture, but it is seems worthy to pursue for reasons described below.

ADAPTIVE INSTRUCTION

We are persuaded by the argument that students' learning will not change without a change in instruction. Simply providing new content and new tests, or even ramping up the accountability requirements, will not necessarily help all students learn to meet or exceed serious proficiency standards

(standards that include the capability to use knowledge and skills to solve new and authentic problems and to pursue further learning). Research is pointing toward the need for teachers to adapt their instruction by monitoring and responding appropriately to each student's progress or difficulties. In addition, there are indications that there is even more to be gained by attending to students' roles in adapting instruction to their own needs and interests and by helping them monitor their own progress, particularly through using technologies or forms of instruction that explicitly afford them choices and feedback responsive to their particular stages of progress and preferences.

We believe in the importance of having valid and precisely specified indices of student progress and problems and having a repertoire of validated "appropriate responses" keyed to the stages of progress and problems identified by the indices. The evidence needed to guide the kind of adaptive, individualized instruction we are describing is preliminary at best and mostly nonexistent. Getting it is no simple matter, but the idea is important to pursue.

Cohen, Raudenbush, and Ball point out that the concept of adaptive instruction implies that instruction should act like a dynamic treatment regime in medicine, one in which the dosage or protocol varies depending on the patient's particular characteristics and symptoms.[30] What they then call "instructional regimes," which may require distinctly different pedagogical treatments or responses from teachers for students in the same classroom depending on each student's progress and particular problems, represent quite complex objects indeed when, and if, they are subjected to experimental evaluation. Recognizing the students' own roles in choosing what they are exposed to or pay attention to complicates the picture even more. Steve Raudenbush has given further consideration to the implications of this complexity, including its implications for rethinking the lessons from the original Coleman study, and we cannot really improve on his argument:

> The Question, then, is how to conceptualize a research agenda that improves educational policy by improving research on instruction. My answer is based on four inter-related propositions.
>
> First, I argue that improving educational policy research requires a new causal model. According to this model, the proximal cause of student progress is the "instructional regime." I define an instructional regime as a more or less coherent plan for achieving explicit goals for student learning by continuously assessing student progress and then tailoring instruction to the results of those assessments. Resources and incentives play a prominent role in this model by facilitating the enactment of proven instructional

regimes. Thus knowledge about the impact of instruction supplies a scientific basis for policy concerning resources and incentives.

The study of classroom instruction therefore plays a role in educational policy that is similar to the study of clinical practice in health policy. Not surprisingly, the clinical trial immediately emerges as a model for testing instructional regimes. However, my second proposition is that, despite important similarities, the social structure of instruction—the fact that it occurs within classrooms nested within schools—distinguishes it from the canonical assumptions underlying the clinical trial in medicine. This distinction has fundamental implications for the design of research—experimental and non-experimental—in education.

Third, a successful agenda for research on the impact of instructional regimes will require a well-orchestrated interplay between experimental and non-experimental research. I argue that we will inevitably see differences between an intended instructional regime and the regime actually enacted. Understanding each of these is essential. A key methodological challenge is that inferences about the impact of instructional regimes students actually experience are not protected by randomization. Better methods are therefore needed for drawing causal inferences in the absence presence [sic] of non-randomly assigned instructional regimes.

Fourth, discovering the impact of multi-year sequences of instruction is the fundamental aim of policy-relevant research on instruction. Most of the cognitive goals we seek for students, including, for example, reading with comprehension, writing an effective essay, or tackling a multi-step math problem, require multiple years of instruction. To understand the impact of sequences of instructional regimes poses special challenges to valid causal inference, particularly in the light of the fact that children's experiences in instruction occur in multiple social settings.

Meeting these challenges requires an ambitious research agenda. It requires highly trained researchers with knowledge about the social settings in which learning emerges: classrooms, schools, families, and neighborhoods. This is intrinsically an inter-disciplinary research agenda, and it requires strong connections between researchers and practitioners. Moreover, it requires substantial investments in educational research. Many of the essential elements for the success of such an agenda are now in view, but I argue that more clarity on its goals and methods are essential to generate positive long-term impact on children's learning.[31]

It is noteworthy that Raudenbush's argument is consistent with the review of earlier research studies such as the Coleman Report.[32] The fundamental point is that while the availability of resources may set constraints on what is possible within instruction, if within classes or schools instruction itself varies in response to the characteristics of the students, either in positively adaptive ways or negative ones (such as when expectations are lowered and teaching is "dumbed down" for students perceived to be of lower ability), there is not likely to be a strong relationship between the general levels of resources available in a school and the outcomes obtained for particular students, particularly if the student characteristics that influence their differential treatment or expectations are controlled for in the studies.

Raudenbush's paper also provides an analytically elegant grounding for the arguments made by others that randomized experimental trials of education "treatments," while a useful component of the research and development required to produce warranted and compelling knowledge, can never provide sufficient guidance for policy or practice. In particular he makes the distinction, which can be found in the evaluation literature, between evaluating the "intention to treat," which can be captured with randomized designs, and the actual "enacted treatment," which can escape randomization and which must be assessed using other qualitative and quantitative methods and observations, including particularly observations of whether the intended treatments are well-implemented and affect classroom instruction.

Murnane and Nelson and Fullan, Hill, and Crevola provide additional examples suggesting that randomized trials are most informative when the treatment is well-specified and relatively easy to implement. However, such treatments are not likely to encompass all of the variability and tailoring required if at-risk students are to get beyond improvement at the most basic level and reach significant levels of proficiency.[33] The Fullan, Hill, Crevola book *Breakthrough* in particular is a remarkably clear and compelling review of the limitations of current research and reforms and an optimistic assertion that we could be on the threshold of a breakthrough in developing the kinds of instructional regimes based on content and skill domain-specific "critical learning instructional paths" (what others of us would call "learning progressions"[34]) that would support formative assessment and adaptive instruction designed to help students move toward success from wherever they might currently be in their learning.

Breakthrough also has a remarkable foreword by Richard Elmore that expresses support for the ideas but also caution based on his long experience with schools and systems attempting to reform. Elmore thinks that what is required is a fundamental change in the culture of American schools (which we would characterize as a shift from expectations based on practices of selection toward adopting the practices of adaptive instruction) and that it may require a long, incremental, and multiplateaued process rather than the "tipping point" anticipated in *Breakthrough*.[35] In a memorable metaphor, Elmore suggests that the work of "deliberately displacing one culture with another" may be more like "moving graveyards. More deliberate and steady than discontinuous." Still, he doesn't fault the description of what technically would be required to support the change, whether it is sudden or steady.

This discussion suggests an elaboration on the distinction we drew above between reform ideas that focus on changing the context of instruction in ways that might free or encourage it to change and those that try to change instruction more specifically and directly, one that offers a different perspective from which to view the history of federal policy and foundation grant making with respect to education reform.

TENSIONS BETWEEN POLICY AND PRACTICE

An emphasis on adaptive instruction highlights tensions between policies and practices. How much leeway do policies give people, and how much do they force them to change? This issue is discussed in depth by Cohen, Moffit, and Goldin, who point toward a fundamental dilemma in the relationship between policy and practice in social service institutions.[36] Solving the problems that policy is called on to address usually requires the people delivering the services to change what they are doing; that is, the people whose efforts are needed to solve the problem are themselves often a prime cause of the problem. If the changes that are required are relatively modest and within the capability of the practitioners, that may not be a big deal; but if they require big changes, and/or the knowledge, resources, and technology to support the required changes are in short supply or absent, then the odds on a policy succeeding go way down.

Cohen and colleagues describe a poignant mutual dependency between policymakers and practitioners. Policymakers cannot in the long run succeed and reap the social and political benefits of successful reform if practitioners do not or cannot make the required changes.[37] To do their jobs, practitioners need the resources that policymakers control, and they have to be cognizant of the authority and legitimacy that policymakers wield by virtue of their office so they have incentives to be responsive to policy. If, however, the demands of policy go too far or exceed what practitioners are capable of, the mutual dependency may produce various forms of dysfunctional or perverse behavior, including pro-forma compliance and cheating. Clearly the shift to requiring that instruction should succeed with substantially all children raises this question of whether it is a stretch too far, at least with current resources.

Looking back on the preceding eras of reform, toward the end of the George H. W. Bush to the beginning of the Clinton administrations, Marshall Smith and his colleague, Jennifer O'Day, wrote a set of analytical essays that tried to come to terms with the policy dilemmas associated with promoting ambitious instruction in an American education system in which authority and responsibility are divided among multiple levels of government and then divided again within each level.[38] They pointed out that the back-to-basics and minimum competency policies seemed to have had some success in the 1970s and early 1980s, particularly with increasing scores for minority students, though, as they note, these also were associated with favorable economic trends and increases in parents' educational attainment. They expressed concern that economic trends were turning less favorable and worried that the growing commitment to increasing educational standards coupled with the "school restructuring" reform emphasis on school-by-school change carried out "bottom-up" by local professionals—a reaction to the perceived stultification and limitations of conventional top-down reform—might leave the students most at risk again falling behind, stuck in schools that wouldn't have the resources and capacity to make the more ambitious changes.

They observed that the success of the back-to-basics/minimum competency period reforms could be attributed to the fact that they simply required an intensification of current practice. There was a de facto alignment between the "teacher-directed, skills-oriented, rote and factually-based curriculum and pedagogy" that teachers were prepared for, and familiar with, and the requirements of the kinds of assessments that were being used to measure change and accountability.[39] They reasoned that it would be unlikely for practice and its outcomes to change toward the levels required by more ambitious reform goals in more than a few exceptional schools unless there were sources of instructional guidance and enabling support that could somehow reach all schools that need them. Their candidate for such a source was the state, rather than the federal or local levels, and they said that the lynchpin of the system should be ambitious state standards in the core subjects, along with performance assessments able to determine whether the standards' expectations were being met. These should be coupled with "curriculum frameworks" that would outline in sufficient detail what course of study—what content and skills—should be covered over the years of schooling to enable students to meet the standards. They chose the states as the focus for these standards and frameworks because, in contrast to the federal government, they have the constitutional authority to maintain education systems, and they have sufficiently wide jurisdictions to make a significant reduction in the cacophony of local choices and priorities (which would have the added virtue of mitigating the effects of student mobility across schools and districts).

States, then, should go further in a conscious attempt to align all of the major factors affecting instruction to support effective teaching within the frameworks for meeting the standards, in effect paralleling the kind of de facto alignment that occurred during the earlier, more conventional minimum competency era. This could include such things within their direct control as standards-based curricula for preservice teacher training in state institutions and for related teacher credentialing, as well as the kinds of in-service professional development they support and the way that their school financing system structures the flow of resources and incentives to local districts. Smith and O'Day emphasized that they were focusing at the state level on issues of *what* to teach, and they recommended leaving the questions of *how* to teach to the local level. This was their concession to the emphasis of the school restructuring approach to reform on bottom-up local creativity and initiative. They agreed that detailed prescriptions on pedagogical approaches would be stultifying, but they felt that the state frameworks could ensure that all students would have the opportunity to learn what the goals require while leaving local professionals the leeway to be creative in adapting their teaching to the particular needs of their students.

Smith and O'Day labeled their recommendation "systemic school reform," highlighting the issue of ensuring coherence of all of the elements of the education system by aligning them with specified ambitious goals or standards and the curricular frameworks that would support them. Under this label, or sometimes using "standards-based reform" or "standards-based, state systemic reform" to encompass the whole package, versions of this cluster of ideas have become the staple of education reform policy in this country over a remarkable run of almost twenty years. In particular, it informed the Goals 2000 legislation and the Improving America's Schools Act of 1994 and, more recently, arguably, the No Child Left Behind Act. In the early years of that period, this spread was mediated by Smith's roles in the Clinton administration and by his and O'Day's participation in the deliberations of the Pew Forum on Education Reform, which was a key part of the education reform program at the Pew Charitable Trusts managed for six years by Robert Schwartz. The Forum's membership included many of the thinkers and policymakers who played key roles in formulating standards-based systemic reform. Schwartz's program funded or shared funding of a number of local and many of the national projects that promoted or enacted elements of the reform, programs such as the New Standards Project, other activities of the National Center on Education and the Economy, the National Alliance for Restructuring Education, and the precursors of Achieve (the organization formed by governors and business leaders to promote the standards ideas endorsed by the national education summits, and which Schwartz then left Pew to head).

At the core of this approach, and probably the aspect that makes it so widely acceptable and persistent, is a kind of "grand bargain" in which in exchange for making a commitment to setting common standards for student outcomes and to being held accountable for their students' achieving them, educators and schools will face reduced regulation on the input side of the equation and will be left free to choose the particular approaches to instruction they will use in helping students meet the standards. This bargain is often framed as a shift from regulation of or accountability for inputs to accountability for outcomes. In the case of the federal programs, it is coupled with a kind of supplementary bargain in which the states receive Title I funding on the condition that they set common standards for all students (not just those eligible for Title I support) and hold schools accountable for reaching them; but they are left free to define the particular content and performance standards they will use within the broad subject areas of literacy, mathematics, and, now, science that the current law specifies must be the focus of standards.

These bargains need to be reexamined. It certainly is true that in most subjects there is insufficient knowledge and evidence to justify any very specific prescriptions about approaches to teaching and instruction more generally. The instinct to specify outcomes and to leave instructional approaches open is understandable and possibly wise in the short run, but it makes real sense only in a context in which there is an ongoing good-faith effort to collect evidence on what instructional approaches do work (and under what conditions and for whom they work) and then to make those results publicly available for refinement with the expectation that as they become warranted others also will use them when they are relevant to their particular situation. Smith and O'Day's conception of systemic reform called for the development of "curriculum frameworks." These frameworks were to be developed by "highly qualified" teachers and disciplinary experts and were to be updated frequently (presumably based on experience with how they worked out, including whether they were too easy or too hard or provided ambiguous guidance). As described, they would leave many issues of timing and order to the discretion of schools and teachers, focusing instead on the essential big ideas to be covered over multiyear blocks of time. Still, the use of terms like "guidance," "qualified," and "expert" implies that there may be at least some knowledge about how things can or should be taught as well as what should be taught—something like "pedagogical content knowledge."

If so, we now think it would be a mistake not to take such knowledge into account and not to try to get more of it. It also is not likely to be possible to develop good assessments of complex or ambitious learning without knowing quite a good deal about how that learning might have been taught or acquired. In fact, assuming that the goals and standards do actually expect students to be able to know and use knowledge at levels and in ways well beyond what has conventionally been expected and tested in the past, it is not clear that there will at first be many people who are expert in what of these things most students may be able to do and what is fair to expect them to do if they have good instruction, since almost by definition we have not been gathering evidence about that. That means that, at best, current state standards are just hypotheses about what students really should be expected to do if they are well-taught, and in practice it is clear that they sometimes are little more than grab bags of everything disciplinary interests would like to see included. More often, however, they are somewhat idealized descriptions of what good students may be able to do under quite conventional conditions, and the discipline of setting priorities and defining performance expectations is left to the state assessments—to the statistical mercies of the psychometricians and to achievement level-setting based on groups of experienced teachers and other experts eyeballing the items the psychometricians have produced and picking those that seem to be consistent with some idea of "proficiency" or "basic." That the assessments and these achievement levels have absolutely no external validation against independent observations of students' performances in the real world, or even in real schools, is one of the genuine scandals of standards- or outcomes-based reform as it is actually practiced.[40]

That aside, the point here is that neither content nor performance standards should be set beyond a kind of first approximation without serious consideration of how students in fact perform under various fairly well-specified instructional regimes. The frequent revision that Smith and O'Day recommended should be based on such an understanding—both of what is likely in usual circumstances and what may be possible with better instruction—as more is learned about what that is. It should go without saying that no formulation of growth expectations or adequate yearly progress beyond a first approximation should be established without serious iterative empirical work of this sort on the relationship of growth to instructional quality.

So, we would not now be so quick to strike a long-term bargain trading away any specification of desired approaches to instruction in return for acceptance of accountability for producing desired outcomes. In fact, we would bend at both ends of the bargain. We would not recommend abandoning accountability in the sense of reporting outcomes measured as well as possible for all relevant student groups; requiring schools to have processes for choosing reasonable and appropriate responses to the information and for gathering evidence on and learning from the results; and intervening with support or sanctions when there is persistent lack of improvement. But we would recognize that no one knows everything needed for ensuring success for all students at the levels we now say we expect. So the accountability should be for transparency and for trying to learn how to do better. Punishment and embarrassment do not motivate complex learning. And we would argue for leaving room to be able to require the use of proven approaches when they have been identified (perhaps always with an option to experiment with potentially better approaches), particularly for schools that are having difficulty.

This brings us back to instructional regimes. While Raudenbush focuses on the need to design and understand the close-in variation of teaching and learning in response to particular students' progress and problems in the midst of instruction in particular subjects, he also makes clear that he recognizes that these interactions take place in complicated and layered contexts and that those contexts can facilitate or constrain the effectiveness of the immediate instruction through the resources, incentives, inhibitions, or just plain confusion they provide. It is probably an open question, answerable only in practical research experience, whether these contextual affordances should somehow be considered part of the regime itself or whether there can be some sort of independent classification or theory of contexts so that what would be studied would include the interaction between regime and context. Certainly in some cases the design of the regime would include specifics on how to try to influence the context so that it falls within some benign range of values on its key dimensions (i.e., there are food programs to deal with student nutrition, there are constructive relationships with parents and the community, there is adequate security, there are not confusing and conflicting standards and accountability incentives or curricular mandates coming from the state and the district, etc.). In that case, it would seem to make sense to include those specifications as part of the regime.

FINAL THOUGHTS

The basic lesson to be drawn from this excursion into the history of education research and policy is that we all have learned a great deal about the distribution of problems that concern us in education and a lot about what doesn't work to solve them. Clearly, education is a multifaceted process. There are most likely many factors, at many levels, that are necessary for success for all students but none that are sufficient alone (just to complicate things, of course, they may have compensatory relationships with each other, so that being very high on one compensates to some extent for being low on some others). That means that a lot of work has to be done on an other-things-being-equal or constrained basis, and then extrapolations can be made about what might happen if the most promising approaches are combined. There are many promising ideas about what might work, and it seems pretty clear that adequate solutions will require bundling interventions focused on many factors and many levels of the system. We assume that it may be possible with respect to each of these factors to identify the range of values or characteristics that seem to be necessary if there is to be success for most students, though we would not expect any of them to be sufficient for ensuring success alone.

The problem of designing systems that would make it possible for teachers and students to manage what would be involved in monitoring and reacting appropriately to each student's progress and problems in each, or any, subject in normal classrooms would represent a prototypical case of producing an instructional regime. The requirements of such a regime include rather well-defined conceptions of how students' learning is likely to proceed, with instruction, including common problems and typical or possible variations. It would need tools—formal or informal assessments, ways of observing or eliciting understanding—for revealing students' progress, and it would require, either from the start or to be built up through codified experience, an available repertoire of appropriate and effective responses to specific information about students' progress and needs.[41] It also would require techniques for organizing instruction and the class to allow time to observe students' progress and to respond to individual or subgroup needs appropriately while keeping the rest of the class on track as well. Depending on what was actually required to maintain progress, the regime might provide rules about when instruction would have to switch to different modes, perhaps including efforts outside the class setting. Work on such designs might eventually show that it is simply impossible to ensure success for all within the constraints of conventional school structures; and if so, it might suggest alternative designs that could work better. Similar design points could be made about other aspects of the school, system, and community context that the design would have to accommodate or influence, including the levels of resources in terms of time, money, and leadership and organizational support that might be required for success.

Just describing the complexity of the kinds of design that might have a chance of succeeding makes it clear that something other than the current ways of doing business in education research and development will be required. While it may be possible to prototype some elements of the required design piecemeal and on a smaller scale, at some point the pieces have to be put together, and they have to be put together in a way very close to the real world of schools and with the intimate collaboration of real teachers and other educators. Beyond that, ultimately the designs have to be tested and used at scale in real systems.

Others have written well and forcefully about the limitations for encouraging the required types of collaborative work of the incentive systems within which most academic researchers work and the lack of an infrastructure of settings and long-term support that would provide access to schools and allow iterative attempts to design and test solutions to problems of practice over the amount of time (and the range of places) that is likely to be required.[42] Tony Bryk and Louis Gomez's *Ruminations on Reinventing an R&D Capacity for Educational Improvement* is a particularly thorough and principled description of the range of capacities and forms of work and social relations that have to be put together and supported over time to carry out effectively what they call "Problem-centered Design, Engineering, and Development (DED) for Educational Improvement."[43] It is based on the work of the Information Infrastructure System Group led by Bryk and Gomez, who are working on designing technological supports for solving the problems of carrying out reflective practice within the sort of instructional regime we have been describing. The John D. and Catherine T. MacArthur Foundation, as a companion project to the one that produced this book, supports this work, as does The William and Flora Hewlett Foundation.

Describing these issues adequately requires a great deal more discussion and thought. The point here is simply that organizing the institutional structures needed to generate the kinds of knowledge that will be necessary for meeting the education system's new goals is itself a massive design problem, and it is one that both the federal government and private foundations should attend to if they are serious about having schools that succeed with all.

We would like to acknowledge the editorial and substantive help from John Bransford and Nancy Vye. They should not be blamed for any remaining confusions or infelicities. We also are grateful for the lessons learned from the members of the MacArthur Research Network on Teaching and Learning and our colleagues at the Consortium for Policy Research in Education (CPRE) Center on Continuous Instructional Improvement, particularly Deborah Ball, David K. Cohen, Tom Corcoran, Susan Fuhrman, Peg Goertz, and Brian Rowan, who continue to push these ideas into the future.

CHAPTER 2

Research-Based Evidence and State Policy

Robert B. Schwartz and Susan M. Kardos

In our uniquely decentralized education system, policymaking is a widely distributed activity. It takes place at the district, state, and federal levels of government and in all three branches as well. Fifty years ago this description of our system, while theoretically accurate, seemed much less consequential, for in most parts of America, schooling was principally the responsibility of local government. Until the Brown decision (1954), the National Defense Education Act (1958), and, most important, the Elementary and Secondary Education Act (1965), the federal government's influence on schooling was marginal. While there were a handful of states with a strong tradition of policy leadership in education (e.g., New York and its Regents Exams), most states took a much more limited view of their role in education. States set minimum standards for such things as teacher qualifications, school construction, and the school calendar but left decisions about curriculum, teacher salaries, and graduation requirements to local school boards.

We are now in a very different world. While the major education governance controversy in 2008 revolves around the federal government's role, triggered by the accountability provisions of the George W. Bush administration's No Child Left Behind Act (NCLB), the big story over the past twenty-five years has been the steadily expanding role of the states in setting education policy. Indeed, the resistance to NCLB comes largely from the states, most of which had put in place their own standards, assessments, and accountability systems well before the passage of NCLB. They are understandably frustrated by the federal government's imposition of a single tem-

plate for measuring "adequate yearly progress" (AYP) on more than fifty different state systems, each with its own definition of "proficiency." Among
the many ironies surrounding the current debate over NCLB is the enormous
buildup of state policymaking activities in education that took place during
the administration of President Ronald Reagan, George W. Bush's true ideological father. In 1983, President Reagan released a report entitled *A Nation at
Risk* while delegating to the states the responsibility to address the burning
national education problem. The states, in fact, responded to Reagan's call
with a blizzard of legislative and other policy initiatives to raise graduation
requirements, increase instructional time, strengthen teacher certification,
and generally increase academic rigor.

Education policymaking and leadership at the state level is highly fragmented, with governors' offices, legislatures, state boards of education, and
state education agencies all playing some role. Perhaps the most striking development during the 1980s was the emergence of governors as major actors in
the education policy arena. Even before the release of *A Nation at Risk,* a few
southern governors had come to see education as a key engine of economic
growth and development. Over the course of the 1980s, an impressive set of
"education governors" emerged, especially in the South, where educational
performance had historically lagged behind the rest of the country. Men like
Lamar Alexander (TN), Bill Clinton (AR), Bob Graham (FL), Jim Hunt (NC),
and Dick Riley (SC) not only built their political reputations inside their own
states principally on their aggressive and ambitious education reform programs but also emerged as major national leaders on this issue. By the end of
the decade, when President George H. W. Bush and the National Governors
Association jointly convened the first National Education Summit in Charlottesville, Virginia, it was hard to find a state chief executive who was not a
self-proclaimed "education governor."

If education policymaking was to become a principal responsibility of
governors, it naturally followed that governors needed to recruit their own
education policy staffs. By the mid-1980s, these positions had become sufficiently widespread to warrant the formation of an informal network of Governors' Education Policy Advisors. Naturally, other units of state government
that had historically seen themselves as principally responsible for setting
education policy—most obviously, legislatures and state boards of education—followed suit. Consequently, by the end of the 1990s, it was not at all
uncommon to find professional education policy staff sprinkled across several different units of state government. In this environment, figuring out

what role research-based evidence plays in the formation of state policy is no easy task, for on any given policy decision there are typically multiple actors, each with his or her own sources of information and advice. Attempts to generalize about the policy process across states are fraught with peril, for each state has its own history, governance and finance systems, political culture, reform context, and constituency groups. How policy decisions are made in any given state at any given time is in large measure a product of the leadership skills and force of personality of individuals, regardless of the particular office they happen to occupy.

Given this background, this chapter examines the gulf that exists between education research and state education policymaking. We begin by summarizing a survey study[1] that describes how and where policymakers get information meant to inform their policymaking. We next describe how the current policy environment has changed since the 1985 survey. On the one hand, policymaking is susceptible to the inertia of politics and ideology; on the other hand, the policy environment seems to demand evidence-based policymaking and seems to have greater capacity to use it. Using several examples,[2] we illustrate the multiple ways in which policymaking and research are disconnected as a result of politics and ideology, scarce resources, complexity of educational problems, and the importance of context and implementation. We elaborate on the class size reduction example to further illustrate how even seemingly clear research evidence[3] is an uncertain guide in education policymaking. We then present a mini–case study of the policy process in action. This case of a governor's task force illuminates the process and circumstances of state education policymaking and the real challenges of bridging the gulf between evidence-based research and the policymaking process. This leads to a discussion of the mismatch between the incentives for education research in the academic versus the policy arenas. Finally, we outline the lessons learned from this inquiry and present some recommendations to increase the likelihood that research-based evidence will inform education policymaking, and vice versa.

THE INFORMATION NEEDS OF STATE EDUCATION POLICYMAKERS: COHEN'S 1985 SURVEY

In 1985, Michael Cohen released the one systematic study we have found on how and where state education policymakers get policy advice. Specifically, his survey examined the kinds of information state education policymakers say they need to make decisions, the sources from which they get information, and the dissemination vehicles used to receive it.

Cohen found that policymakers' positions in the governance structure tend not to predict the kind of information they needed. In fact, there were broad similarities regardless of the specific respondent groups or their issue areas. State policymakers wanted most to know about other states' challenges and policy solutions—what was tried and what the results were. In addition, there seemed to be little of the needed information available about implementation strategies, cost of particular polices, and analyses of impact of policies on populations at greatest educational risk.

Cohen found that state policymakers most frequently relied on sources of information within their own states, specifically from their state education departments. In addition, they relied on education associations and school districts. Notably, they relied least frequently on higher-education institutions. The survey found that chief state school officers were the most likely actors to make use of national (as compared to state) sources of information, followed by governor's education aides, legislators, and state board members. Similarly, state policymakers depended on information from individuals within their states and rarely on individuals from national organizations or from other states. One striking finding from the survey was how infrequently state policymakers relied on prominent researchers, leading scholars, or other individuals active in national research and development networks for information, even when these individuals were in their own states. Last, the survey found issue networks undeveloped, though potentially valuable.

What might account for this reluctance to utilize these available resources? First, Cohen's survey brings to light the importance of framing education questions in ways that "come to grips with the particular mix of governance, fiscal, distributional, and programmatic concerns which characterize state policymaking."[4] Clearly, state policymakers require analyses that address their most salient concerns. Scholars and education researchers often frame their inquiries in ways that are more theoretical or more pointed than state legislators or aides find useful. Of course, this all presupposes that education researchers are addressing issues of public interest in the first place.

Next, it makes sense that state policymakers would rely on state-specific information that is easily attainable from their departments of education, associations, and districts. But why they would not avail themselves of the rigorous—often state-specific—analyses from education scholars in their states at first seems puzzling. In fact, as Carol Weiss explains, policymakers "prefer to get their analysis from interest groups rather than from objective academic analysts."[5] While Weiss is actually referring here to members of Congress and their staffs, the analysis still applies. She explains that policymakers know what each interest group's position is on any given issue; thus, policymakers can apply the appropriate filter. In contrast, Weiss says, they are far less certain of scholars' and academics' positions: "They assume that academics, like everyone else, are pushing their own political values, but since they don't know what these are, they can't compensate for them." One can see why a policymaker might then avoid such uncertainty.

Cohen's survey found that information that was easy to access, received in a timely fashion, directly applicable to specific state or policy contexts, and inexpensive was the most likely information to reach state policymakers. This is not surprising, but it is an important point that is often overlooked.

WHAT HAS CHANGED SINCE COHEN'S SURVEY?

Writing early in the post–*Nation at Risk* period, Cohen observed that "while political agendas at all levels of government are notoriously ephemeral and often defy long term predictions, there are signs that this wave of educational reform will remain on state agendas for some time to come. If so, we anticipate that general government policymakers . . . will continue to demonstrate active concern over the quality of education."[6] Cohen's prediction at the start of the reform wave was accurate; state policymakers are even more engaged today with complex questions of education excellence and equity than they were more than twenty years ago. Our question, however, is whether research-based evidence is playing any greater role in state education policymaking today than it did during the period of Cohen's survey.

In the twenty-plus years since Cohen's survey was published, there have been several major developments that have influenced the demand for evidence-based information and advice from education policymakers. The major development, of course, has been the evolution and growth of the standards movement, which has had several different effects—not all salutary—three of which are especially relevant here. First, the movement has shifted the conversation about educational quality from focusing principally on inputs to a much closer examination of results. Second, it has pushed policymakers and practitioners to redefine success as improving the educational performance of all students, not just those from groups that schools have typically served well. Third, it has cast a searchlight on student work and, in an increasing number of schools and districts, has stimulated conversations among teachers about those instructional practices that seem to routinely produce higher-quality student work in particular classrooms. Taken together, these effects, in an environment characterized by a rising degree of externally imposed accountability for results, have focused the attention of both policymakers and practitioners on data and evidence in unprecedented ways.

A second, related development since the Cohen survey has been the emergence of education as a significant national political issue. At the time of Cohen's survey, no one could have predicted that by 2000 education reform would consistently show up in public opinion surveys as one of the top two or three domestic policy concerns of American voters. This has led to a substantial increase in media coverage of education, which in turn has increased public demand for more and better information on school performance.

The increased public attention to education has led to the phenomenon cited earlier: the buildup of professional education staff, especially in statehouses, where most of the policy action has been centered over the past two decades. At the time of the Cohen survey, it was not uncommon in governors' offices to find general-purpose policy staff members that were responsible for several issues, one of which was education. Today, virtually all governors have education policy advisers with training and experience in the field, and there has been a similar professionalization of staff on the legislative side.

One indication of the rising demand for professionally trained staff has been the growth of master's programs specializing in education policy. Another is the increasing inclusion of education as a specialization within graduate programs in public policy. These developments should add up to a policymaking environment in which research-based evidence plays an increasingly significant role. Indeed, it is in this environment that the authors of No Child Left Behind—the law marking the transition of standards-based reform from *de facto* to *de jure* national policy—sprinkled 111 references to "scientifically-based research" throughout the act, and the federal government's education research agency underwent a status change from the Office of Education Research and Improvement (OERI) to now the Institute for Education Sciences.

This portrait of the changes affecting educational policymaking is incomplete, however, for it omits the increasing ideological, cultural, and political polarization that has come to characterize American life. As education has become a prominent political issue, it has also become a popular battleground on which to fight larger cultural and ideological wars. Consequently, debates that in quieter times might have been carried out largely within the profession—debates over the use of calculators in math classes, the inclusion of open-ended response items on state tests, the consequences of zero-tolerance policies, the appropriateness of homework, or the need for recess, for example—are now fought in the op-ed pages of the *Wall Street Journal* and on talk radio by political commentators with larger axes to grind.

On one level, this is hardly a new phenomenon in American educational history. Education policy has often been caught up in larger cultural wars, especially during periods of deep division. Today's phonics versus whole language debate, for example, can be seen as the continuation of an argument that goes back at least to the controversy generated by the 1950s bestseller *Why Johnny Can't Read.*[7] Indeed, the proponents of the movement for evidence-based policymaking and scientifically based research would argue that they are trying to overturn precisely this tendency to ground educational decisions in dogma rather than data. Unfortunately, the rhetoric and policy decisions of some of the leaders of this camp within the Bush administration have led skeptics to view the movement, especially as it applies to the implementation of the federal government's reading policy, as one more example of ideology masquerading as science.[8]

ADDITIONAL EFFECTS ON STATE POLICYMAKING

The growing ideological and cultural polarization of the last decade has affected state education policymaking in a variety of additional ways. While the standards movement has provided a striking example of bipartisan "big tent" politics, as best exemplified by the decision of liberal Democrats Ted Kennedy and George Miller to join conservative Republicans John Boehner and Judd Gregg in co-sponsoring NCLB, standards-based reform is hardly the only game in town. There is strong political support nationally and in many states for more market-based reform strategies, including charter schools, vouchers, and other mechanisms to increase parental choice in education. There is also a growing homeschooling movement. Although standards and choice are not mutually exclusive—in fact, some choice advocates like Chester Finn and Diane Ravitch argue that both strategies are essential and interdependent—the constituencies behind these reforms are largely separate.

The market-based reform movement can be viewed as the education wing of a larger conservative movement that fueled Ronald Reagan's path to the White House and that generally stands for free markets, less regulation, and smaller government. The intellectual energy behind this movement has been provided by a network of such Right-of-center think tanks as the Heritage Foundation, the T. B. Fordham Institute, the Hoover Institution, and the

American Enterprise Institute, which in turn have been subsidized by a network of Rightist foundations like Bradley and Olin.[9]

These think tanks now constitute an important part of the policy research and advocacy landscape, providing an alternative source of information and advice for the growing number of young conservative governors and legislators who were swept into office in the Gingrich revolution in the mid-1990s. Such officials tend to be deeply suspicious of information emanating from the established education organizations ("the blob," as they sometimes call them) or from education schools, which they generally view as hotbeds of political correctness and "progressive" education ideology.

So while the standards movement (and especially NCLB) has in fact created greater demand for more evidence-based policymaking, and there is greater staff capacity in state houses today to respond to data and research-based analysis, education policy has become increasingly caught up in the larger political and cultural wars that divide the country. In this climate, only research findings that unequivocally support one policy choice over another are likely to be sufficiently powerful to trump the power of ideology. Yet even in those rare cases where such findings exist, policymakers need to take care to read the fine print before rushing off to act on those findings.

HOW WELL CAN RESEARCH GUIDE POLICYMAKING?

In his book *Children as Pawns* Timothy Hacsi takes on the question "How well can research guide policymaking?" by examining several important and high-profile educational issues. Through his analysis of Head Start, bilingual education, social promotion, school finance, and class size, Hacsi reaches the following conclusion about the relationship between evidence and policymaking:

> One lesson for politicians is that if they really want to find out what works in education, they should seek nonpartisan reviews of the evaluation evidence. In most instances, the evidence is not clear-cut. Even when it seems relatively straightforward, it often lacks the specifics needed to describe exactly how programs should be implemented. But in almost every case the evidence has something to say, even if that is simply that advocates of one approach or another are speaking from their emotional or political positions, not from evidence.[10]

Thus, he concludes, although evidence cannot always guide policymaking unequivocally, it should always, at least to some extent, guide policymaking.

Hacsi's discussion sheds particular light on the gap between education research and education policymaking. First, policy debates are often influenced more by politics and ideology than by the presentation of evidence. This phenomenon can often lead to policy debates that are focused on the wrong issue. For example, since its emergence in the 1960s, the debate about bilingual education has been hotly mired in politics. Hacsi explains that although proponents on both sides of the issue will claim that evidence is on their side, the *actual* evaluation evidence shows two things: Teaching language-minority children effectively, especially those from poor or working-class backgrounds, is very difficult; and our schools do a poor job of teaching language-minority children, whether in English, in their native languages, or in combination. Hacsi suggests, then, that while the debate has focused on the nature of bilingual programs, attention has been diverted from what matters most: program quality and teacher quality.

Second, education research often points to the need for more resources, which policymakers either do not have or do not want to allocate. For example, Hacsi explains that the school finance evidence is persuasive. Money does matter. Money spent directly in classrooms makes a difference for students. It should be no surprise, however, that ever since the Coleman report suggested that the socioeconomic background of a student and his or her classmates was a more important determinant of educational achievement than anything money could buy, researchers (mainly economists) whose findings have supported the thesis that money doesn't matter have found a ready audience among policymakers.[11] This argument, of course, has an element of truth, for more money alone, absent an intelligent plan for how to spend it, is in fact unlikely to produce gains in achievement. However, because education is always competing for resources with other important functions at all levels of government, Hacsi's conclusion from the evidence that money does in fact matter is not what policymakers want to hear.

Third, policymakers and the public seek simple solutions to complex problems. Consequently, policy solutions often are not aligned with the problems they aim to solve. The issue of social promotion is an example of a policy solution not matching the problem. In other words, prohibiting social promotion is a simplistic way to appear to be dealing with a complex problem of low student achievement. Presumably, retaining students who fail promotion tests or do not meet promotion standards will force teachers and students to work harder to meet those standards. This policy solution has arisen in response to the equally flawed practice of promoting students based on time served, independent of whether or not they have mastered the knowledge and skills necessary to succeed at the next grade level. The policy debate has been framed as if these are the only two policy choices. However, as Hacsi points out, teaching struggling learners is what our schools are historically weakest at; therefore, teaching these students more effectively will take more than sporadic remediation, summer school, and the fear of grade retention.

Finally, policymakers often do not consider the importance of the context in which they are trying to implement research findings. The class size reduction issue (described in several chapters in this volume and in some detail below) is an example of an issue about which the evidence is persuasive. Smaller classes have a positive and long-lasting effect on student learning. In the case of class size reduction, however, the appropriateness of this policy solution to education problems is less a question of convincing research evidence and more a question of context and implementation. Yet the class size reduction example stands in stark contrast to the other examples in important ways. It is not surrounded by the same sort of ideological energy as, for example, bilingual education or social promotion are. Intuitively, people seem to believe that smaller classes are better for students. Parents, teachers, and students all seem to prefer smaller classes. Policymakers are generally predisposed to find research justification for policy decisions that they think will have political benefits, and the evidence for class size reduction is indeed compelling. However, in the case of class-size reduction, we will learn that even strong research evidence depends very much on its applicability in a different context and the creation and implementation of the resulting policy solutions.

Taken together, Hacsi's examples illustrate the complicated relationship between education policymaking and education research. The business of education research is knowledge creation, and the business of education policymaking is knowledge use. Education researchers necessarily present incomplete information (research inquiry is guided by a narrow band of questions) to policymakers who want to act on complete information. Education researchers create knowledge in particular contexts for policymakers who seek to adapt it to the circumstances of other contexts. According to Hacsi, we will never know that a particular curriculum is the best we can offer students, nor will we know exactly how to train teachers most effectively. There will be no one-size-fits-all answer for how to teach language-minority children well or how to help children who are falling behind in first grade. Education, and people, are too complicated and varied for that to be possible. Educators and policymakers, therefore, must act on incomplete knowledge. This is surely better than acting solely on what "feels right" or is politically popular.[12] However, as the class size reduction example below will further illustrate, even clear and compelling research evidence is an uncertain guide. What works for certain students and teachers at particular times in particular contexts may not work for students and teachers in other times and places.

THE CLASS SIZE REDUCTION EXAMPLE

As noted earlier, class size reduction stands out as a prime example of the difficulty policymakers have utilizing educational research. Despite the fact that Tennessee's Project STAR (Student/Teacher Achievement Ratio Study), the most well-known study on the effects of class size, was rigorously designed and its findings were conclusive, decisionmakers were unable to create successful education policy based on its results. The usability of this research was mitigated by failures to consider seriously context variation as well as by poor program implementation.

Project STAR

Tennessee's Project STAR examined the effects of class size reduction on student achievement.[13] The study, a randomized, controlled field experiment conducted in Tennessee in the early 1990s, is regarded by prominent social science researchers as "one of the great experiments in education in U.S. history" and it is touted by the educational research establishment as providing "resulting scientific evidence" that is among "the most credible available."[14] It is highly regarded because of the size of this statewide study, its duration and follow-up, and its experimental design. Notably, it yielded substantial and unequivocal findings about an educational issue that had been debated for decades.[15]

Over all, the study found that smaller classes (13–17 students) were associated with improved test scores in math and reading and that the gains were greatest for students who began their schooling in smaller classes. The study also found that smaller classes had the greatest effect on minority students in urban schools.[16]

Context and Implementation: Triumph in Tennessee, Chaos in California

According to Frederick Mosteller and colleagues, Tennessee is a good example of how "a policy decision may be made based on the definitive results of a well-designed and implemented experiment."[17] Since it would have been far too expensive to implement such a vast reduction in class size across the entire state, and since the STAR study showed such great gains among minority and urban students, policymakers in Tennessee decided to implement class size reduction measures in the state's seventeen poorest districts, where the research showed the intervention would be the most effective. Thus Project Challenge was born, and it seemed to stand as an example of how educational research could be used to create effective education policy.[18] Project Challenge reduced K–3 class size to approximately fifteen students in the seventeen Tennessee districts with the lowest test scores and lowest average incomes in the state. The project was credited with improved student achievement test scores in math and reading.[19] However, California's attempt to follow Tennessee's example and implement a large-scale class size reduction program proved much more problematic. When California began large-scale class size reduction in 1996, the state was forced to hire throngs of emergency credentialed new teachers and create new classroom space where none existed before. Particularly for schools serving poor and minority students, reducing class size meant declines in teacher qualifications and more inequitable distribution of credentialed teachers. Finally, analyses of the relationship between reduced class size and student achievement were inconclusive.[20]

While the results of Project STAR are instructive for education policymakers and practitioners everywhere, disregard for the specifics or careless application of the findings could lead to shortsighted or misdirected policy solutions. For example, where Project STAR showed gains for students when classes were reduced to fifteen students, California reduced classes to twenty. Where Project STAR classrooms were staffed primarily with experienced teachers, California classrooms are disproportionately staffed with new teachers, and this problem tended to be most prominent in urban and rural schools. As Hacsi explains, "STAR's findings showed that low-income children benefited the most from small classes, but if low-income children in California receive inferior teaching, they may actually gain *less* from small classes than middle-class children."[21] California seems to be an example of the misalignment of conclusive research findings and a policy solution, or, as Hacsi has written, "careless, widespread implementation." Indeed, context and careful implementation do matter, and haphazard policy solutions may actually cause the reverse of the desired effects, "a shameful legacy from an idea with so much promise."[22]

A Governor's Task Force: Policymaking on the Fly?

One possible explanation for California's "careless" implementation of the class-size initiative is that the policy initiator, Governor Pete Wilson, had virtually no responsibility for implementation, which was in the hands of the state education agency and local school districts. This pattern is increasingly common. While there are always a handful of states in which—because of tradition, governance arrangements, political culture, or sheer force of personality—the chief state school officer or state board of education is the principal initiator of policy proposals, the current dominant pattern in most states is that governors set the agenda. In the skirmishing for visibility and perceived leadership on high-profile public policy issues like education, governors have an enormous advantage over other actors. They can much more easily command media attention. They typically have much more sophisticated and well-staffed communication operations than the other actors. They have annual high-profile public events, especially their state-of-the-state addresses that are tailor-made for launching public proposals. And because state education agencies are typically not under their direct control, they can make bold proposals without fear of being held accountable for their implementation.

Given this context, it should not be surprising that gubernatorial-initiated policy proposals are seldom deeply grounded in a thoughtful analysis of the relevant research and experience. One of us, Robert Schwartz, had occasion in 2003 to get a first-hand view of the development of a gubernatorial-sponsored policy initiative. Although there are obvious dangers in attempting to generalize from one particular case, there are several features of this example that are illustrative of the process and circumstances under which gubernatorial policy proposals often arise. Our focus in this story is on the policy-making process and what it tells us about the challenge of bridging the gulf between that process and research-based evidence.

THE MINI–CASE STUDY

On October 29, 2003, readers of the *Boston Globe* learned that Massachusetts governor Mitt Romney planned to announce the appointment of a fourteen-member task force to address the problems of the state's role in underperforming school districts. Under an elaborate set of review procedures and criteria established in the commonwealth's education reform law, the commissioner of education was expected to recommend to the state board of education at its November meeting that at least two Massachusetts school districts be declared "underperforming." Although the Massachusetts Department of Education had some prior experience with intervention in low-performing schools, there were no policies or procedures in place to guide state action in districts declared to be underperforming.

The task force that the governor and his staff assembled was an impressive group. Chaired by the president of The Boston Foundation, it included, among others, the co-chairs of the Legislative Committee on Education, two respected urban superintendents, two former urban principals, the state's social services commissioner (a former New York deputy schools chancellor), and a state college president (and former state commissioner of education). It also included one of the two principal architects of the Massachusetts Education Reform Act (a former legislator then serving as chair of the Massachusetts Business Alliance for Education) and the then chair of the state board of education, who at the time also served as the governor's education policy adviser. Schwartz was asked to serve on the task force largely because of his prior experience as president of Achieve, a national organization created by governors and corporate leaders that conducts studies of state education policies.

At the first meeting of the task force (on November 24, about a month after the initial announcement), Governor Romney gave the group the following charge:

> Based on findings from research and practice, the task force will develop recommendations on state intervention in under-performing school districts. The work of the task force will focus on designing a framework for state-local partnerships, based on organizational and educational strategies that hold the greatest promise for strengthening schools and significantly raising student achievement. The goal of such collaborations is to enhance each district's internal capacity to effectively implement reforms and ensure continuous improvement. The task force will identify the essential elements of a district turnaround strategy, along with common barriers to successful implementation. The task force will also recommend where and how the state might add the most value to these new partnerships, and will consider any statutory or regulatory changes that may be required.

In addition to receiving the charge, the task force was informed that it had about a month to complete its work, since the governor wanted to include an appropriations request based on its recommendations in his January budget submission to the legislature (as it turned out, the final task force meeting was in mid-January). The group also learned that, while it would receive part-time staff support from the administrative assistant to the state board chair, it was essentially on its own for research support.

A few days before its first meeting, Schwartz was asked by the task force chair, Paul Grogan, to kick off the group's discussion by offering a short summary of what is known about the characteristics of effective school districts.

Grogan's idea was to help the group develop a shared conception of what a high-performing district looks like, to focus on an analysis of the barriers that constrain persistently low-performing districts from improving, and to then forge a state-sponsored strategy for helping such districts remove the barriers.

Grogan's decision to begin with a discussion of high-performing districts was based on the premise that there is in fact a substantial base of research and experience on this topic and that it would be relatively easy to secure consensus on a short list of key characteristics. His prediction was accurate. When Schwartz suggested at the end of the first meeting that it would be helpful to pull together what is known from the experience of other states that have attempted to intervene in low-performing districts, another member reported that his organization had undertaken such a search in the process of preparing a position paper on this topic and that there was little that Massachusetts could learn from others. This was the closest the task force came in its five meetings to a discussion of whether there was any relevant research or experience on the core question it had been asked to address: state intervention in underperforming districts.

As it happens, the briefing book prepared by the board of education staff person for the first meeting contained several relevant articles, including the executive summary of a study of New Jersey's takeover of the Newark School District; a summary of an intensive examination of six cases of state takeover and eight cases of mayoral governance control undertaken by Kenneth Wong and Francis Shen entitled "Do School District Takeovers Work?"; an excerpt from a Fordham Foundation report summarizing the types of intervention strategies attempted to date to fix failing schools; and a report from the Learning First Alliance on effective districtwide improvement strategies.[23] After the initial meeting, staff circulated a recent Kara Finnegan and Jennifer O'Day study of schools on probation in Chicago.[24] Of these several readings, only the Chicago study was ever referenced in the deliberations of the task force.

In reflecting on why research played such a marginal role in the work of the task force, there were at least three contributing factors. The first was the very tight timeline under which the group was working. In a more rational world, the development of state strategy for intervening in underperforming districts would have begun well in advance of the initial need to implement such a strategy, not on the eve of the first cases of intended state action. Given the press of daily events in a governor's office and the number of issues competing for gubernatorial attention, however, this kind of policy timeline is not uncommon. Even with a more leisurely timeline and more staff capacity available to support the work of the task force, the outcome might not have been much different, for it is not clear how much guidance a state could realistically derive from the available research.

While there is now an ample body of research and experience on intervention in low-performing *schools*, the literature is considerably sparser when it comes to districts, and little seemed relevant to the particulars of the Massachusetts situation. The task force member who dismissed the relevance of experience from other states was not entirely off the mark, for neither the financial bankruptcy examples in the literature nor the "educational bankruptcy" takeovers in three New Jersey cities seemed very applicable to the Massachusetts situation.

This leads to the third, and most important, reason why research had so little bearing on the deliberations of the task force: the power of context. For better or worse, most members were deeply grounded in the specifics of education reform in Massachusetts. They understood the political dynamics at play in the first two underperforming districts and in the next wave of districts likely to be so designated.[25] They also understood that the Department of Education was fully stretched in carrying out its current responsibilities under the commonwealth's education reform law and had virtually no capacity to provide on-the-ground assistance to troubled districts. They also knew that Massachusetts had a rich array of nongovernmental resources that might be tapped for this purpose, given its wealth of higher education institutions, nonprofit education organizations, and management consulting firms.

In the final analysis, the principal recommendation of the task force— that Massachusetts create a cadre of individuals and organizations who could serve as "turnaround partners" with underperforming districts—drew much more heavily on local knowledge than on research-based evidence. In the real world of state policymaking, the combination of factors at play in this case—a politically driven timeline, a relatively weak research base, a belief in the uniqueness of the local context—closed off any possibility that evidence from the experience of other states would be seriously introduced into the task force deliberations. The challenge of injecting research-based evidence into the deliberations of bodies like this one, even with a more relaxed timeline, is not to be underestimated, especially when the research evidence is less than compelling.

SCHOLARSHIP AND POLICYMAKING: COMPETING CULTURES

If we stand back from the Massachusetts example and ask a more fundamental question about why state policy seems to be influenced so little by the findings of education research, at least part of the explanation may lie in the mismatch between the incentives for education research in the policy world versus the academic world. These differences manifest themselves along several different dimensions.

Time

The difference in the academic and policy timetables contributes to the mismatch in the two worlds. While academicians and researchers often find themselves on rushed deadlines and hectic schedules, the "hurry-up-and-wait" nature of journal and book publishing—with the seemingly endless draft, revision, review, re-revision, and press time—contributes to an overall pace suited to one with great endurance and patience. And while policymaking is not exactly done in triage, it hardly can wait the standard year to eighteen months it might take a university scholar to release findings. Yet academicians are often discouraged from publishing original findings anywhere other than in peer-reviewed scholarly journals, since it is these journals that have the most professional currency among their colleagues and when tenure review time approaches.

Audience

In addition to time, education researchers write scholarly articles for other researchers, sometimes for practitioners, and rarely for policymakers. Journal articles often publish research studies with rigorous but complex designs and with interesting but complicated findings. Editors encourage detailed discussion of the analytic framework of the inquiry, the methodology, the analysis, and the findings. Researchers often describe the contributions their work makes to the knowledge base and the implications for future research. However, researchers rarely address in detail that which is actually most important to policymakers: the implications and recommendations for policy based on a contextualized discussion of the findings. Forty-page academic articles are not easily digested by policymakers or their aides; the language, and, in fact, the journals themselves are not easily accessed by those who make policy decisions.

Complexity

Finally, in scholarly work, there is a premium on nuance and complexity. Rarely do research studies guided by straightforward questions and answered with simple statistics get published in research journals. Instead, findings are complicated and context dependent. There is nuance and inference and conjecture involved. Researchers try to be measured in their analysis and even-handed in their conclusions. They are appropriately cautious about posing unequivocal policy recommendations from their work, thus often leading to the less-than-satisfying conclusion "it all depends." In fact, even in those rare instances when research seems to be definitive, context variables and poorly conceived implementation can doom adaptation in alternative settings.

Reiterating the "Two Culture" Problem

The problem of the two cultures cannot be minimized, for as long as research-ers and policymakers operate under such different systems of incentives and rewards, there will continue to be a gulf between the two communities. But in our conversations with leading policy researchers and state-level policy advisers, we are encouraged by the shared recognition of the importance of finding better ways of introducing evidence into the policy process. People in both communities offered examples of recent research findings that have quickly made their way into state policy discussions; a notable example is the work of Richard Ingersoll and Susan Moore Johnson and colleagues on teacher turnover, induction, and support.[26] The Internet has clearly had a huge impact on shortening the cycle from publication to dissemination, as has *Education Week*, which was in its infancy at the time of the Cohen survey.

In an American Educational Research Association (AERA) talk in 2000 entitled "Education Policy: What Role for Research?" Susan Fuhrman offered a compelling explanation of three major sets of studies that had such a sig-nificant impact on policy: the Perry Preschool research, the STAR class-size study, and the reading study of the National Institute of Child Health and Development. In her view, these studies

- addressed an important topic,
- confirmed conventional wisdom,
- had preexisting constituencies,
- were led by persuasive policy brokers,
- were longitudinal,
- were successfully replicated, and
- produced usable research syntheses.[27]

The importance of policy brokers was a theme that recurred in our con-versations with people in the field. For state policymakers, the messenger seems to be at least as important as the message. Several researchers in the Consortium for Policy Research in Education (CPRE)—e.g., Susan Fuhrman,

Tom Corcoran, Richard Elmore, Michael Kirst, and Allan Odden—show up repeatedly at the national and regional meetings of the state-based membership organizations and in state capitals. While their credibility with state policy advisers is based primarily on the quality and relevance of their work, it is not incidental that several of them have worked inside government, and all have had considerable experience interacting with state policy leaders.[28]

In addition to his role at CPRE, Kirst has for the past twenty years served as codirector of the preeminent state policy center Policy Analysis for California Education (PACE).[29] PACE is funded by a combination of foundation grants and state government contracts and is jointly led by senior professors from the University of California and Stanford University. In many ways, PACE exemplifies the kind of long-term partnership between state education policymakers and policy researchers and analysts that critics of the research community call for. Because its core operating support is private (mostly from the William and Flora Hewlett Foundation), it has been able to maintain sufficient independence to publish periodic reports entitled *Conditions of Education in California*, a publication whose contents are often less than flattering to the state. PACE also undertakes independent analyses of such controversial public policy initiatives as the 1993 statewide voucher initiative, smaller scale analyses of policy proposals on a wide range of topics, and occasional evaluations of state reform programs.

In describing PACE's work, Kirst points to five dimensions that influence the fate of efforts to disseminate research findings to policymakers and practitioners.[30] The first is the *source* of communication. Kirst argues that the fact that he and his senior PACE colleagues have had substantial state governmental experience and are very familiar with the political culture of Sacramento gives their work credibility with state policymakers.

A second dimension is the *communication channel*. Here Kirst discusses the importance of building policy issue networks around specific issues. The best national example of such an issue network was the school finance network built by the Ford Foundation in the 1970s, in which lawyers, economists, and policy analysts forged strategies that led to greater finance equity in several states.

A third dimension is *format*, and here Kirst underscores the value of moving beyond the typical technical research report to short, pithy, jargon-free policy briefs. PACE does not limit itself to the written word, always seeking opportunities to provide oral briefings to busy policymakers. PACE also uses the media to get its message out to policymakers, both through op-ed pieces and issue briefings for reporters and editorial writers.

A fourth dimension is the *message* itself, and here Kirst emphasizes the importance of crafting the message to fit the user's context. This leads to the final dimension, which is the importance of understanding the *characteristics of the recipients*. This kind of knowledge can only be developed out of extended back-and-forth conversations between the research producers and the intended consumers, a strategy PACE invests in heavily.

FINAL THOUGHTS

The PACE example is both inspiring and sobering—inspiring in the relationships it has built and sustained between education research and education policymakers and sobering in that, despite its work, education policymaking in California over the past two decades has hardly been exemplary. The California story is yet another reminder of the power of ideology and politics in the policymaking process.[31]

But there are important lessons to be derived from the work of PACE, CPRE, and other thoughtful policy research organizations, lessons that if carefully applied could, over time, begin to narrow the divide at the state level between research and policy. One is that, even absent a PACE-like organization, states can create venues where researcher and policymakers come together regularly to exchange information and ideas and to generate a user-driven agenda for future work. A second lesson is for states and universities together to invest in the development of a next generation of policy brokers. This could involve identifying talented young analysts or advisers in state government who might be recruited into specially designed graduate programs or providing funded internships in state government for promising doctoral candidates. On the university side, if policy brokering is to be seen as a worthy professional activity, it must be given legitimacy in the promotion and tenure process. Similarly, if replication studies and research syntheses are important factors in influencing state policymakers to act on research findings, then these kinds of projects need to be valued more highly within the academy. Our bottom-line conclusion is that the yawning gulf between research and policymaking can only be bridged by a bold, concerted, deliberate realignment of structures, incentives, and ways of doing business in both research and policymaking institutions.

CHAPTER 3

What's the Evidence on Districts' Use of Evidence?

Cynthia E. Coburn, Meredith I. Honig, and Mary Kay Stein

Contemporary education policies of various types increasingly demand that school district central offices use "evidence," variously defined, to ground their educational improvement efforts. In the 1980s and 1990s, the standards-based reform movement pushed school systems to assess student performance against federal, state, and local standards and to use student data to guide their choices of improvement strategies. More recently, the federal No Child Left Behind (NCLB) Act[1] has significantly raised the profile and the stakes of student-achievement data as well as the importance of research-based programs. School districts are required to collect and analyze standardized test data and disaggregate them according to ethnicity, free- and reduced-price lunch status, special education, and language status. NCLB further requires that in order to receive Title I funds, districts must be able to show that curriculum adoption, instructional programs, professional development, and other forms of support to schools are rooted in "scientifically based research." Thus, the use of evidence in district central office decision-making is emerging as a critical arena of educational leadership and administrative practice. But what do we know about districts' use of evidence? And what does that suggest for the promise and prospect of current attempts to encourage districts to use evidence in their ongoing practice?

In this chapter, we turn to the research literature for answers. Drawing on a comprehensive review of research on evidence use in school district central offices, we argue that central office administrators do use evidence in their decisionmaking but in ways that stretch much beyond the model promoted by recent federal policy. Rather than the linear model of decisionmaking assumed in policy design, the actual process by which district personnel draw on research is a complex and at times messy one that is mediated by individual and collective interpretation and is shaped in fundamental ways by organizational and political conditions. We further argue that it is only by understanding the underlying processes of decisionmaking and the conditions that shape how decisionmaking unfolds in complex social and political systems that we can begin to craft policies and interventions that can help districts realize the promise of evidence use. To that end, we offer key lessons for encouraging evidence use in districts—lessons that are rooted in the understanding of the social process of evidence use in school districts that our literature review has uncovered.

This chapter draws on a comprehensive review of research literature related to district central offices and evidence use. Given our charge, we limited our search to publications related to district central office staff (e.g., superintendents as well as midlevel and frontline administrators) and deliberately did not include research on elected officials, such as school board members. After an exhaustive and systematic search of the literature, we ultimately identified fifty-two books, peer-reviewed articles, and academic conference papers that were relevant to the questions of which evidence central office administrators use in their decisionmaking and the process by which they use it.[2] These works formed the basis for our analysis. Members of the research team read through each article, wrote summaries, and coded the articles. We then assessed the articles for key themes and characteristics of evidence use in school districts, as well as places where there were controversies and contradictions in the research.

EVIDENCE USE IN DISTRICT CENTRAL OFFICES: TOWARD A MORE COMPLEX PORTRAIT

As evidence from the business world accumulates on the benefits of using evidence in decisionmaking as a way to improve organizational performance, policymakers and others have increasingly called for school districts to use evidence more routinely and systematically in their decisionmaking. Yet underneath the calls for school districts to use evidence exists a set of assumptions about the nature of evidence and evidence use that may not accurately reflect the realities of decisionmaking in public bureaucracies such as school districts. More specifically, federal policy initiatives rest on assumptions that there is a relatively straightforward and linear pathway between evidence and district decisions intended to improve educational outcomes. That is, they assume that evidence is clear, unambiguous, and available; that decision makers use evidence in an instrumental fashion, weighing the merits of alternate courses of action and choosing the solutions that best fit the problem; and therefore that evidence leads directly to decisions.[3]

However, our review of existing research on evidence use in district central offices suggests that the process is much more complex than perceptions of evidence use in recent policy would suggest. First, appropriate evidence is not always available to central office decision makers for a variety of organizational and political reasons. Second, even if the appropriate evidence is available, evidence does not speak for itself; rather, it must be accessed, noticed, and interpreted as it is used, and these underlying processes of evidence use are mediated by individual and collective beliefs and worldviews. Third, two decades of research on the role of evidence in district decisionmaking reveals a host of roles for evidence that go beyond those imagined by the instrumental model of decisionmaking. Finally, our review suggests that all aspects of this process are profoundly and perhaps necessarily shaped by the organizational and political context within which they unfold. In the subsections that follow, we elaborate on each of these arguments in turn. Rather than have a separate section on the role of organizational and political contexts, we weave our discussion throughout, emphasizing how these factors shape each facet of the relationship between evidence and decisionmaking.

THE NATURE OF EVIDENCE

With the rise of accountability policy and increased emphasis on scientifically based research, school districts increasingly find themselves inundated with evidence. Social science and evaluation research are becoming an increasingly prominent part of the district landscape. There is so much data that some districts are overwhelmed by it.[4] However, despite these trends, district administrators often lack the *right* evidence—evidence that addresses the question or issue at hand in a form they can access and use at the time that they need it. District administrators have a particularly difficult time accessing findings from research or evaluation studies. Often there are not studies that address the pressing issues that the district is grappling with, and when the studies do exist, they may not be easy for district leaders to find and access.[5] Existing studies may also present contradictory findings or come in a form that district administrators find too abstract or technical, providing little concrete guidance for decisionmaking and action.[6] There are also problems with achievement data. Data are not always in a form that allows district administrators to answer the questions they have. For example, the state of California does not collect data using unique student identifiers, thus it is not possible to track individual student progress over time, limiting the kinds of questions that district administrators in California can ask of their data.

These problems of access and availability are exacerbated by a serious mismatch between the rapid pace of decisionmaking in districts and the relatively slow process by which research and evaluation findings and, in some cases, test scores are released.[7] For example, in their study of evidence use in three midsize urban districts, Corcoran and colleagues found that even district central office staff inclined to engage in evidence-based decisionmaking often made decisions about program adoption in the absence of evidence.[8] The district central office administrators reported that they could not wait for evaluation results or pilot studies before acting given intense pressure to respond to pressing needs or the need to appear decisive.

Organizational and Political Factors That Shape Availability

The nature and availability of evidence in a given district is influenced by features of the local organizational and political context. At the most basic level, district central office administrators are unable to use data in decisionmaking when they lack the technological infrastructure to access it. Although there has been considerable effort in the last decade to develop the local technical capacity to create adequate access to data, many districts still fall short in this regard.[9] But beyond technical infrastructure, access to data and evaluation may also be related to the position of the research office vis-à-vis central office decision makers. In some districts, the research office is a separate and often marginalized unit. In these situations, decision makers may not have access to data or research when they are making decisions, even if the evidence actually exists in another part of the district central office.[10] Access to research depends in part on the available research resources in the local community. Districts vary greatly in both the presence of universities or independent research organizations in their community and the nature of their connections to these organizations.[11] Finally, in recent years there have been increased efforts to address issues of availability of high-quality research using public policy. The What Works Clearinghouse is one of a number of efforts funded by the federal government to create a synthesis of research findings on key topics of interest to educational leaders and to disseminate them widely. It will be important to track the extent to which these initiatives influence local districts' access to high-quality research that helps them to address their pressing needs.

Social Processes That Underlie Evidence Use: Search and Interpretation

Even if the appropriate evidence is available and accessible in a timely manner, district central office personnel must still look for it, notice it, and attend to it—a set of processes that some scholars call "search." How the search process proceeds is crucial because it shapes what evidence is even considered by district personnel. Furthermore, evidence does not speak for itself; district personnel must interpret and make meaning of it in order to use it. Both of these processes—search and interpretation—are influenced by individuals' preexisting beliefs and experiences. In this section, we review the research on these two social processes that underlie evidence use. We then discuss the organizational and political factors that shape them.

Search

Studies of district central office administrators suggest that their search processes are active and continual, in that district personnel are continually seeking information from a wide range of internal and external sources.[12] However, search can also be unsystematic and shaped in profound ways by preexisting beliefs and knowledge. Kennedy found that the district administrators in her study "tended to look indiscriminately at everything that came their way and . . . could not describe exactly what it was they were looking at."[13] Studies consistently show that central office administrators tend to search for and pay greater attention to evidence that resembles what they already know and expect to find.[14] This happens at a very subtle level as it influences what administrators notice as they review data or research studies. Simply put, administrators tend to see aspects of the data or research that support their beliefs, assumptions, and experiences and do not notice those aspects of the data that might contradict or challenge these beliefs. This phenomenon may be exacerbated during conditions of data overload that many districts are currently experiencing. Under these conditions, administrators, like other decision makers, tend to narrow the range of evidence they pay attention to because they simply cannot attend to it all given the real limits of their time and attention.[15] All of this suggests that rather than evidence leading directly to decisionmaking, it is always mediated by the individual worldviews that shape search.

Interpretation

Once a given piece of evidence has been "found," decision makers engage in a process through which they decide whether and how to use the information. Spillane and others have referred to this process as "sensemaking" or "interpretation."[16] Sensemaking theorists argue that the meaning of information is not self-evident; rather, individuals need to construct their understanding of the meaning and implications of evidence at hand. They do this by fitting new information into their preexisting understandings or cognitive frameworks.[17] Kennedy calls these frameworks "working knowledge," or "the organized body of knowledge that administrators and policymakers use spontaneously and routinely in the context of their work. It includes the entire array of beliefs, assumptions, interests, and experiences that influence the behavior of individuals at work."[18]

Thus, like search, interpretation of evidence is mediated by an individual's beliefs and experiences. In fact, Kennedy reports that in her close analysis of instances of decisionmaking in sixteen districts, she found no instance where evidence had an independent influence on decisionmaking. Rather, decisions were always influenced by individual and group interpretations of evidence, which in turn were influenced by working knowledge.[19] As with search, this can be a subtle process. For example, Kennedy illustrates how working knowledge shapes interpretation by showing how district central office administrators in one district interpreted low rates of college attendance among students as pointing to a need for increased vocational education options. The administrators then used the interpretation—the need for vocational education—rather than the statistics themselves as the basis for subsequent policy decisions. But the influence of working knowledge on interpretation can also be stark. Study after study reports that district administrators tend to discount various forms of evidence when the evidence does not support their preexisting beliefs.[20] For example, in her study of the use of Title I evaluations in fifteen districts, David found that district administrators consistently discounted evaluations that challenged their perceptions of the programs, questioning their validity, the appropriateness of the methodology and measures, and the degree to which the evaluations measured valued outcomes.

When central office administrators interpret evidence, they also tend to simplify it.[21] Central office administrators rarely receive information in discrete, manageable packages. Rather, they face complex pieces of evidence that may be interpreted in a variety of ways, none of which point unambiguously to how to strengthen objective performance outcomes. In such situations, district administrators appear to focus on discrete pieces of information that they understand or believe they understand at the sacrifice of others. Similarly, district central office administrators may break multiple complex pieces of evidence into component parts.[22]

While some important aspects of evidence may be lost as part of this process, simplification may be an inevitable part of the interpretation process given the limits of time and attention.[23] Simplification may in fact enable evidence use because it converts evidence into a form that district central office administrators may actually be able to apprehend and find relevant to their decisionmaking. In her study of district central office administrators involved in school-community partnerships in Oakland, California, Honig shows how central office administrators were able and willing to use evidence in these ways when they translated complex local challenges into discrete, familiar action steps.[24]

In summary, evidence-based decisionmaking is sometimes framed as an antidote for ideology-driven decisionmaking. However, as the research base makes clear, people make decisions precisely by drawing on what might be considered ideology—including their prior knowledge—as a fundamental part of the decisionmaking process.

Organizational and Political Factors Shaping Search and Interpretation

Thus far, we have emphasized the ways in which search and interpretation are mediated by individual working knowledge and cognitive capacity. However, district administrators are engaging with evidence within a complex organization that is located in a broader and often highly political environment. These organizational and political contexts create conditions that appear to shape search and interpretation in important ways.

First, the search and interpretation processes are influenced by the organizational structure of the district. Typically, decisionmaking in districts is a profoundly social process. It is highly interactive, involving many people in and across a series of meetings (e.g., task forces, committees, teams) and informal conversations that stretch over time.[25] The organizational structure of the district—the configuration of subunits and task forces—influences who tends to interact with whom in the course of their daily work. This is significant because people develop shared beliefs and understandings as they interact with one another, including common ways of framing problems, common understandings about the nature of different demands, and common images of particular programs. These shared ways of thinking can subsequently influence both search and interpretation.[26] For example, in their longitudinal case study of decisionmaking in one midsize urban district, Coburn and Talbert found that individuals in different subunits in the same district central office had very different understandings about what constituted valid evidence, high-quality research, and appropriate evidence use.[27] In the absence of formal structures or a tradition of interaction across units, people in units developed shared understandings that grew further and further apart over time. As a result, people in different units interpreted findings on the efficacy of particular instructional approaches (both research findings and performance data from schools) in dramatically different ways. This suggests that organizational structure is likely to shape patterns of interaction in ways that influence how district personnel interpret research evidence and data.

Search is also influenced by political pressures.[28] Decisionmaking in districts exists in highly politicized and highly changeable environments.[29] District central offices have multiple constituencies to serve and multiple layers of governance—above as well as below—to whom they must be responsive. Multiple interest groups inside and outside the district with different stakes and, at times, different values pressure district administrators to make particular decisions. These political pressures appear to play an important role in search processes as the very decision to seek further evidence or commission an evaluation study can emerge from political motivations.[30] Political processes also shape search in a more subtle way. Shifts in political circumstances often bring new issues to the fore, changing perceptions about what is important to pay attention to. As new issues become salient, district administrators notice and attend to different sources of information. For example, Kennedy recounts how political controversy relating to personnel matters brought a longstanding program to the attention of district staff in one of the districts in her study.[31] In the course of addressing the personnel issue, staff noticed and attended to previously "dormant" evidence. Thus, political processes shifted notions of what was important to pay attention to, which in turn raised the profile of certain kinds of evidence and not others.

Role of Evidence in Decisionmaking

We have just discussed the microprocesses that underlie evidence use and the political and organizational factors that shape how these processes unfold. Here, we take a step back and look at the overall role that evidence plays in how central office administrators make decisions. We organize our discussion by drawing on categories that have been developed by scholars of evaluation use over the last two decades. These scholars typically identify four roles that evidence plays in decisionmaking: instrumental role, conceptual role, symbolic role, and no role.[32] Recent work by Carol Weiss and colleagues argues that new demands by the federal government that districts adopt programs that are certified to be rooted in scientifically based research has created a new role for evidence, a sanctioning role.[33] Here, we use these categories to analyze the research on how district central office administrators use evidence in their decisionmaking. We then discuss how political and organizational conditions influence how and when district administrators use evidence in one manner rather than another.

Instrumental Role

When policymakers exhort districts to use evidence in their decisionmaking, they often seem to envision that evidence will play an instrumental role. That is, they imagine that district administrators will use evidence directly and centrally to provide guidance to decisions related to policy or practice.[34] Weiss describes the image of instrumental use in the following way: "A problem exists; information or understanding is lacking either to generate a solution to the problem or to select among alternative solutions; research [or other forms of evidence] provides the missing knowledge; a solution is reached."[35]

However, our review of research suggests that it is not common for evidence to play such a role. In Kennedy's in-depth analysis of fourteen decisions made by central office administrators in sixteen districts, only two decisions appear to have been made by using data or evaluation research to directly inform decisions.[36] Similarly, David's analysis of thirty-five decisions related to Title I in fifteen districts found that only one-quarter of these decisions involved the use of evaluation data to make changes in their programs, and most of those changes were relatively minor.[37] In their study of the role of overwhelmingly negative evaluations of the drug abuse–prevention program DARE, Weiss and colleagues identified only three out of sixteen districts that used the results of the evaluation in an instrumental fashion, closing down their programs specifically in response to the negative evaluations. However, even in these instances, the influence was not always direct, as it was often long-delayed and diluted.[38] Finally, Corcoran and colleagues found that only one of three districts in their study was able to institute structures and procedures such that they could draw on research evidence in their decisions about curriculum or program adoption.[39]

It is important to note that even when evidence does play an instrumental role in decisionmaking, the interpretive processes described earlier are still at play. For example, Kennedy reports that the two decisions in her study where evidence was used instrumentally involved what she described as "rather creative interpretation of the evidence."[40] Furthermore, evidence is rarely the sole factor that central office administrators consider when making a decision in this manner. They also consider budgetary issues, political issues, and administrative issues along with evidence use. Thus, there is not a one-to-one relationship between evidence and decision, even in situations where evidence seems to play an instrumental role.[41]

Conceptual Role

To say that evidence is rarely used in an instrumental fashion in decision-making is not to say it is not used at all. Research outside of education suggests that in fact the most common role that evidence plays in policymaking is what Weiss calls "conceptual use"—that is, interaction with evidence provides decision makers with new ideas, new concepts, or new generalizations that influence how they view the nature of the problem.[42] Thus, evidence plays a role in influencing individual and shared working knowledge, even when it does not influence a specific decision.

It is difficult to ascertain the frequency with which evidence plays a conceptual role in decisionmaking because most studies of evidence use at the district level have not paid attention to it. However, we have hints about its importance in the few studies that do attend to this phenomenon. In their survey of forty superintendents, deputy superintendents, and assistant superintendents in Delaware, Fillos and Bailey report that 78 percent of these individuals reported that evidence typically provides general background information on various issues rather than guiding particular decisions.[43] Weiss and colleagues report even more dramatic findings in their study of school district responses to negative evaluations of the DARE program. They argue that fifteen of sixteen districts showed evidence of conceptual use of DARE evaluations in that extensive media coverage of the evaluations caused individuals in districts to develop a sense of the approach as ineffective. Thus, the evaluation studies (through the widespread media coverage of their findings) influenced how people thought about the program, even in cases where it did not directly influence a decision in the short term. Sometimes the manner in which researchers conceptualize their studies—rather than the findings themselves—can play a role in how administrators think about their work and the issues at hand. In this case, research provides a fresh perspective on long-standing problems or a new language for communicating about experienced but unarticulated patterns of practice.[44]

Conceptual use of evidence is a potentially powerful way for research and data to become a part of ongoing district practice. If, as we have suggested, evidence is always mediated by individuals' working knowledge, then a key way to influence decisionmaking is to influence the working knowledge of those who are involved in the decisionmaking process. Yet, policy makers and many researchers rarely acknowledge this role for evidence at all, which potentially leads to an underestimation of the degree to which evidence actually plays a role in district central offices and a lack of attention to potential avenues for encouraging a role of evidence so defined.[45]

Symbolic Role

District central office administrators also use research and data to justify pre-existing preferences or action. Weiss refers to this usage as "symbolic" because the main function of the evidence is to create legitimacy for solutions that are already favored or even enacted.[46] Multiple studies show that evidence frequently plays this role in central office administrators' decisionmaking.[47] For example, in one account, Robinson described how central office administrators used social science research in school board presentations to influence opinions, even when that research was not used directly to inform the development, selection, or implementation of those programs. Kennedy reports that evidence was used to justify decisions that were already made in seven out of the fourteen decisions in her study. Weiss and colleagues document symbolic use of research in four out of sixteen districts. Finally, Corcoran and colleagues found symbolic use to be widespread in the three districts in their study. They describe as a typical pattern, "The champions of specific reforms typically examined literature selectively and found theories and 'evidence' to justify their approaches, or they recruited 'experts' who were advocates of the preferred strategy."[48]

Although it may be less intuitive, symbolic use may facilitate other, more substantive forms of evidence use. Because decisionmaking in districts is often a profoundly social process, it is enabled by the development of shared understandings and common ways of framing the problem. District decision makers may use evidence symbolically to generate such shared understandings.[49] Furthermore, symbolic use may be a necessary feature of moving improvement agendas forward in the complex political environment that comes with being a public institution, since research-based decisions can backfire without adequate attention to political considerations of the environment.[50] For example, Massell and Goertz report an instance where district staff adopted a research-based curriculum without considering or planning for the potential opposition among the teaching staff.[51] When the test scores declined in the first year (a predictable outcome for new and challenging curricula), individuals who had been opposed to its adoption used the decrease in test scores to organize opposition and eventually cause the district to stop using the curriculum. Massell and Goertz argue that greater attention to political realities might have led to a different decision or a different approach to implementation.

Sanctioning Role

Given increased federal and state requirements that school districts use programs that have particular kinds of research evidence, we may see an increased incidence of districts adopting policies or practices solely because the programs meet this mandate.[52] Evidence plays an interesting role in this process. Typically, district decision makers themselves do not review research and evidence. Rather, individuals at the state or federal level review available evidence on program effectiveness and use it to create lists of programs that are deemed "research-based" and thus approved for use with state or federal funds. District personnel choose programs from these lists in order to receive federal or state funding.[53] We call this new role for evidence *sanctioning*. In their study of sixteen school districts, Weiss and colleagues identified two districts in which evidence played a sanctioning role in the decision to discontinue DARE.[54] These districts discontinued DARE and selected other programs not because they believed negative evaluation findings but because the other programs were on the list of approved programs and DARE was not. Thus, evidence was used to sanction some choices and not others, which shaped district decisions about program adoption.

It is important to note that in this scenario, evidence has only a limited opportunity to influence district administrators' working knowledge, because district personnel do not read or review the evidence themselves but instead rely on those who have created the lists. Indeed, in Weiss's study several districts adopted programs that they did not particularly support solely as a way to maintain their federal funding, suggesting that the act of picking a program from a list did little to shape their view of the problem or appropriate solutions.

No Role

Finally, there is also evidence that districts often make decisions without reference to research, evaluation findings, or systematic data.[55] In David's analysis of thirty-five decisions about Title I programs, 25 percent of all decisions were made on the basis of political or financial concerns alone. An additional one-third of the decisions were based on what David calls "subjective information," which she defines as impressions or anecdotal information. Thus, evaluation findings played no role in well over half of the thirty-five decisions in the study.[56] Kennedy reports that five out of fourteen decisions were made without any reference to research or systematic data.[57] Similarly, in their exploration of why six districts continued to use the DARE program in spite of uniformly negative evaluations, Birkeland and colleagues found that individuals in these districts dismissed the evaluation either because they thought the evaluations measured the wrong outcomes or because they had anecdotal information that suggested that the program was working in their district.[58] Thus, their decision to continue to use the DARE program was based on other considerations rather than on the results of the evaluation studies. Finally, Corcoran and colleagues suggest that the degree to which district personnel use research or data in their decisionmaking may be related to the kind of decision they are making.[59] In his study of three districts, one out of three used such evidence in curriculum adoption, and all three used it in evaluating internal initiatives; but none used research evidence or data while making decisions about professional development.

Organizational and Political Factors Shaping the Role of Evidence

When and under what conditions do school district personnel use evidence in one manner versus another? At least three factors seem to play a role: political pressures, organizational capacity, and public policy.

As discussed earlier, decisionmaking in district central offices unfolds in highly politicized environments. Political pressures sometimes push district administrators away from using evidence altogether (no role) since district staff sometimes make decisions that contradict evidence in order to be responsive to these political realities.[60] Thus, even if individuals in the district interpret the evidence in ways that support a particular action, they may not feel able to take action given a prevailing political situation. District staff may also respond to political pressure by using evidence in a symbolic manner as a way to bolster the legitimacy of their position or generate support for a course of action.[61]

Interestingly, advocates of research-based programs and evidence-based decisionmaking often position their use as an antidote to overly politicized and ideological decisionmaking on the part of school and district leaders.[62]

Yet it appears that research and evidence do not take decisionmaking so much as they become tools in the very political processes they are meant to circumvent.

Organizational capacity also influences how district personnel use evidence in their decisionmaking. Evidence-based decisionmaking asks district central office administrators to play new and sometimes unfamiliar roles. Demands to use data as part of accountability requirements, for example, require a shift in orientation from collecting data for compliance reporting to the government (using evidence in a symbolic manner) to collecting data and making it accessible to inform ongoing decisionmaking (instrumental role). Evidence use also requires research literacy and skill in data analysis and interpretation. However, many districts appear to lack these capacities, which frustrates their attempts to use evidence in decisionmaking.[63]

District personnel also seem more likely to use evidence in instrumental or conceptual ways when district culture and norms encourage it. For example, in their study of three district central offices, Corcoran and colleagues found that evidence use was greater in district central offices and subunits within district central offices where norms, expectations, and routines supported ongoing engagement with empirical research.[64] They also showed that evidence played a minor role in decisionmaking in district central office subunits that did not maintain such norms and expectations.

Finally, public policy appears to be increasingly influential in raising the profile of data and research in school districts. Multiple studies report a greater role for data at the central office level in the wake of high-stakes accountability policies. For example, Massell reports that since passage of state accountability policies in the mid 1990s, the majority of the twenty-three school districts in her study had begun to use student performance data as a regular part of decisionmaking, at least in some of the ways discussed above. Similarly, requirements that tie federal funds to programs that are identified as "research-based" appear to have increased the adoption of those programs, if not the direct use of evidence in making the selection.[65]

However, policy that encourages data use or the use of "scientifically based" research does not guarantee that districts will use research and data in instrumental or conceptual ways. For example, early studies of evaluation use showed that federal mandates to participate in Title I greatly increased the number of evaluations that district central offices conducted but did not increase the degree to which districts actually used them to inform program improvement. Similarly, in their longitudinal case study of one district's attempts to foster evidence-based practice, Coburn and colleagues found that increased policy pressure to use research in decisionmaking led to increased symbolic use rather than increased instrumental use of social science research.[66] District administrators increasingly used the language of research ("research says") to justify their preexisting positions rather than actually reviewing and drawing on findings in their decisionmaking.

Public policy seems to foster instrumental and conceptual use only to the degree that it helps build or reinforce the capacity for central office administrators to use data and research in this manner. For example, Massell found that districts were more likely to respond to accountability policy by using data in substantive rather than symbolic ways when they had local norms that supported instrumental use, including a philosophy that saw data as a key lever for system improvement. Without such capacity, it appears likely that districts respond to calls for evidence use in uneven, symbolic, or superficial ways or fall back on old patterns of engaging with data and research that work against evidence use.[67] The question, of course, is how policy can build this capacity in places where it does not exist.

LESSONS FOR ENCOURAGING EVIDENCE USE AT THE DISTRICT LEVEL

Given what we know about the complexity of the evidence-use process and the factors that shape it, what steps can be taken to help school district central offices enhance their use of various forms of evidence in their decisionmaking with the goal of helping improve their performance? Our review suggests several answers.

Lesson 1: Collaboration with External Organizations Can Facilitate Access to the "Right" Evidence

Earlier we discussed the challenges that districts face in accessing, noticing, and otherwise obtaining research and data. Collaboration with external organizations and researchers can help facilitate this access. These connections can be a particularly effective means of accessing information and interpreting it in ways that meet local district needs. They also can provide schools and districts access to social science research, research-based practice, and practices for gathering and analyzing local data. These organizations often have credibility with school and district personnel because they are able to integrate research knowledge with an awareness of local needs and conditions, thus supporting its effective use.[68]

Collaborations with researchers can also mitigate some of the challenges of access and relevance. When researchers and district personnel collaborate to design research and evaluation studies, it is more likely that the research will address issues that are relevant to the district. Ongoing conversation about findings between researchers and key stakeholders can also bring research to decision makers' attention and provide opportunities for researchers to help create links between findings and district personnel's preexisting beliefs and understandings. For example, Bickel and Cooley describe how their long-term research partnership with a large urban school district led to these outcomes.[69] Because they involved top-level district leaders in decisions about the focus and design of the study, the officials were more likely to pay close attention to the findings. They also engaged in in-depth discussions about the findings with individuals at multiple levels of the central office over the course of the project. These conversations provided the opportunity for the researchers to check their interpretations, and to learn how to frame findings so that they were meaningful to the people in the district. As a result of their efforts, their findings played a key role in policymaking in the district.

Lesson 2: Districts Can Develop Structures or Processes to Fund and Support Search

Another way to ensure that districts access the evidence that they need is to take deliberate steps to support the search process. As discussed earlier, search processes in central offices are typically active and continuous but can be unsystematic, since district personnel look at whatever crosses their desk and tend to notice only those things that confirm their preexisting beliefs. Two strategies for deliberately supporting search emerged in our review of the literature. First, districts may be able to lessen the degree of haphazardness and the overall intensiveness of the search process by designating particular people to be responsible for search. Honig reports on one district's use of this approach.[70] This district designated specific central office administrators to specialize in search. These administrators spent a majority of their workday with their evidence sources—school and community leaders—to gather information about implementation progress. This division of labor among staff seemed to enable search by making it a regular responsibility of particular individuals who had the skills, inclinations, and resources that spanning organizational boundaries to collect information requires.

Second, districts can enable search by creating structured protocols to guide the process. Learning Walks, promoted by the Institute for Learning, are one such protocol. Learning Walks involve district administrators and school level leaders in structured observations of multiple classrooms to collect evidence about teaching practice and student learning. These walks are guided by observational protocols and rubrics, and district staff are encouraged to use the data they collect to inform decisionmaking about instruction and professional development at the school and district levels.[71] Research suggests that such standardized protocols for data gathering work best when there is a clear, coherent, well-articulated, and shared vision across the district regarding what good instruction looks like in order to guide how the people involved in learning walks interpret the evidence they collect.[72] That is, learning walks and other search strategies may be most effective when they function as tools to develop and sustain shared understandings of high-quality practice.

Lesson 3: Foster Conditions for Collective Interpretation

Individual and collective interpretation is at the heart of evidence use in school districts. While interpretation—and the central role of preexisting beliefs and understandings in shaping it—may be a fundamental part of the evidence-use process, it seems possible that districts could create conditions that mitigate the tendency to discount evidence that contradicts preexisting beliefs and working knowledge. The questions are: When and under what conditions can research and other forms of evidence be used in ways that help people question their assumptions and challenge their frames of reference rather than just provide a means to reinforce preexisting ways of doing things? And how can districts foster these conditions?

We know of no research that addresses these questions at the district level, but research on evidence use in schools is instructive. This work suggests that teachers are more likely to engage with new information in ways that cause them to question their assumptions when they engage with information in a social interaction, which, in turn, can foster greater access to expertise that exists within the system.[73] Furthermore, especially when it involves diverse points of view, social interaction around evidence requires participants to negotiate among and between diverse interpretations, which can bring to light assumptions and contribute to the development of shared understandings that move beyond individual ways of thinking. This process is more likely to push people to rethink their frames of reference when there is adequate time to delve deeply into the meaning and implications of the evidence and structured protocols for looking at evidence that helps people work through conflicts in interpretation.[74]

Structuring such conditions at the central office may prove challenging, given limited time and the complex organizational structure of school districts. District leaders must be able to create adequate time and focus for administrators to engage in the collective interpretation of evidence. Without adequate time to sift through and interpret evidence, this activity is likely to get swallowed up in the multiple time commitments, numerous priorities, and large amounts of information that characterize district administrators' work. District leaders must also consider how to organize and otherwise convene their staff around evidence in ways that are likely to increase its use.

The fact that district decisionmaking is often stretched across multiple workgroups or subunits poses something of a dilemma for district leaders. On the one hand, these subunits support evidence use by providing ongoing opportunities for people to gather and interpret various forms of information and to build a culture that is favorable to evidence use. Such group processes sometimes increase the expertise brought to bear on the evidence at hand and build trust among district staff, which is essential for exploring new possibilities. On the other hand, workgroups can become cut off from the rest of the central office in ways that limit the expertise brought to bear on particular decisions and that foster the development of dramatically different interpretations of the meaning and implications of common evidence. Particularly troubling is the tendency for the district research office to be cut off from decision makers in other areas of the district. This suggests that central office leaders must think carefully about how to convene key actors from different areas of the district to engage in conversation about the meaning and implication of research and data related to pressing district issues and needs.

Lesson 4: Develop Political Support for Evidence Use

Like interpretation, politics may be an inescapable part of decisionmaking in public organizations.[75] The question for those concerned with fostering evidence use is how to create conditions for ongoing and substantive evidence use in highly politicized and highly changeable environments. One possible answer is to create political support both for evidence use itself and for jointly developed interpretations and action steps. Marsh studied two mid-sized California school districts that attempted to build political support for evidence use.[76] These districts convened community-wide planning groups to examine and help interpret student performance data and to share their own evidence about the need for districtwide improvement and strategies for achieving it. In these school-community dialogues, district central office administrators drew on student performance data as well as parent-community input to craft both a districtwide improvement agenda and community and professional support for that agenda. Marsh shows how the high levels of trust between district central office administrators and community residents developed through this process helped to increase the availability of various forms of evidence, including community feedback, and marshaled the political support essential to certain district central office decisions.

Lesson 5: Develop New Strategies for Building Central Office Capacity for Evidence Use

If, as we have argued, capacity is key to fostering sustained and systematic evidence use at the central office, the key question is how to foster the development of capacity in districts where it does not yet exist. Existing research offers only limited answers to this question. Case studies of school districts that appear to use data in a consistent manner report that these districts invest in professional development on data use for individuals throughout the system, including those at the central office level.[77] However, these studies do not specify what this professional development might entail, nor do they evaluate it.

Our analysis of the social processes underlying evidence use provides some initial guidance for areas on which to focus capacity-building efforts. It suggests a central focus on interpreting and making meaning of various forms of evidence. This interpretation process is likely enabled with greater research literacy, including the ability to critically evaluate research studies, analyze and interpret relevant data, and draw implications for policy and practice. It is also likely enabled by content knowledge in the area that is the focus of decisionmaking.[78] Given the social nature of decisionmaking, district personnel also need to develop the ability to access expertise within and outside the district and to bring it to bear on decisions at hand. They also need the ability to develop structures and protocols that bring diverse individuals together to jointly negotiate a shared understanding of the meaning and implications of the evidence.

Using evidence in the ways we highlight requires profound shifts in the basic nature of central office administration. Our portrait suggests a model of central office administration that moves beyond standardization of practice to a more dynamic model of central office administrators as problem solvers in complex and sometimes ambiguous contexts. Central office administrators need new models of professional practice that include evidence use as part of their daily routines. They need different supports to take risks inherent in the endeavor. Ultimately, as Davies argues, in order for evidence to be used in an ongoing and substantive way, these capacities need to be integrated into notions of professional competence for district-level personnel.[79]

FINAL THOUGHTS

In recent years, educational policy has created new pressures and incentives for districts to use evidence to assess their policies and practices and to adopt improvement strategies rooted in research. Yet these policies seem to be based on a vision of evidence-based decisionmaking that assumes a direct linear relationship between the evidence and a decision that will improve educational outcomes. In contrast, the portrait of district central office evidence use that emerges in the research literature is much more complex, political, and nuanced than that suggested in policy designs. This portrait suggests that there are considerable challenges to providing districts with relevant evidence in the forms and within the timelines that they need it. Even if the appropriate evidence is available, the degree to which district administrators access it is shaped by the nature of their search processes. The available research also suggests that evidence, once noticed, is likely to play a range of roles that stretch far beyond the instrumental role envisioned by policymakers and that some of these additional roles may indeed be productive and thus should be encouraged. At the core of evidence use are interpretive processes whereby individuals and groups make meaning of evidence in ways that are profoundly shaped by their preexisting beliefs and practices and day-to-day limits on how they direct their attention. Finally, all of these processes are influenced by the structure and organization of district central offices as workplaces and the pressures and priorities in the environment.

As we begin to craft second-generation policies to encourage and support ongoing evidence use at the district level, we must begin to design policy strategies in ways that are rooted in research-informed understanding of the nature of decisionmaking in central offices. This suggests moving beyond a focus on creating greater availability of high-quality research to one supporting the development of district capacity to effectively engage in search activities so that district personnel attend to and access this research. The availability of appropriate research is a necessary, but not sufficient, condition for getting research into the hands of central office decision makers. It also suggests moving beyond incentives and mandates for evidence use to strategies that support the capacity of district central office administrators to engage with evidence in ways that influence their working knowledge and ability to effectively solve problems. Finally, it suggests crafting policy supports that help districts foster organizational and political conditions that are more conducive to substantive and ongoing evidence use.

Ultimately, unless policy makers, district leaders, and researchers find ways to effect some of the deeper processes involved in evidence use at the district level, it seems likely that the movement for evidence-based decision-making, like so many other reform efforts, will be taken up in substantive ways only by those districts with existing capacity and compatible cultures. We need new policy strategies carefully targeted to key capacities and organizational conditions in order to move beyond the level of "policy talk" to foster substantive and sustained evidence-based practices at the central offices in more than a handful of districts.[80]

The authors thank Tom Corcoran, Tom Hatch, Erin Murphy-Graham, and Deborah Stipek for comments on an earlier draft of this paper. We also thank Carolina Belalcazar and Mika Yamashita for research assistance and Marlene Mullin, Scott Mergl, and Michael O'Neill for administrative assistance. In addition to funds from the MacArthur Network on Teaching and Learning, this chapter was supported by the Spencer Foundation.

CHAPTER 4

Evidence-Informed Change and the Practice of Teaching

Andy Hargreaves and Corrie Stone-Johnson

Among all the contemporary initiatives in educational reform, one of the most common and compelling ideas is that changes and improvement efforts should be driven and supported by evidence of student learning. This quest for evidence comes from many sources: mounting dissatisfaction with the limited impact of successive prior reform efforts, a sense of urgency to increase standards of student learning, the drive to narrow the achievement gap between students from different cultures and backgrounds, and desires to strengthen the knowledge base of teaching in order to enhance professionalism and professional recognition among teachers.[1] However, people differ in what they mean by "evidence," in the kinds of evidence they demand as proof of successful practice, and in the status of evidence or certain kinds of evidence as justification for changes in practice compared to other sources of knowledge and insight.

The call for teaching and learning to be more evidence-based has not been without controversy. One view of evidence-based education has been that education should be a science or profession, much like medicine, with randomized trials and strict scientific research procedures producing guidelines for successful practice. In this view, the knowledge base for education has been weak.[2] Only strict adherence to scientifically rigorous and replicable research procedures will remedy this deficiency and produce evidence about what works, evidence that should then be applied in a systematic way (perhaps even by mandated means) to practice.

By contrast, many educators have argued that teachers have their own unique knowledge of the craft or art of teaching. This, they say, should define the knowledge base for education. Respected craft knowledge can be drawn on by those who are familiar with the school and its surrounding community and used by teams of teachers working in professional learning communities in their own settings.[3] In this second view, evidence-based strategies for successful teaching cannot be standardized or universalized but must vary and be adapted and contextualized according to the local needs and demands of particular groups of students and their schools.

Scientific or practical, general or local, universal or particular, top-down or bottom-up—these are the polarities that typically accompany debates about evidence-based practice. These debates embody different views about what works, who knows best, and who should be in charge of teaching. Like all controversial issues, this one is more complex. First, the extent to which stronger and better evidence might advance the quality of teaching and its impact depends on the nature of evidence itself—on how it is defined, used, interpreted, and made legitimate. Second, the relevance and impact of evidence-based practice in teaching also depends on what conceptions of teaching and learning are being employed, how evidence applies to each of them, and how these conceptions shape the conditions under which evidence itself will be used or misused.

This chapter explores the relationships of evidence to teaching and the culture of teaching by examining both teaching as a multifaceted and multilayered practice and the role of evidence in each of these facets. Specifically, it reviews the role of evidence in teaching as

- a technical practice
- an intellectual practice
- an experiential practice
- an emotional practice
- a moral and ethical practice
- a political practice
- a situated practice
- a cultural practice

The review culminates in a research-informed vision for teaching that is embedded in a set of professional learning principles that create positive synergy among the many practices of teaching by stimulating and supporting teachers to critically review and judiciously apply the evidence of research and experience together in ethical and professional communities that are dedicated to the continuous improvement of all students' learning.

THE PRACTICES OF TEACHING

Teaching—like medicine, law, or dentistry—is a professional practice.[4] It consists of systematically organized and thoughtfully as well as ethically grounded activities among a community of professionals that is dedicated to the service of others.

The practice of teaching is complex. It is not mechanical or predictable. Nor does it follow simple rules. Indeed, teaching is an assemblage of many practices, each affecting, drawing on, or intersecting with the others.[5] Each of these practices relates to evidence in its own distinctive way.

The Technical Practice of Teaching

The belief that there could be and should be a scientific evidence basis for teaching began with the process-product research on effective teaching in the 1960s and 1970s. Following Gage's 1963 call for better observational studies of teaching, and aided by new technologies such as tape recorders that helped capture life in classrooms, investigators examined and evaluated experimental approaches to teaching that built a knowledge base for the field. Process-product research demonstrated the variable nature of teachers' impact on classroom learning through such behaviors as the use of wait-time, pacing and coverage of content, and other instructional strategies.[6]

Process-product research blazed the trail for the view that how teachers taught should not be based on personal style or philosophical preference or, even less, unquestioned traditions but, rather, on scientific evidence. Yet the evidence of teacher effectiveness in the process-product paradigm had its limitations. It could not explain variations and differences between classrooms, its implementation strategies (such as mailing teaching manuals to thousands of teachers) were simplistic and ineffective, and it mainly demonstrated differences between more or less effective forms of teaching within existing parameters of traditional, whole-class teaching.[7]

The evidence base of process-product research rested on an essentially *technical* view of teaching: teaching involved the mastery and employment of technical skill. If the technical perspective could document how teachers taught, and even demonstrate what ways teachers taught best, it could not explain why teachers taught the way they did or how they learned to do so. Thus, in the technical perspective, the evidence base of teaching might show how teacher behaviors and their effect on student outcomes differed between traditional and progressive or formal and informal teaching, but it could not explain how and why those behaviors and outcomes came about.[8] If the researchers could not explain the origins of teachers' behaviors, then there was no way to understand how to get the behaviors to change. As a result, the effort to establish a knowledge base for teaching moved into an (often more qualitative) exploration of teachers' knowledge, thinking, expertise, decisionmaking, beliefs, and emotions.

Yet, despite more than two decades of research of this kind, the knowledge base for teaching and learning, according to many critics, remains in question.[9] As a result, researchers and policymakers, impatient with the seemingly disappointing results of this largely qualitative interlude, returned to advocate for and practice more experimental research that pinpoints the most effective teacher behaviors.[10] In the United States, this push for more scientific research is supported through the No Child Left Behind (NCLB) Act of 2001, which calls for (and only funds) research on teaching that is deemed to be scientifically "rigorous," where rigor is defined as reliable, quantifiable, large-scale, blind-controlled methods of observation or experimentation.[11]

Many argue that this is the approach that has been adopted by medicine, and that the educational analog is to perform randomized experiments in classrooms and schools with sample sizes large enough to show commonalities in and among classrooms and schools that can be generalized to the population at large in such a way as to identify common and variable patterns of cause and effect.[12] This more contemporary view of evidence-based educational change raises more sophisticated questions than its process-product predecessors about the warrants for teachers' methods and decisions because of its comparisons to medical decisionmaking. Yet its view of teaching, and why teachers teach the way they do, remains grounded in a predominantly technical view of the work, where high-quality teaching results from learned knowledge, skill, and other technical expertise acquired through initial and continuing professional training. Poor teaching, it is supposed, results from a lack of awareness of or training and practice in "what works."

Medicine may have changed in leaps and bounds over the decades in ways that teaching has not. Yet outside America, even David Hargreaves (no relation), one of the staunchest advocates for evidence-based educational change along medical lines, acknowledges that while randomized trials and new technologies form part of the basis of professional judgment, physicians make their own decisions according to other criteria as well based on "what is known from natural science (basic laws and causes), from medical sciences (e.g. the effects of drugs on organs), from tradition (inherited within the specialty), from what one was taught (early professional socialization) and from personal experience (what therapeutic action one has learnt works with what kind of patient in what situation)."[13]

Others note that medical judgments are influenced by intuition, ethics of care for the suffering of patients that sometimes supersede what is technically the most effective treatment, and even the perpetuation and defense of professional self-interest. Medical professionals routinely draw on intuition and accumulated knowledge derived from experience and repeated practice in making judgments that affect patients, and they select and apply technologies according to particular patients and circumstances. Nurses, especially, find that their dedication to an ethic of care is often compromised by bureaucratic cost-cutting and hierarchical demands that are not in the best interests of their patients. Indeed, an overly technical view of nursing as management of data and information often leads, in the eyes of nursing staff, to the neglect of personal relations that define the core of their work. Thus, effective medical judgment and practice is not merely informed by technical, or even intellectual evidence, but also by practical, emotional, situational, ethical, and political criteria that make up other forms of evidence and constitute the conditions supporting or impeding its use.[14]

It seems clear that the nature and role of evidence and conditions for its use in teaching must be as sophisticated as this broadened understanding of evidence-based practice in real medicine. To misunderstand the nature of teaching (or medicine) as merely or mostly a technical practice of what professionals should know and be able to do is not only an injustice to the complexity of the work but also leads to misdiagnoses of the problems of practice and mistakes about how to improve it.[15] Avoiding these mistakes requires engaging with the other forms of practice.

Teaching Is an Intellectual Practice

Teaching also involves increasingly complex work that is highly cognitive and intellectual. Particularly since the advent of cognitive science, and its attention to the different ways in which students learn, educational researchers have elucidated the sophisticated nature of teacher cognition and its importance for student learning in relation to areas such as teacher decisionmaking, thinking, subject content knowledge and pedagogical content knowledge, and expertise.[16]

A detailed investigation of the responses of twenty-nine reform-committed seventh- and eighth-grade teachers to initiatives in interdisciplinary curriculum, alternative forms of assessment, and standards-based reform found that even these highly capable reform enthusiasts experienced change as hard intellectual work.[17] The reforms were not self-evident, the standards often appeared too vague to understand, learning to plan backwards from the standards was difficult to accomplish without support, and developing new curricula was intellectually taxing and sometimes draining. It took many months for even the best and most committed teachers to understand and become comfortable with implementing complex reform demands. As Fullan notes, change often produces "implementation dips" in performance that can lead many people to prematurely revert back to their previous (safer) practices.[18]

Schools that see teaching and learning as ongoing intellectual practices often seek to become *learning organizations* that process knowledge and learning effectively, understand the relationship of cause and effect across an organization through developing capacity for systems-thinking, involve everyone in the big picture of change, and develop the capacity to reason their way through complex challenges and problems. These schools focus on learning at all levels in the organization—students, teachers, leaders, parents, and the organization in general.[19]

When teaching is interpreted as an intellectual practice, evidence of what works is not decided by gurus, governments, or oligarchies of external researchers and then imposed on teachers in hierarchical systems of power and dependency. Evidence, rather, becomes a source for improving student learning through enhancing teachers' learning about the effects of their teaching; the interests, strengths, and needs of their students; and alternative strategies that have some externally validated track record of success. Willingness to change means willingness to learn as well as opportunity to learn.[20]

Teaching Is an Experiential Practice

Viewing teaching as an experiential practice highlights the point that formal evidence of a systematic, codified nature can be overrated as a guide to professional practice. Teachers have understood this for a long time. In his classic 1932 text *The Sociology of Teaching*, Willard Waller wrote, "The common-sense understandings which teachers have of their problems bites deeper than the maunderings of most theorists. Teachers will do well to insist that any program of educational reform shall start with them, that it will be based on, or it shall include, their common-sense insight."[21]

Scientific evidence and practical experience provide legitimate and, at the same time, imperfect bases for professional judgment and knowledge. Marilyn Cochran-Smith and Susan Lytle identify three relationships between knowledge and practice. In *knowledge-for-practice* outside experts generate what goes into the knowledge base of teaching and transmit this information to teachers. *Knowledge-in-practice* centers around teachers' own practical knowledge, in which teachers learn by doing and, through various teaching opportunities, gain a deeper understanding of their own work. *Knowledge-of-practice* blends the previous two types with classroom teachers constructing their own knowledge and engaging it with the larger field of educational study through school-university partnerships and action. In this interactive construction, practical experience is as important as research-driven knowledge.[22]

Examples of Experience-Based Practical Knowledge

The 1980s and 1990s witnessed a proliferation of research and writing on the nature and value of teachers' experience, practical knowledge, and voices. Research on teachers' personal practical knowledge sought "to capture the idea of experience in a way that allows us to talk about teachers as knowledgeable and knowing persons." Experience was regarded as central to teachers' expertise and a source of valid theory. Personal practical knowledge, or craft knowledge, consisted of the routine and situated knowledge that teachers have of curriculum materials and development, subject matter, teaching strategies, the classroom milieu, parents, students, etc. This knowledge, its advocates claimed, was communicated through the images, metaphors, and stories through which teachers represented their work to themselves and others. These forms of practical knowledge can constitute as valid a source of evidence and insight for professionals as formalized research. Student work and student-teacher interaction are often the most reliable data a teacher uses to make decisions on a daily basis.[23]

Usefulness in practice, or what Doyle and Ponder call the "practicality ethic," is one of the key criteria teachers use to evaluate change initiatives. Research on knowledge utilization indicates that a teachers' adoption of an innovation or reform depends in part on their perceptions, as a user, of what needs the research will fill, whether it is workable in their local reality, and whether it will make their practice better or easier.[24]

Of course, the use of practical knowledge can also be deeply flawed. In a study of teachers' experiential knowledge, for instance, it was found that teachers privileged and even retreated to claims about their own experiential knowledge not only in the absence of awareness of research findings but also as a way of discounting the evidence of other teachers' experiences in other schools. Teachers whose work is performed repetitively and largely alone tend to use experience mainly as a way of recycling practice from year to year as they avoid looking at the long-term and respond conservatively to change. In Deborah Britzman's words, for these teachers "practice makes practice." In the expertise literature, it is often said that practice (without opportunities for feedback and revision) makes permanent.[25]

Without opportunities for feedback and reflection, teachers' practical and experiential knowledge can become partial and parochial knowledge. Some of this knowledge can be sexist and racist knowledge, perpetuating erroneous beliefs that minority children cannot learn or that detracking does not serve students' interests. Or teachers' knowledge and voices may be arbitrarily privileged over and against the evidence of experience among students or parents, or even other teachers elsewhere. The evidence of teachers' practical knowledge and experience is therefore significant but not sacrosanct. Its validity depends on the conditions under which it is produced as well as the community communication processes through which it is validated. Many argue that teachers need to become adaptive experts who actively seek to check existing ideas and view lifelong learning (which includes unlearning) as a major part of being a professional.[26]

Teaching Is an Emotional Practice

Like all other work that involves interacting with people, teaching is not only a technical or intellectual practice but also an emotional one. In the words of sociologist Norman Denzin, an *emotional practice* is "an embedded practice that produces for the person an expected or unexpected emotional alteration in the inner and outer streams of experience. . . . Emotional practices make people problematic objects to themselves. The emotional practice radiates through the person's body and streams of experience, giving emotional culmination to thoughts, feelings, and actions."[27] As an emotional practice, teaching activates, colors, and expresses teachers' feelings and actions and affects the feelings and actions of others with whom they work and form relationships. Teachers can enthuse their students or bore them, be approachable to parents or alienate them, feel supported by their colleagues or mistrusted by them.

In enacting teaching as an emotional practice, teachers may show passion for their subject matter, care and concern for their students, frustrations with reform requirements, or even anger at injustice. Good teachers, says Robert Fried, are passionate about ideas, learning, and their relationships with students. In teaching for understanding, one of the tasks of teaching is to draw on and develop emotional understanding. Emotional understanding proceeds not only gradually but also instantaneously, at a glance, as teachers reach into their own feelings and past emotional experiences to make sense of and respond to those around them.[28]

Caring is central to the emotional practice of teaching and learning—as a moral contribution of some of it and an emotional condition of all of it. Indeed, caring and feeling relationships are at the foundation of student success. Change movements can destroy these foundations when they demoralize teachers by undermining their purposes, turn teachers into disappointed reform enthusiasts, exhaust educators with "repetitive change syndrome," and deprive educators of time for relationships with students because of the technical requirements of assessment demands or reform implementation.[29]

If teaching is acknowledged as an emotional practice, the implication for evidence-based change in education is that indications of evidence of learning and success must include the emotional goals and processes of learning (e.g., empathy, resilience, self-esteem) as well as the emotional conditions for learning (e.g., safety, security, order, attendance). It is also essential, in any learning community, that reviewing, analyzing, or basing improvements on evidence is not just conducted through "going through the motions" task-centered teams. Evidence-based education must also "go through the emotions" and strengthen the relationships of the groups and communities that produce it.

Teaching Is a Moral and Ethical Practice

The fact that teaching is an emotional and intellectual practice does not automatically make it moral and ethical. Callous genius can be the mastermind of evil and wickedness. Emotional manipulation can lead people into mass hysteria or lure them into sects and cults. Yet teaching and learning are never amoral; they are always ethical and moral practices, either in a good or bad way, by design or by default.

By example, through group development or by direct instruction, teachers promote and produce virtues such as justice, fairness, respect, and responsibility—or their opposites. Knowing and appreciating the measure and importance of these virtues, and being able to exercise them in practice, requires what Campbell calls "emotional knowledge." Yet strangely, as Fenstermacher points out, all advocacy and adumbration of the knowledge base of teaching, of what teachers should know and be able to do, "is nearly devoid of talk about the moral nature of teaching, the moral duties and obligations of teachers, and the profound importance of teachers to the moral development of their students."[30]

In respecting teaching as a moral craft, as a moral and ethical practice, what kinds of ethical knowledge do teachers need and how should they exercise it in their judgment about evidence-based educational change, about how evidence is produced, used, or interpreted? Even if they are legally forbidden to do so, should teachers explain culturally biased test items to those that do not understand them when, for instance, the tests refer to picket fences that urban children have never seen or to birthdays, which Muslim families do not celebrate? Should teachers make clandestine use of bilingual education practices that are strongly supported by research evidence even if state proposition mandates have legally outlawed them?[31]

The literature on how schools can and should operate in professional learning communities says little about how they should operate as ethical learning communities. Explicit articulations of the core ethical values that underlie decisions (e.g., "It's about every student's success, not just about us") can be very important in guiding conversations, inquiry and decision-making. There is long-standing evidence that when teachers work together, they all too often protect themselves, exercise norms of noninterference, and turn a blind eye to unprofessional conduct that harms students rather than confronting colleagues about issues such as bullying their students, treating them unfairly, inflicting undue punishment, or failing to evaluate their work respectfully.[32] The moral is that professional learning communities must also be *ethical* learning communities that hold colleagues collectively accountable for the integrity of their practice and the varieties of evidence that supports their work.

Teaching Is a Political Practice

Teaching is also political in the sense that, in some measure, it is always a relationship of power. Willard Waller described schools as "despotism[s] in a state of perilous equilibrium," and in their bureaucratic, hierarchical nature, too many schools sadly still fit his description.[33] Yet whatever particular organizational form it takes, institutionalized education will always have political dimensions, such as the authority and experience of the adult compared to the child and the pressure of collective will over individual freedom. These universals are then overlaid with the exercise of particular political agendas and interests over the rights and responsibilities of teachers and students—governments, school boards, business interests, and many more.

Educational reform analysts and advocates, says Seymour Sarason, ignore these power relations at their peril.[34] Applying and analyzing evidence as a way to improve school practice is not a neutral and rational technology of change that can be cleansed of all political impurities. Politics is irretrievably at the heart of all education, including how evidence is created and used.

Governments use evidence selectively and ideologically. For these reasons, officially sanctioned research evidence should never be taken at face value, and part of the culture of evidence-based practice should be directed to supplying teachers with the time and equipping them with the skills to evaluate the validity, veracity, reliability, and contextual relevance of research-driven initiatives with which they are presented and about which they are often asked to make choices. In the underfunded and overpressed work of schools and change implementation, these conditions are often lacking. For example, Datnow, Hubbard, and Mehan's evaluation of Comprehensive School Reform initiatives found that teachers were pressed to make decisions about adopting research-based literacy initiatives on the basis of information they had no time or opportunity to review, and mediated by principals they sometimes did not yet know or whose judgment they did not trust.[35] It is essential that teachers have the professional capacity to review, critique, make informed decisions about, and adapt the evidence accordingly. Ideally, they will also carefully monitor the effects of new innovations on their students' abilities to learn.

Teaching Is a Situated Practice

Teaching varies depending on what is taught, who is taught, and how learning is assessed.[36] Teachers should not be pure scientific rationalists whose decisions are influenced solely by "incontrovertible" evidence of "what works" best for most students' learning. Evidence for practice must take into account the contexts in which teaching takes place.

An obvious but important point about context is that in most schools student numbers are large, resources are scarce, and time is always tight. Earlier work conducted by Andy Hargreaves asked why teachers resisted or compromised "progressive" or "child-centered" methods that might assist student learning. The practice of teaching, he argued, was organized around *classroom coping strategies* through which teachers tried to achieve their purposes in ways that accommodated a wide range of institutional and social constraints such as parental expectations, large class sizes, and standardized assessment requirements.[37] Over time, teachers' individual and collective adaptations to these constraints were interpreted and drawn on as accepted methods of "what works" in teaching—indeed, as the accepted definition of teaching itself. The question-and-answer method of classroom "recitation" between teachers and large groups of students that persisted across generations, the hands-up method of student participation that maintained students' attention through competitive participation while allowing transmission of knowledge, and the practice of having children working individually *in* groups rather than working together *as* groups so as to maintain curriculum coverage and individual accountability were among the many coping strategies teachers developed.[38]

The organizational efficiency of these coping strategies led to their institutionalization within the teaching profession. As they were passed from generation to generation, teachers, students, and parents (who had also once been students) came to see them as comprising "real school" or as a fundamental "grammar of schooling" that should not be weakened or compromised. This accumulation of coping strategies defined all that was true and "practical" for teachers; it comprised a seemingly unshakeable evidence base of hardened experience against which the change proposals of academics or prognostications of bureaucrats stood little chance. Few teacher preparation ideas survived in the face of these persistent pressures and overwhelming constraints on classroom life and the ingrained coping strategies that experienced colleagues had developed in response to them. Moreover, most teachers could not convert even the most inventive and insistent reform efforts into familiar routines and practices once they were behind the doors of their classroom sanctuaries—another persistent element of the context of teaching.[39]

While many of the situational constraints on teachers' pedagogical choices are historically and systematically pervasive, others are more variable. For instance, innovative and inquiry-based strategies that teachers feel they can employ successfully in white, affluent communities are often rejected in favor of more traditional and didactic approaches to instruction and discipline in working-class, urban, or ethnic-minority settings, where the demands of custody and control are more intense.[40]

If evidence-based improvement is to be effective, the contextual contingencies around it must be addressed, not avoided. These include setting "realistically patient" rather than "politically expedient" timelines for sustainable interpretation and implementation, reorganizing the school day or school week so that teachers have scheduled time to meet and engage in efforts at evidence-based improvement, and undertaking restructuring of the education workforce to provide teachers with support from other paid adults in ways that promote stronger professional learning and collaboration among teachers themselves.[41] As a situated practice, it is not just instruction but also the context of instruction that should be subjected to evidence-based principles.

Evidence and "Systems Issues"

It is also noteworthy that evidence-based change does not take place in isolation from other commitments and initiatives, and these pressures often block strong and sustainable change. For example, while a change to evidence-based instruction requires long timelines for sustainable implementation, Adequate Yearly Progress requirements push teachers and schools into selecting solutions based on limited understandings of their legitimacy and implications and on insufficient timelines to evaluate alternatives.[42]

Furthermore, mandating reforms according to an evidence base that has been compiled from large-scale studies of existing practice, rather than exemplary exceptions to it, necessarily confines solutions to those that are available within the current range of teachers' coping strategies and within current resources and other conditions that perpetuate the existing grammar of schooling. Such models of evidence-based change capitulate to rather than challenge the existing contexts of public school teaching. In light of all these considerations, it is vital that evidence-based educational change initiatives acknowledge, address, and analyze the conditions of their own use.

Teaching Is a Cultural Practice

Over time, as teachers' coping strategies become ingrained and accepted, they form part of the professional culture of teaching. Culture has *content* and *form*.[43] The *content* of culture refers to the substantive attitudes, beliefs, values, and ways of life that members of an organization, or a subgroup within it, hold in common. The content of a teacher culture may be found in allegiances to subject knowledge, commitments to child-centeredness, acceptance of low standards, placing a strong focus on care and community, concentrating on the academic elite, giving pride of place to sports and to its "jocks," valuing or disvaluing published data and evidence, etc.

The *form* of teacher culture describes the patterns of relationship and association among members of the culture. These forms may be *individualized*, with teachers working independently and in isolation from each other; *collaborative,* with teachers working together and sharing ideas and materials as a single professional community; *balkanized,* with teachers separated into and working together in different subgroups, such as grade-levels or subject departments, that are at best indifferent and at worst actively hostile to one

another; or characterized by *contrived collegiality*, with collaboration mandated, imposed, and regulated by managerial decree in terms of measures
like compulsory coaching or required collaborative planning.[44]

Reba Page wrote that "understanding the cultures of schools is crucial
to understanding the work of teachers." Cultures of teaching frame teachers' work, filter educational change, and have important consequences for
student learning. In general, cultures of collaboration among teachers produce greater willingness to take risks, learn from mistakes, and share successful strategies with colleagues that lead to teachers having positive senses
of their own efficacy, beliefs that their children can learn, and improved
outcomes in that learning. How strong the professional cultures or communities of teaching are in particular departments, schools, or even whole systems is crucial in determining how committed they are to improvement and
how well students achieve in them. These collaborative principles apply to
school districts as much as to schools themselves.[45]

Cultures of collaboration are essential preconditions for thoughtful application of evidence-based practice. Their promotion of norms of continuous improvement opens teachers to the potential influences of outside or
inside evidence. Their informal elements of mutual support, reciprocity, con-
fidence, and trust create the social conditions of security that enable them
to adapt to and prosper from the anxiety-provoking challenges of educational change. As a precondition of evidence-based change, effective culture-
building requires time and patience as well as high-quality leadership that is
increasingly distributed across an entire teaching staff that shares responsibility for improvement.[46]

Collaborative teacher cultures are a necessary condition for thoughtful
implementation of evidence-based educational change, but collaboration
alone is not always enough. Collaborative cultures do not always have a sufficient sense of urgency. In the UK, Hay/McBer & Associates recently found
that, by themselves, collaborative cultures do not always produce the best
learning results because teachers are reluctant to challenge each other to
make difficult changes to their routines and practices. By themselves, collaborative cultures may also place excessive or exclusive weight on practical or experiential knowledge at the expense of more formal types of data
and evidence. In addition, collaborative cultures may not necessarily have a
clear enough focus on or understanding of students' learning in their quest
to secure improvement. In his investigation of underperforming schools, for
example, Richard Elmore argues that teachers collaborated in a dedicated
and energetic way to improve their students' learning, but their collaborative

efforts were based on their passion and enthusiasm for teaching and not on analyzing and understanding their students' learning.[47]

Last, evidence on the implementation of evidence (what used to be called knowledge utilization) provides little guidance on how to reconcile a culture's existing beliefs and assumptions with the challenges posed to it by disturbing data. Most existing claims about effective knowledge utilization strategies are neither clear nor universal. For instance, the widely argued position that changes in teachers' practice have to be engineered or forced before teachers will change their beliefs may only work under conditions of imposed change. Similarly, the popular view that successful change requires both pressure and support is of little value unless, on evidential and/or ethical grounds, more specific claims can be made about the balance, sequence, type, and tone of pressure and support, respectively.[48]

In summary, teaching is a cultural practice that creates or fails to create the professional belief systems and working relationships that are the preconditions for evidence-based improvement. Evidence-based educational initiatives require significant investment in the culture building processes. They can also push collaborative teacher cultures to focus more persistently on student learning needs, especially when this might create professional discomfort for teachers themselves. A systematic connection between professional culture and evidence-based inquiry in caring and trusting relationships of ethical integrity is at the heart of one of the most powerful principles for implementing evidence-based improvement: professional learning communities.

PROFESSIONAL LEARNING COMMUNITIES

Professional learning communities (PLCs) bring professionals and evidence together through formal and informal means in order to create deliberate improvements in practice and results.[49] Efforts to convert schools into PLCs are proliferating rapidly in the United States, Great Britain, and Canada, and emerging qualitative and quantitative evidence are providing important understandings of how professional learning communities can operate effectively as vehicles for organizing and implementing evidence-based educational change.

Important dimensions of teacher learning communities can be clarified by returning to the basic forms of teaching practices that were discussed earlier. However, here we view these new forms as collective, rather than individual, practice. For the sake of clarity and brevity, we have regrouped these into three broader categories.

Professional Learning Communities as Technical, Intellectual, and Experiential Practices

As a technical, intellectual, and experiential practice, professional learning communities require the means to collect, sort, analyze, and review technical and experiential data in ways that promote continuous improvement. They also require the technical conditions of time, space, organization, and resources to make their functioning feasible and sustainable.

Successful PLCs depend on data—copious amounts of it. Standardized tests or examination data provide the most easily accessible evidence in this respect, and despite criticism of its biases, or of the narrowed view of learning it represents, standardized testing nevertheless provides a data base that can pinpoint areas of practice requiring attention. Many other kinds of data are also technically helpful as a basis for decisionmaking in professional learning communities. Quantitatively, these can include teacher-designed assessments (often more useful diagnostically than externally administered standardized tests), course allocation patterns, behavioral incident and attendance data, rates of extracurricular participation, results of satisfaction and engagement questionnaires, etc. Qualitative data might include exhibitions, displays of student work, teacher comments and written feedback, etc.

Multiple forms of data give better insight into the performance of a school, department, class, or child, but, as Milbrey Wallin McLaughlin and her colleagues found in their study of eighty-six schools in the Bay Area that were seeking to become PLCs, the overall spectrum of data can lead to feelings of information overload. Given the intellectual challenge of integrating and processing data, McLaughlin's team found that provision of technical expertise from consultants helped educators cope with feelings of overload, as did the emergence or appointment of someone on the staff of the school who would be knowledgeable about data management and who also knew how to access the evidence of outside research. These educators, who work as boundary spanners between the organization and the outside, can locate research that is presented in the concise and accessible forms that busy teachers value or can translate it in a way that achieves accessibility.[50]

Another way of reducing overload is to create an integrated technological system of data and evidence management. At Noumea Primary School, which is located in a highly disadvantaged part of Sydney, Australia, principal Jenny Lewis and her colleagues designed a now widely used data management program called *Schoolmate*.[51] Lewis wanted a system that would help her staff learn quickly how to respond to their children's needs and problems. The program collects student achievement and behavioral data, along with teachers' comments on students' work and welfare information, which are entered on an ongoing basis into the database on a computer rather than into teachers' notebooks or students' agendas. The data can then be disaggregated by teacher, class, age group, or individual child, as well as by ethnicity and socioeconomic status. Teachers use the data routinely as part of their instructional and whole-school decisionmaking. When there is a rise in behavioral problems, for example, it is possible in an instant to see in which classes, year levels, ethnic groups, or genders the problems are concentrated (these results do not always square with teachers' first intuitive responses).

Professional learning communities appear to work best when evidence-informed change is incorporated into regular cycles of planning, implementation, inquiry, and review focused on learning, which is reminiscent of the classic cycles of action research and is now becoming institutionalized as a part of school inspection and self-evaluation process in the UK. Although this planning and review process may look rather mechanistic as a school emerges into a professional learning community, it works best when it evolves into a routine way in which the school and teachers operate—so that whenever a problem is experienced, the school's first response is not "what do we *do* about this?" but "what do we *know* about this?"[52]

At their most advanced stage, strong PLCs also engage in networked learning opportunities with other schools in ways that enable lateral transfer of knowledge and practice from one institution to another. Some networks, like the National Writing Project, which connects thousands of individual teachers, or the Coalition of Essential Schools, which networks innovative schools, have a longstanding existence.[53]

Professional Learning Communities as Cultural, Emotional, and Ethical Practices

The "hard side" of professional learning communities is found in their technical, intellectual, and practical aspects—in structures, strategies, plans, procedures, and processes that are used to review and apply evidence and knowledge in order to improve practice in the specific situations and with particular students that professionals know best. The soft, relational side of PLCs attends to equally important aspects of morality and meaning in evidence-informed decisionmaking.

The strongest PLCs are characterized by cultural norms and relationships that make processing and application of research and data possible. Marvin Wideen and Ivy Pye, for instance, found in their study of an exceptional Canadian elementary school that a strong professional culture gave teachers a robust relationship to outside evidence as well as to the messages of visiting speakers.[54] The culture empowered teachers to engage critically and confidently with, rather than react dependently toward, these sources of data.

The backbone of a strong professional culture and a professional learning community is trust. The pursuit of improvement, management of change, and rectification of underperformance all create difficult emotions of anxiety, fear, threat, and loss. Confrontations with disturbing data that challenge people's sense of their own effectiveness magnify these feelings. Successful change efforts do not eliminate these difficult emotions and anxieties but create a holding pattern for them so they do not become unbearable, or flood the teacher so he or she is unable to cope. The heart of this holding pattern is a web of trust.[55]

Trust makes difficult conversations about improvement possible. Strong professional learning communities are therefore characterized by strong cultures of trusted colleagues who value each other personally and professionally, who are committed to their students, who are willing to discuss and disagree about evidence and data that can inform them about how to improve their practice in ways that benefit their students, and who are willing to challenge one another's practice in doing so. The ultimate hallmark of such strong and trusting professional cultures is that while they will do their utmost to understand and learn from colleagues who resist change efforts, ultimately they will ostracize persistently resistant teachers who oppose change that would substantially benefit students simply to protect their own interests.[56]

In this latter respect, a strong professional learning community is also an ethical learning community. It is a place where teachers are prepared not only to challenge their colleagues' and their own technical shortcomings but one where they are also ready to question their colleagues' moral judgment where necessary. In her discussion of ethical learning communities, Elizabeth Campbell documents how teachers all too often comply with a professional code of noninterference when they see colleagues do harm to students through sarcasm, favoritism, unfair grading, failure to return work promptly, etc.[57] Campbell not only chastises teachers for these shortfalls of ethical conduct, she also actively advocates for teaching to become a community of inquiry where, as well as debating with the technical implications of achievement scores or research articles on instruction, teachers also develop their *ethical knowledge* by openly discussing and deliberating on the ethical demands and dilemmas of their work.

Professional Learning Communities as a Situational and Political Practice

Neither professional learning communities nor the evidence on which they draw are innocent or pure. What is professional is also political; it is inextricably bound up with power relationships. PLCs are positively political when they empower students to be not just objects or targets of data analysis but active participants in it so they can review and take responsibility for their own learning, performance, and improvement. PLCs are also political when they empower teachers to have the scope and to develop the skill to exercise discretionary judgment in situations of unavoidable uncertainty. Districts, states, and nations that give their teachers considerable latitude for curriculum creativity and instructional flexibility establish the discretionary condition for professional learning communities. *Low trust* political environments that standardize curriculum, prescribe instruction, and use "alignment" as a synonym for micromanagement eliminate the elements of discretionary judgment that are essential in PLCs. These distinctions are best captured in comparisons that Andy Hargreaves has drawn between *professional learning communities* and *performance training sects*.[58]

According to McLaughlin and Talbert, the flexibility and professional discretion that characterize professional learning communities tend to flourish in more affluent communities whose schools meet the measured standards and enjoy the freedom to explore beyond them. Datnow, Mehan, and Hubbard similarly found that schools that adopted the more flexible and open-ended models of Comprehensive School Reform tended to be located in more affluent districts.[59]

Poorer districts, meanwhile, are more likely to adopt reform models of a more prescriptive, micromanaged nature—evident in a number of tightly scripted, widely adopted, and officially sanctioned literacy programs. These programs combine a contractual insistence on performance standards using prescribed classroom teaching techniques with a cultural emphasis on required teacher collaboration, intensive coaching and technical assistance, and closely monitored therapeutic sessions among implementers devoted to the disclosure and remediation of "problems." Such literacy and math programs and their associated procedures of intensive and closely monitored implementation yield positive results, according to large-scale research, in terms of short-term gains in measured student achievement, and in relation to basic literacy skills for younger age groups. Due to their dramatic short-term impact, they can have startling effects on the belief systems of teachers who previously believed their students were incapable of learning, and they can provide unconfident teachers who may be poorly or newly qualified with an intensive instructional repertoire that is theirs for life.[60]

These patterns of change have become a source of great hope in poor communities, which require urgent attention to the improvement of achievement and the narrowing of achievement gaps in contexts where there may be great shortages of highly qualified or even minimally qualified teachers. However, these uses of evidence-based improvement also have many limitations. Their benefits are less strong or even negligible with older students in relation to more sophisticated literacy and math skills, their achievement effects seem to plateau after only two to three years, they exert high collateral damage on other less structured and prescriptive areas of the curriculum such as arts and humanities, and they tend to promote patterns of teacher dependency on and fear of outside-in evidence and programs that are the antithesis of discretionary judgment in a professional learning community.[61]

FINAL THOUGHTS

It is right and timely that the study and practice of educational change should be driven by a quest and even a demand for evidence. Evidence takes many forms, and all of it should be grist for the improvement mill. Teaching is not only a technical and intellectual practice of what teachers should know and be able to do where research evidence can be applied in a relatively straightforward way. It is also an experiential, emotional, ethical, cultural, political, and situational practice that requires complex and knowledgeable decision-making in variable situations of rich and sometimes difficult relationships. Given the multidimensional nature of the practice of teaching, one of the stronger approaches to evidence-informed improvement lies in professional learning communities, which utilize both research-based and practically grounded evidence to make technical, emotional, ethical, and even political judgments about improvements in the classroom, the school, and education at large that will benefit all students whose lives their teachers affect.

The more prescribed and tightly regulated performance training sects of evidence-based literacy and math improvement that characterize many districts serving poorer communities may sometimes provide a necessary place to begin if time is pressing, capacity is weak, and student needs are great. But if an apartheid of improvement is to be avoided, the challenge must be to move beyond the plateaus these strategies quickly reach in order to develop the professional learning community approach to evidence-informed change already being enjoyed in many more affluent communities. The necessity for such a developmental approach to evidence-informed change is educationally and ethically evident. The evidence of what such a developmental model might look like is not yet strong, however. Thus, while we are becoming increasingly clear about what successful and sustainable models of evidence-informed improvement in the shape of PLCs look like, the evidence of how to get there developmentally from more basic beginnings still has to be, and urgently needs to be, developed.

Nonprofit Organizations and the Promotion of Evidence-Based Practice in Education

Mark A. Smylie and Thomas B. Corcoran

This chapter explores the roles of nonprofit organizations in working with schools and school districts to promote innovation and improvement. Specifically, we examine the role of nonprofit organizations in promoting evidence-based practice. A particularly salient theme in our analysis is how nonprofit organizations may consider and use evidence in doing their work, in establishing and sustaining relationships with their funders and with schools and school districts, and in navigating their way through the volatile and sometimes contentious contexts in which they operate. As we will see, the heightened press for accountability within the nonprofit sector and across the educational system as a whole may encourage nonprofits to adopt evidence-based practice inasmuch as funders, clients, and the broader environment may be defining accountability in those terms. This new accountability may require more than making simple and sometimes highly selective references to previous research to support a nonprofit's strategies. It may require producing evidence of results.

While hard estimates are difficult to come by, the number and diversity of nonprofit organizations working with schools and school districts are enormous. In his analysis of the school improvement industry, Brian Rowan estimated that more than 80 percent of all school systems in the United States contract with more than 3,700 outside organizations for some professional and technical service in any given year. In addition, more than 400 outside organizations, not including universities, perform research and development (R&D) functions. While he does not break out nonprofit organizations in these counts, Rowan deems them "numerous."[1]

The size and diversity of the nonprofit sector make it difficult to generalize about the varied organizations that populate the sector. It is also difficult to develop a typology that would capture the most salient dimensions of the numerous types of nonprofit organizations. The implication for our analysis is that while we seek a general understanding of the potential role of nonprofit organizations in promoting evidence-based practice, we must also explore how this understanding may vary across different organizations within this sector.[2]

PROMOTING EVIDENCE-BASED PRACTICE

It is difficult to explore the role of nonprofit organizations in promoting evidence-based practice until we determine what we mean by evidence-based practice. So, we begin with a discussion of various meanings of the concept and what we think is required to promote it. The definition and demands of evidence-based practice have important implications for understanding the likelihood that nonprofit organizations—indeed, any type of organization—will be able to promote it effectively.

Meanings of Evidence-Based Practices

Typically, in education, decisions about the design or adoption of improvement initiatives have not been based on careful reviews of evidence of effectiveness. It has been commonplace for education innovations and improvements to be justified on the basis of their logic, their consistency with particular philosophies or value systems, past practice, anecdotal and promotional stories ("gee-whiz reports," as Robert Slavin calls them) provided by users, or simply the "good word" of developers.[3] Where evidence has been considered, it has been used in several different ways. Most typical have been selective appeals to literature that justify the strategies being pursued. Often these justifications have been based on specific polemics, normative essays, or theoretical arguments rather than on original empirical evidence. However, organizations citing such sources typically have referred to them indiscriminately as "research." When empirical evidence has been examined, decisionmakers have often relied on a single study or the work of a particular researcher rather than examining the larger body of evidence. Another approach is to rely heavily on the clinical experiences and perceptions of practicing educators. Here, indicators such as levels of use, teacher satisfaction, professional opinion, and appeals to experts (e.g., accomplished teachers) have been used to justify a program or practice.

Sometimes systematic reviews and syntheses of literature have been used to guide the design or adoption of strategies or programs. A good example of this use of evidence was in the development of original New American Schools designs.[4] Unfortunately, using evidence this way is not widely practiced, perhaps because it is often hard to find relevant reviews.

Even more rarely have reformers conducted rigorous empirical evaluations of program effects before scaling up their work. This use of evidence is currently favored by the U.S. Department of Education, and the recent reauthorization of the Elementary and Secondary Education Act (ESEA), referred to as No Child Left Behind (NCLB), gives preference to those educational practices and professional development activities that are supported by "scientifically-based" research. NCLB defines "scientifically-based" as research that "employs systematic, empirical methods" and uses "experimental or quasi-experimental designs" with a preference for random assignment experiments. While the U.S. Department of Education has received considerable criticism for espousing a narrow definition of what counts as "science" and "bona fide" research in education, the federal government's stance has been quite influential.[5] It has created an impetus for a "product-oriented" interpretation of evidence-based practice, putting a premium on validation and transportation of discrete programs and practices and emphasizing fidelity of implementation over mutual adaptation in context.

In addition to the issue of what constitutes evidence to support new practice is the issue of how new practice is introduced to schools and school districts. Perhaps the most prevalent approach is "technology transfer." These practices are considered exogenous to the context in which, and to the people by which, they are to be implemented. This is an approach by which research prescribes practice. Specification of what to do—"What Works"—and implementation fidelity—"Just Do It!"—are its guiding principles.

An alternate view of evidence-based practice—the definition we advance in this chapter—is more complex, interactive, and dynamic. This perspective envisions policymakers and practitioners using the best evidence available to make decisions about how to work with students and engaging in a continuous process of data collection and review to improve programs and practices over time. This approach places the practitioner at the center of instructional decisionmaking rather than the program developer and demands that practitioners make full use of the knowledge available to them to make the best possible decisions about diagnosis and treatment of their students' learning needs. This approach recognizes that research in education seldom specifies the precise actions that need to be taken to meet the needs of all students in all situations. It also recognizes that useful evidence-based knowledge can be derived from clinical experience as well as from scientific studies.

This perspective sees value in both theory, formal and applied, and research. In this view, local decisions and action should be guided by experience as well as by principles derived from theory and research, and it should not be constrained by narrow empiricism. This view requires more than the validation of the effectiveness of educational programs and products through clinical trials; it requires the development of practitioners' capacities to assess and make use of knowledge gained from different sources to provide the best possible learning opportunities for their students. This approach requires practitioners to monitor and study their practice in order to strengthen their understanding of what works under various conditions. It incorporates an ongoing, reflective process of developing new evidence and knowledge from the thoughtful, disciplined study of practice. This establishes a dynamic process of discovery and action. Claims based on past research may serve as an initial basis for decisions and action, but those claims may be trumped by evidence of outcomes associated with those decisions and actions in local context. For external organizations promoting evidence-based practice in schools, initial evidence might "get you in the door," but developing evidence about the outcomes attained in the local context would be important to sustain the work.

The issue of fidelity is not irrelevant to this view of evidence-based practice. However, fidelity is something to be considered in relation to strength of evidence, the similarities in the original and new settings, the need for flexibility and adaptation of practice to context, and ongoing inquiry. In general, the greater the specification of the practice and the more persuasive the evidence, the more fidelity should be stressed. Only when the evidence of effects is overwhelming and the replicating conditions are the same would insisting on high levels of fidelity make sense. Where practices are not well specified, where the evidence is mixed or shows only modest effects, or where the contexts differ significantly, deliberate, evidence-based adaptation is more appropriate.

The assumption is that even the most robust intervention can be improved and that variations in effects among students and across contexts can be reduced through analysis of student responses and modifications in the program. This approach presumes that practitioners have the flexibility to make adaptations when new evidence calls for them. If this more dynamic, principle- and process-oriented view of evidence-based practice is conducive to meaningful educational practice and improvement, then we need to consider the things that are required of organizations (and, for the purpose of this paper, external, nonprofit organizations) that seek to promote it.

Demands on External Organizations

In order for external, nonprofit organizations to promote evidence-based practice as we have defined it, they must possess and exercise a number of different capabilities. They must be able to identify, define, and understand problems in schools and classrooms and be able to identify outcomes to address those problems. They must develop and sustain strong connections to the knowledge base—scientific and practitioner—in the domains in which they are working. They must be able to work collaboratively with practitioners to collect evidence, diagnose problems, and, where required, make adaptations. They must be able to assess the contexts in which they work and evaluate the available scientific evidence and professional expertise concerning the appropriate actions to take in these contexts so as to achieve the desired outcomes. External organizations must be able to tell weak evidence from strong and the relevant from the irrelevant. They must be able to think theoretically and operate with regard to sound theories or "maps" of change. Uncritical reliance on evidence as information about what to do can be problematic without good theory and problem definition as guides.

These organizations must have the capacity for continuous inquiry, analysis, and adaptation.[6] They also must have the capacity to monitor and evaluate the conduct and effects of their own work. And they should have the willingness and ability to be flexible and to alter directions when the evidence warrants it. They must be more pragmatic than ideological, more problem-oriented than product-oriented. These organizations should be able to engage in this inquiry and analysis in a way that is credible and persuasive to schools and to funders. It is not enough to simply justify or legitimate their goals, services, and actions by appealing to values, philosophies, or popular but untested theories; inquiry and analysis should be conducted in a way that makes credible contributions to the broader base of evidence concerning the improvement of schools, teaching, and student learning.

Our definition of evidence-based practice also points to particular capacities external organizations must have for working with schools. These organizations must be able to develop and sustain over substantial periods of time commitment and engagement of the schools and school districts with which they work. This may require that they be able to work with schools and school districts as contributing partners and participants in planning and decisionmaking. Thus, coconstruction may not only be required to adapt work to a specific context but also to promote commitment to and engagement in the work itself.

In addition, external organizations must be able to provide a great deal of "process support" to schools over time. It means working alongside educators to enhance their readiness for change, the implementation of new practice, and their capacity to diagnose problems and design interventions. It may also mean providing support for developing the organizational and human resource capacities of schools and school districts to engage in and benefit from this form of evidence-based practice.

All these requirements suggest that a successful external organization must be able to acquire and sustain adequate and stable levels of financial resources and recruit and retain a professional staff that can work well with schools. It must have the capacity for research and development and be able to connect with the knowledge base and the field of action. External organizations may thus need to develop the understanding and commitment of their sponsors and to sustain supportive relationships with them. Like working with schools and school districts, this may require external organizations to enter into relationships in which sponsors are active partners in coconstructing the work.

It is not clear that external organizations need all of these capacities to work effectively with schools and school districts or, depending on the context, whether some capacities may be more salient than others. Our argument and the research reviewed in the next section suggest that all are important in one way or another. In addition, it is not clear whether external organizations that lack certain capacities can "make up" for them by collaborating with other organizations, such as universities or other research organizations, to build overall capacity for inquiry and analysis. While such relationships carry the prospects of added capacity and economies, the literature on interorganizational coordination for children's service provision indicates that such relationships may also introduce new complexities, conflicts, and costs, which may compromise any added value.[7]

A LOOK AT NONPROFITS

If such capacities are important to promoting evidence-based practice as defined here, how likely are nonprofit organizations to possess, develop, and exercise them? How do their defining characteristics, those that distinguish them from for-profit organizations and government agencies, for instance, affect their ability to develop such capacities and to promote evidence-based practice? How do common behavioral tendencies of nonprofits affect these abilities? And finally, what trends and issues in the nonprofit sector may affect how they perform this kind of work with schools and school districts?

Legal and Structural Characteristics

Nonprofit organizations are defined by several legal characteristics that distinguish them from other types of organizations. They are exempt from federal taxation and are eligible to receive tax-exempt gifts. They provide services to benefit their members or persons beyond the organization, often public services in partnership with government. Many nonprofits organize their missions and strategies around particular principles and values and are driven more by altruistic than self-serving motives.[8] Nonprofits are controlled by private, independent boards of directors and must abide by the "nondistribution constraint." Nonprofits are not prohibited from making profits; rather, they must devote any profits they do make to financing future services or distributing them to persons in noncontrolling positions within the organization.

The literature is not clear whether these characteristics are advantageous or disadvantageous to nonprofit performance, their ability to achieve their missions, or their ability to compete with for-profits or government agencies for clients and funding. For instance, Burton Wiesbrod contends that the nondistribution constraint may reduce nonprofits' access to the market for equity capital that may be used to support and expand services, build organizational capacity, and support experimentation and innovation. In contrast, some observers argue that nonprofits carry lower administrative costs that give them some advantage over government organizations. Others suggest that such savings may be offset by costs accrued by carrying "free riders" and from the need to devote sometimes considerable resources to securing donations, building organizational membership, or competing for grants and contracts. Richard Steinberg elaborates on this idea of a "trade-off," arguing that while nonprofit and for-profit organizations possess different internal structures and operate under different conditions, they perform quite similarly in production, marketing, and the distribution of services. He contends that these similarities can be explained by a "theory of compensating differentials." For instance, the tax advantages held by nonprofits may balance out the advantage for-profits hold in their access to financial capital.[9]

Resource Dependency

Resource dependency is a theoretical perspective used widely in the literature to explain the behavior of nonprofit organizations. In brief, this perspective views relationships among organizations in terms of self-interested exchange and mutual benefit. Organizations enter into and maintain relationships as long as they find them beneficial. Organizations will adapt to sustain those relationships if they believe that they will continue to benefit from them. If a relationship ceases to provide benefit, and if one or more organizations in that relationship are unwilling or unable to change in order to restore that benefit, the relationship will likely end. The implication is that an organization will change to meet the expectations of other organizations so as to optimize the benefit of relationships with them. Furthermore, an organization will change its goals, structures, and behavior in order to continue to receive resources it needs.[10]

Nonprofit organizations depend on external sources of revenue and other resources for their operation and survival, and, according to Weisbrod, "no source of revenue has unambiguous effects." The character of a nonprofit's behavior and output will be related to the character of its revenue. Nonprofits may prefer revenue from unconstrained sources, but when that revenue becomes scarce they will shift to sources that impose more obligations and constraints. As resource dependency theory would suggest, nonprofits often find it necessary to adapt to the interests and expectations of their donors, funders, and stakeholders.[11] Indeed, nonprofits with multiple diverse funders and stakeholders may need considerable flexibility to satisfy multiple and diverse interests.

The literature also suggests that the sources on which nonprofits depend most for support exert the most influence over their behavior. Nonprofit organizations tend to respond more to the goals of their strongest constituencies than those of their weaker constituencies. Historically, foundations and government agencies have been among the largest and most influential sources of support to nonprofit organizations. It is well established that foundations can exert substantial influence over organizations they fund. They can choose the organizations they will support, concentrate their resources in particular types of organizations, and use their resources to "lever" particular behaviors and outcomes. Government agencies can influence nonprofits in similar ways. Donations can also be a source of influence. An unrestricted donation does not constrain a nonprofit in pursuing its goals. But, according to Weisbrod, not all donations are unrestricted.[12] When donations are made with conditions, they may exert influence similar to foundation grants or government contracts. Donations may also be akin to sales or fee-for-service arrangements, attained only if the nonprofit offers something that the donor is willing to purchase.

These dynamics may trigger a number of issues. The degree of change required of nonprofits to obtain needed resources may create conflicts between a nonprofit's mission and goals and its funders' missions and goals. Adaptation may be "bounded," with nonprofits only willing and able to go "so far" in their relationships with particular funders and stakeholders. Adaptation also may take a conservative course. Walter Powell and Rebecca Friedkin contend that when financial resources are in short supply, or when they are controlled by a small number of sources, nonprofits are inclined to adopt more mainstream and acceptable approaches rather than more confrontational, controversial, or innovative ones that may be more consistent with their mission and goals.[13] When nonprofits must look for support to a large number of funders with diverse interests, their response may be similar—abandon the innovative for the acceptable.

The issue of resource dependency has come into sharper focus as competition for traditional sources of funding increases in the nonprofit sector and as the sector becomes more commercial and market-oriented. Paul Light tells us that this is the "best of times and the worst of times" for the sector. During the past twenty years, there has been substantial growth in dollars attracted by the sector and the total employment within the sector. At the same time, there are increased demands for service and accountability and greater financial stress and uncertainty. Government budget cuts and increased privatization and outsourcing have shifted traditional flows of resources from nonprofits to a broader range of organizations, which has resulted in greater competition for funding among nonprofits and between nonprofits and other organizations as well as a growing sense of financial insecurity.[14]

As resources have become scarcer, funders and clients of services have become more demanding, expecting nonprofits to demonstrate economic efficiencies and results. For instance, government agencies are able to be increasingly selective in awarding grants and contracts, attaching more restrictions, greater reporting requirements, and higher expectations and performance standards in the process. This pushes nonprofits toward providing more and better service and toward greater accountability. It may also push them away from innovation and toward seeking safer, more acceptable changes in the schools. And because nonprofits generally provide services rather than products that are easily "market-tested," they can lack a credible basis for demonstrating the value of what they do.[15]

Pressure also comes from the diversification of the human service "market." Through privatization and outsourcing, for-profit firms increasingly are competing for work and revenue traditionally controlled by nonprofits. According to Light, for-profits are likely to expand their market share and engage in more direct competition with nonprofits for clients and funds. This may be especially true in education. Twenty years ago the idea of a school district outsourcing key services to a for-profit firm was anathema, but it is now considered to be innovative, even standard, practice. As competition has increased, nonprofits' operating margins have been squeezed severely threatening their ability to support mission-related activities.[16]

In the face of what Lester Salamon calls "a permanent state of budgetary stringency," many nonprofits have had to reduce their services (despite increasing demands), create new operational efficiencies, or find alternate sources of funds. For the most part, the sector has pursued the third course. Nonprofits have reduced their reliance on donations and government funds and have moved toward grants, fees, and more commercial sources of income. This has brought them into increasingly complex relationships with the rest of the economy and into greater competition with for-profit organizations. For example, many of the new curricula and improvement programs developed in the past decade by nonprofits, including universities, using federal financial support have been sold to for-profit firms. This move into the commercial market is not universal across the nonprofit sector, and, as Salamon reminds us, nonprofit activity in this market is not new. What is new is the extent to which nonprofits have become involved in commercial activity in search of resources and the projections that commercial activity among nonprofits will become more intensive.[17]

Isomorphic Behavior

The literature tells us that nonprofit organizations have a tendency toward isomorphic behavior: They tend to change in the direction of institutional conformity. Isomorphic behavior is related to, but goes beyond, adaptations associated with resource dependency. It refers to changes that nonprofits make to reflect broader social and institutional norms and expectations of their environments. These environments include the fields of service nonprofits provide (e.g., education and social services), the nonprofit sector as a whole, and the particular niches in which nonprofits operate. Growing competition for resources pushes nonprofits harder to provide services and adopt organizational practices that are expected of them in the larger environment. Nonprofits' legitimacy, support, and perhaps survival are related to the extent to which they look like and operate as others expect them to. Isomorphic changes are not necessarily innovative or ensure improved performance and effectiveness.[18]

Weisbrod argues that as nonprofits pursue revenue in the same ways and in the same markets as for-profit firms, they tend to emulate those firms. Nonprofits are shaping themselves more and more in the image of business-oriented firms to attract "customers" and donors who value that image. Findings from Joseph Galaskiewicz and Wolfgang Bielefeld's study of nonprofits are consistent with this observation. Those nonprofits took on the managerial, political, and legitimation tactics of the arenas from which they were most heavily dependent for resources. The more they used the predominant tactics of other organizations in those arenas, the more resources they reaped. These nonprofits also emulated the tactics of organizations from which they received their resources. The irony is that while nonprofits may enhance their legitimacy and support by adopting goals and practices of other organizations, particularly the market and business-oriented practices of commercial organizations, they may also undermine the distinctive roles and fundamental justifications for the special social regard and legal privileges they have traditionally received.[19]

While their legitimacy and support are related to the degree to which they reflect external expectations, nonprofits are not completely reactive. Rosabeth Kanter argues that crucial to nonprofits' survival is their ability to shape external definitions and expectations for their mission and to shape expectations for what counts as credible evidence of their effectiveness. James Wooten's historical case study of nonprofit legal education in New York City showed that while nonprofit law schools adapted under the influence of their environments, they also were able to exert substantial influence on those environments in pursuit of their own interests. In more recent research on the characteristics and behaviors of "high performing" and "innovative" nonprofits, Light and his colleagues found that the effectiveness of these organizations was associated with aggressive interaction with their environments and their efforts to challenge and shape those environments to their own benefit. They were also selective about the resources they would accept and the sources from which they accepted them, seeking those that aligned most closely with their missions and operations and carried as few constraints and obligations as possible.[20]

Autonomy and Accountability

Historically, nonprofits have enjoyed substantial autonomy and freedom from accountability. Their traditional sources of funding—donations and grants—were not necessarily tied to specific outputs and evidence of performance. "Mission vagueness" often made nonprofit accountability difficult. Moreover, nonprofits have generally provided services as opposed to goods, making the impact much more difficult to assess. Kanter observes that nonprofits have historically lacked "market tests" of their services and accomplishments. It has been easy for nonprofits to find noncompetitive niches in which to operate, something particularly true of small local nonprofits.[21]

Michael Useem argues that certain conditions are associated with the levels of autonomy and accountability experienced by a nonprofit.[22] He contends that autonomy is likely to be greater, and accountability lower, if a nonprofit's reliance on external resources is low, if outside contributors are large in number and diverse in goals, if no outside contributor accounts for a disproportionate share of a nonprofit's resources, or if there is an ample supply of alternative revenue sources. However, autonomy is likely to be lower and accountability greater if a nonprofit is highly dependent on the resources of a small group of contributors with well-formed preferences.

Lack of accountability carries with it important costs. It may bring welcome autonomy to a nonprofit, but it may also make it more difficult for that nonprofit to attract resources. According to Useem lack of accountability means greater risks for potential investors.[23] In situations where demand for nonprofit service and service quality is high, lack of accountability may bring about external accountability standards, reduce nonprofit autonomy, and perhaps threaten the missions of nonprofits. As competition for scarce resources increases, nonprofit accountability is also likely to increase.

Private foundations are demanding more evidence and accountability from the nonprofits that they fund. Many expect nonprofits to become more "businesslike" in their operations. And as nonprofit services become more commercial, they may well be subjected to new external regulation and market-oriented accountabilities. Two very important questions are whether nonprofits have the capacity to meet the new accountability demands being made on them and whether they can demonstrate through the generation of credible evidence that they are acting and producing in ways that are expected by those that make them. We continue this discussion later as we explore the impact of using evidence-based practices in nonprofits' work.

Capacity for Experimentation and Innovation

Because of their traditional autonomy and the wide variety of interests represented in the sector, nonprofits have been thought to have considerable flexibility and facility for experimentation and innovation. Indeed, some observers contend that in this area they have the edge over for-profit organizations. Yet, there are organizational rigidities that may limit nonprofit flexibility and capacity for experimentation and innovation. These rigidities operate in relation to but also independently of the pressures toward conservatism and conformity associated with resource dependency and isomorphism.[24]

One of the most important sources of rigidity in nonprofit organizations is the centrality of their missions. Dennis Young observes that preservation of mission and goals is one of the strongest internal motivations influencing nonprofit behavior. Reid Lifset argues that nonprofits have both normative and financial interest in preserving their mission and goals, inasmuch as donors and other sources of revenue invest in the achievement of those missions and goals. And nonprofits tend to act accordingly. In a study of large national nonprofits in the areas of youth services, health charities, community and recreation services, and advocacy programs for children and older Americans, Young found that these organizations behaved in ways that preserved their missions, sustained consistency between their mission and their activities (including commercial activities), and preserved their legal status as nonprofits.[25] They were selective in the funding they accepted, opting for sources that imposed the least obligations. They worked hard to avoid activities, particularly commercial ones that posed serious risks to their missions and to their public reputations for charitable and public service. Preserving mission and goals may be easier for large, well-established, and well-supported nonprofits than for smaller, newer, and less-well-funded ones.

The literature identifies several other sources of rigidity that could limit nonprofit flexibility, experimentation, and innovation. Kanter and David Summers argue that the larger the number of funders or stakeholders claiming to define the mission and operation of a nonprofit, the more difficult it is for that nonprofit to experiment and innovate. In addition, nonprofits in which professionals play important roles may be constrained by the norms and standards of practice "imported" by those professionals from sources outside the organization. According to Kanter and Summers, those external norms and standards can interfere with a nonprofit's ability to develop new responses to changing constituent needs and other external demands. They contend that normative-oriented nonprofits have a tendency to believe in their own value independent of external reference.[26] In these organizations, failure to achieve goals is not necessarily taken as a sign of weakness or as an indication of a need to change or innovate.

Internal Stresses and Crises of Identity

Resource dependency, growth of competition and commercialism, increased accountability, and organizational rigidities are all sources of internal stress for nonprofits. Increased competition for traditional funding sources and growing commercialism pose serious challenges to the ways nonprofit organizations operate and to popular conceptions about how they are supposed to behave. By becoming less "charitable" and more "market-oriented" and "businesslike," they may appear to be compromising their public service missions and altering the ways in which they operate, and these changes may raise questions about their legal "protections" and thereby incur even more financial risk. According to Edward Skloot, competition and commercialism can diversify a nonprofit's revenue base and perhaps spawn new programs and services. At the same time, they can promote conflicts over goals and priorities, resource allocation within the organization, and staff activities. Skloot also contends that nonprofits in greatest need of new revenue sources may be the least able to create commercially viable ventures. These nonprofits tend to be small, serve the neediest clients, and lack the internal capacity and operating margin for marketing, service innovation, and organizational flexibility.[27]

These conditions put traditional missions and the charitable and advocacy roles of nonprofits at risk. They create new complexities that require a wide range of more sophisticated technical, legal, and financial expertise. This in turn creates new and heavier demands on nonprofit leadership and sets up the potential for conflict between professional and managerial staff and nonprofessional volunteer staff, donors, and other stakeholders who may hold tightly to traditional missions and roles.[28]

Some observers believe that these changes are leading to a split between donative nonprofits and commercial nonprofits and that this split is creating a "massive" identity crisis for the sector. The crisis may be felt within nonprofit organizations as they experience tension between traditional missions and roles and successfully competing for resources and clients in an increasingly commercial market. It may also manifest itself in the threat it poses to public trust in the sector. As nonprofits become more commercial, they can be perceived as acting and advocating less on behalf of the clients and communities they serve and more on behalf of their own self-interests. And this creates a problem of public perception and legitimacy, as Salamon suggests, a conflict between the "distinctiveness imperative" of nonprofit organizations and the "survival imperative," with the latter seemingly getting the upper hand.[29]

IMPLICATIONS FOR EVIDENCE-BASED PRACTICE

We now explore a number of possible implications of the characteristics and behaviors of nonprofits to use and promote evidence–based practice. We organize this section much like the last, looking first at the implications of structural characteristics of nonprofits, then implications of resource dependency and isomorphic behavior, and so forth.

Structural Characteristics

The structural characteristic of nonprofits most salient to the promotion of evidence-based practice may be their mission of public service.[30] This focus on service could draw nonprofit organizations toward evidence-based practice, particularly if the current trend toward evidence-based decisionmaking in the public sector continues and proves to be fruitful. And if nonprofits were persuaded that evidence-based practice would help them achieve their goals, they would be even more likely to adopt it. At the same time, however, nonprofits with strong normative or value-based missions and goals might eschew evidence-based practice because it could threaten their missions and strategies and because of the flexibility and adaptation it may require. Being evidence-based implies a willingness and a capacity to alter directions when the evidence warrants it. It could require levels of reflection and self-evaluation that might be difficult for an ideologically based nonprofit to achieve, particularly if it is a small organization that lacks the capacity for R&D and cannot easily develop new strategies or services. What may matter most here is the degree to which a nonprofit is "results-oriented" rather than committed to a particular value, principle, objective, or strategy.

Being evidence-based would also require that a nonprofit have the capacity to monitor, evaluate, and justify its actions and outcomes to funders and stakeholders differently. A nonprofit's goals and strategies could no longer be legitimated to others by appealing only to values, philosophies, or popular but untested theories. Instead, nonprofits would have to show that their actions are warranted by credible and persuasive evidence. And this might require a fundamental change in how they represent themselves, their actions, and the outcomes of their work. Such changes might deter nonprofits with particularly strong ideological orientations and weak research and develop capacity from becoming involved with evidence-based practice.

There are several other structural characteristics of nonprofit organizations that we did not introduce earlier because they are not defining of nonprofits per se, though they may make some difference in the ability of nonprofits to promote evidence-based practice: size and locale. Brian Rowan observes that most nonprofits working with schools and school districts are small in size and lack resources for research and development. Small nonprofits may have difficulty monitoring their practice, collecting evidence, keeping up with research, and making changes in their services and operations. Promoting evidence-based practice may require a nonprofit to expand its staff to build R&D capacity, or it may require a nonprofit with relatively few resources to reallocate staff resources (e.g., to trade staff members who provide direct service to the field for R&D staff). These changes could create internal tensions that may undermine the ability of the nonprofit to function efficiently and effectively. In addition, they could prove to be a disincentive for small nonprofits to promote evidence-based practice.[31] Another important implication of size is that small nonprofits with a weak or unpredictable resource base may have greater difficulty developing and sustaining the long-term relationships with schools and school systems required to engage in evidence-based practice. Nonprofits might be deterred from evidence-based practice if they are uncertain that they could "stay the course" and effectively promote it over time.

Locale is another structural characteristic that could have implications for a nonprofit's ability to promote evidence-based practice. Robert Kronley and Claire Handley found that local reform support organizations (RSOs) often have intimate knowledge of a community's educational issues. They tend to provide a broader array of programs and services tailored to their specific settings and are more flexible in how they work with schools and school systems. Trust and legitimacy grow out of proximal familiarity. Because much of their support comes from close by, local RSOs have an incentive to adapt in order to sustain goodwill. Kronley and Handley contend that imported RSOs have much less knowledge of a local community's issues, needs, and interests.[32] Such organizations are more generally identified with a specific program or practice, and their legitimacy is often derived from their national experience and reputation, and so they are more likely to be "wedded" to their particular programs and practices and less likely to expand or adapt them or the ways in which they operate as organizations to local needs.

These findings suggest that local nonprofits may find it easier to engage schools and school districts in evidence-based practice and the changes that may be suggested by it, if they are willing to go along with it. However, local nonprofits may find it more difficult to share "bad news" from evidence and put relationships and resources on which they depend at risk; they may be reluctant to be "public critics" of their primary sources of support and legitimacy.[33] As such these nonprofits may be reluctant to press for changes that may be called for. Imported nonprofits may face a different set of issues promoting evidence-based practice. Their broader reputations may provide some impetus for local schools and school systems to adopt evidence-based practice, and their distance and relative independence from the locale in which they work may make it easier for them to share evidence and suggest changes. At the same time, because of their distance and independence, imported nonprofits may have difficulty establishing the trust relationships so important to processes of ongoing assessment and change. Moreover, if tied to particular programs and practice, imported nonprofits may have difficulty adapting their services and modes of operation should local context or evidence warrant it.

Finally, the affiliations nonprofit organizations are able to develop may make a difference in their willingness and ability to promote evidence-based practice. Research on nonprofits suggests that proximity to and strong relationships with civic and organizational elites have positive effects on the ability to raise donations and gain volunteers.[34] If these elites emphasize evidence-based practice, nonprofits may have substantial incentives to promote it. But if elites reinforce something else, there may be weaker incentives for nonprofits. Moreover, the types of organizations with which nonprofits are affiliated may affect their capacities for evidence-based practice. For instance, nonprofits associated with universities or other research-oriented organizations may be better positioned than more autonomous nonprofits— say community-based organizations—to promote evidence-based practice successfully.

Resource Dependency

Because of growing competition for resources, many nonprofits may need to diversify their resource bases to stabilize their operations. This could lead to greater variety in preferences about mission, strategy, and program exerted by their sources, which could introduce a higher level of fragmentation in expectations and accountability demands, compromising the depth and coherence of effort needed to promote evidence-based practice successfully. Nonprofits that have flexibility in choosing among funding sources and clients may find it easier to control their own future, whether or not that future includes evidence-based practice. And, depending on their own preferences, the ability of nonprofits to shape the values and preferences of those who support them may make it easier for them to promote the practice. It might be argued that evidence-based practices will make it easier for nonprofits to shape the preferences of their funders. If evidence of effectiveness becomes the primary currency of legitimacy, then those nonprofits that have it will secure more funding.

The collection of evidence about performance and outcomes that is part of evidence-based practice also may pose risks to nonprofits and their ability to sustain financial and political support. Collecting evidence that reveals that they are having little impact may lead to a reduction in nonprofits' funding and clients. If the emphasis funders and clients place on evidence of outcomes increases, the nonprofit sector could face significant changes. Growing demand for evidence of impact could lead to a winnowing out of small nonprofits that are not successfully working with schools or that are not capable of generating evidence that is seen as credible. In addition, growing demand for evidence of impact could lead to a growth in large nonprofits that have the R&D resources and staff to be able to provide more "effective" service and to develop credible evidence of impact. With such capacity, large nonprofits might become preferred providers and come to dominate the service market, or at least the nonprofit portion of it. Such a trend might make nonprofits more conservative in their search for and production of evidence and more likely to overstate the validity and importance of the available evidence. Indeed, this might also encourage nonprofits to undertake more conservative, easily measured, "sustaining" practices rather than risk more innovative and "disruptive" ones.

Growing competition for resources may not only require nonprofits to change the types of services they offer and produce greater evidence of outcomes, but it might also change the ways in which they operate. As we argued earlier, competition for resources is likely to increase nonprofit accountability not only for what they achieve but also for how they achieve it. Nonprofits are being pushed by funders to adopt more businesslike operations. The question is whether these practices, adopted to satisfy accountability demands, may promote or impede the promotion of evidence-based practice. The move toward business-oriented practices may draw scarce resources from the "service" side of a nonprofit to the "management" side, reducing the ability of the nonprofit to engage in the long-term, process-oriented work required of evidence-based practice. Yet, the adoption of business-oriented practices may sharpen the focus within a nonprofit on performance, outcomes, and evidence thereof, each consistent with evidence-based practice.

Another consideration is the extent to which dependency on schools and school districts as clients would affect the willingness of nonprofits to promote evidence-based practice. To gain access to schools and school districts to do the "socially useful" work that they want to do (and to also gain revenue), nonprofits must offer something educators value. That something might be the provision of resources (financial, personnel, material), legitimation or status, or the promise of real improvement. If schools or school districts continue to stress expediency and visibility more than evidence of effectiveness, it will be difficult for nonprofits to gain access by arguing that their value is that they are "evidence-based." However, to the extent that federal and state policies, especially No Child Left Behind, encourage schools to adopt evidence-based practices, nonprofits working in education may also have to move in that direction.

But what form of evidence-based practice will the federal and state accountability pressures push schools and school districts, and their nonprofit partners, to adopt? It is certainly possible that high-stakes accountability pressures might push schools and school systems toward a more expedient "technology transfer" form of evidence-based practice. Indeed, the push for short-term, measurable improvement in test scores may serve as a disincentive for the schools and school systems that need it most to engage in the longer-term, process-oriented evidence-based practice that we advance here. As a consequence, nonprofits offering highly specified programs of improvement supported by evidence of increased test scores will have an advantage over those seeking to help schools build professional cultures that foster continuous improvement.

Isomorphic Behavior

Beyond relationships with particular funders, stakeholders, or clients, the broader norms and expectations of the education and policy environment— indeed, the school improvement market— may have substantial influence on whether and how nonprofits promote evidence-based practice. It is more than an issue of gaining access and resources from particular sources. It is a matter of developing and sustaining legitimacy, vitality, and competitiveness in the broader environment. In public education in the United States, evidence-based practice, however it is defined, is gaining greater credence in the school improvement market and in the broader environment as it is being promoted by federal and state policies. Nonprofits may be "pushed" away from promoting more faddish or innovative products that have a weak base of evidence to a narrow form of evidence-based practice, not only to be more competitive for resources but also to establish and sustain broader legitimacy. This could discourage innovation and disadvantage small nonprofits. Only large nonprofits might be able to mount the sorts of R&D initiatives required to test new ideas in scientifically credible ways, and these larger nonprofits could become more dependent on federal grants and thus federal approval of their research and evidence. In turn, this could reduce the special value of nonprofits in the broader pluralist environment.

At issue is what counts as evidence-based practice in the broader environment as well as in relationships with funders and client schools and school districts. Many nonprofits that work in education claim to be "evidence-based," but it is not clear how many of them really are (this depends in part on how evidence-based practice is defined). In the introduction to this chapter, we described some of the different ways that external organizations claim to be "evidence-based." Corcoran and his colleagues found that of the 700 organizations in Kentucky that were accepting state funds to provide professional development services for teachers, only sixty could produce any evidence to support their claims of impact.[35] Only a handful had evidence that would meet minimum standards of research and evaluation methodology. For the vast majority of these organizations, the mere claim of being evidence-based was sufficient to receive funds for services.

Promoting evidence-based practice may help nonprofits establish credibility and legitimacy in the broader environment, which may help them become more visible and competitive in crowded markets in which they operate. Where markets are not so crowded, the issue of wider credibility and legitimacy may not be so important, as least in the short term. Organizations and programs like Success for All, the Merck Institute for Science Education, the National Center for Education and the Economy, the Boston Plan for Excellence, and others like them illustrate how nonprofits have funded large-scale, independent evaluations of their work because they believed that credible evidence would help them improve the quality of their programs and services, enhance their legitimacy, promote their visibility and reputations, and expand their work with schools. Nonprofits that serve smaller markets with little competition have had less need to produce evidence to establish reputations in their environments. For example, the El Paso Collaborative for Excellence in Education and the Fund for Excellence in Baltimore have national reputations but only recently have begun to invest in the collection of data on the impact of their work. Similarly, the International Baccalaureate Program has never conducted systematic evaluations of its work but has earned an international reputation for quality; but now under pressure from new federal mandates, this program has begun to develop a research program to collect evidence of its effectiveness.

Autonomy and Accountability

Competition for scarce resources and the push toward accountability may provide important new incentives for nonprofits working in education to promote evidence-based practice. Norms of organizational autonomy and freedom from accountability among nonprofits are being challenged in the current environment. The heightened press for accountability may encourage nonprofits to adopt evidence-based practice inasmuch as funders, clients, and others may be "defining" accountability in those terms. This new accountability may require more than making simple (and sometimes highly selective) references to previous research to support a nonprofit's strategies. It may require producing evidence of results. Again, depending on the definition of accountability, and depending on the competitiveness of the market in which they operate, nonprofits may lose school and district "clients" to other "providers" if they cannot demonstrate that their services contribute to school performance.

This raises the important issue of the capacity of a nonprofit to develop evidence of its own effectiveness. To provide such evidence, it must have staff with the technical capacity for R&D or partners with such expertise, and the resources to support this work. There must also be incentives in place for nonprofits to overcome the aversion to engaging in self-evaluation that might reveal evidence of ineffectiveness or inconsistency across contexts. Finally, there is the possibility that heightened accountability may lead nonprofits to be more selective about the schools and school districts with which they work. They may avoid those with poor track records and few resources—the "tough cases"—for the risks they pose to achieving successful outcomes. Instead, nonprofits might seek schools and school systems with better records and stronger capacity that present them with success.

Flexibility and Capacity for Experimentation and Innovation

As we advance it here, evidence-based practice requires adaptation as evidence warrants. The autonomy and freedom from accountability traditionally associated with nonprofit organizations may thus make them particularly well-suited to promote evidence-based practice. In theory, those nonprofits able to develop and sustain adequate levels of resources and to attract professional R&D staff will be able to gain the independence needed to experiment and innovate. However, our analysis suggests that there are a number of factors that may severely constrain nonprofits' ability to be flexible and adaptive. Indeed, these factors may promote conservatism and persistence in nonprofit behavior rather than experimentation and innovation.

These factors include the tendency for nonprofits, particularly norma- tively oriented ones, to act in ways that reinforce and preserve their missions and primary strategies. Nonprofits are prone to isomorphic behavior, which may encourage conformity over innovation. Nonprofits may also be influ- enced in conservative directions by the expectations of those organizations that support them. Heightened accountability, which on the one hand may provide an incentive for nonprofits to adopt evidence-based practice, may, on the other, push them toward less risky school clients and less risky, per- haps less effective, practices. None of these influences are necessarily condu- cive to promoting the forms of evidence-based practice we believe hold the greatest value for schools.

Internal Stresses and Crises of Identity

The internal stresses and crises faced by nonprofits also have implications for their promotion of evidence-based practice. Competition for scarce resources; tensions between the need for revenue generation and the provision of qual- ity service; increasing and conflicting demands on leadership; tensions and power differences among volunteer, professional, and managerial staff; con- flicts among efforts to meet demands and expectations of diverse funders and stakeholders—all these issues may make it difficult for nonprofits to devote the resources and sustain the commitment necessary to promote evidence- based practice over time.

Among these sources of discord and stress, the tension between growing commercialism and the preservation of the public service function may hold the most important implications for the promotion of evidence-based prac- tice. The trend toward commercialism may push nonprofits' work toward a product orientation rather than a service orientation. This would be con- sistent with the federal administration's view of evidence-based practice as "technology transfer," and NCLB offers incentives for nonprofits to move in this direction. However, "going commercial" carries its own costs and requires the commitment of internal resources. There are both direct and opportunity costs. Resources that might have gone into working with schools must be put toward product development, marketing, and advertising. Ironically, going commercial to become more competitive may invite more competition from other nonprofits and for-profits, and this may intensify internal tension and stress.

A product orientation and its attendant costs may reduce the ability of nonprofits to promote evidence-based practice as we have defined it here. This form of evidence-based practice requires long-term process-oriented relationships with schools and school districts that may be viewed as inefficient and costly. Facing financial stringency, nonprofits may have to reconcile the tension between developing and selling products, having immediate impact on test scores, and generating more revenue and providing services that may be less profitable but more effective in achieving their mission and goals in the long run. This conflict is clearly illustrated in the case of comprehensive school reform developers who have found that there was more money to be made in selling model components to private vendors than in providing long-term process-oriented services to schools. This choice has often been justified as a more effective dissemination strategy so that "effective" programs could reach more users. However, this strategy may not necessarily be the most effective one for promoting continuous improvements in schools.

As we suggested earlier, "going commercial" may also threaten public and political perceptions of nonprofits' motives and their claims to altruistic public service. It may challenge their credibility and "moral" capital and compromise their legal protections and financial support. In addition, commercialism may introduce a new and different form of nonprofit accountability—the market. These conditions may create incentives for nonprofits to embrace evidence-based practice. If a nonprofit can provide credible evidence that its services are effective, it may do better marketing its products and services to schools in the commercial market. More fundamentally, if a nonprofit can show that through evidence-based practice it is providing a high-quality service and is achieving the outcomes expected of it, it also may enhance its public image. It can demonstrate that the focus of its efforts is on the client rather than its own interests. In doing so a nonprofit can help preserve its reputation for altruistic service and preserve the public trust.

FINAL THOUGHTS

Our analysis suggests a number of observations about nonprofit organizations and the promotion of the form of evidence-based practice we advance here. First, there seems to be nothing inherent in the organizational or legal structure of nonprofits that creates incentives for them to promote evidence-based practice. However, there are other characteristics of nonprofits, notably their missions and sources of legitimation, that have more significant implications for their willingness and capacity to do so. Our analysis suggests that nonprofits that have relied on the salience of educational problems and on passion and charisma to legitimate their actions and attract support may have difficulty moving to evidence-based practice. For these organizations, politics, connections to the communities they serve, and persuasive philosophies have been and may remain more important than evidence justifying their actions. Our analysis suggests that nonprofits are more likely to promote evidence-based practice if their funders and client schools and school districts insist on it. Nonprofits are also more likely to promote evidence-based practice if it is expected in the broader social, political, and policy environments in which they operate.

Our analysis suggests that large, well-funded nonprofits may find it easier to promote evidence-based practice. These organizations may be better able to support the staff and dedicate the resources to stay connected to the knowledge base, to develop evidence of their effectiveness, and to engage in continuous adaptation of strategy. Because of this, larger, professionally based nonprofits may be more capable of promoting evidence-based practice than community- or volunteer-based nonprofits. It is always possible that small, less technically capable nonprofits could collaborate with other organizations to enhance their analytic capacity, but such interorganizational relationships are complex and may introduce new problems that diminish the value added. And problem-oriented nonprofits may be more likely to promote evidence-based practice than those that are organized around specific ideologies, products, or solutions. Their pragmatic stance regarding solutions equips them better for the demands of evidence-based practice.

The development of an evidence-based environment could lead to more nonprofit failures and to consolidation within the sector as some nonprofits struggle to develop evidence of their effectiveness. Large regional and national nonprofits with the capacity to provide evidence of their effectiveness are likely to gain the greatest market share, while smaller, local nonprofits are more likely to fail in such an environment. Pressure to demonstrate effects may raise personnel, R&D, and operating costs, which may encourage consolidation in the sector. This, in turn, may provide an incentive for commercialization to generate new sources of revenue. And this may undermine the overall impact of the shift to evidence-based practice by focusing attention more on the "product" by deemphasizing the "process" or support side of evidence-based practice and by raising questions about nonprofits as "protected" public service organizations.

Finally, increasing demand for evidence of effectiveness, among other dynamics that shape their behavior, may make nonprofits more conservative and risk-averse, which may lead nonprofits to look for "safe" places to work that would increase their chances of success and to favor "sustaining" innovations rather than more "disruptive" ones. This would create an ironic situation where schools and school districts that might benefit the most from evidence-based practice might be least likely to avail themselves of it and where strategies that might be most conducive to school improvement are sacrificed to the self-preservation of the agent or to the stability of a relationship of mutual dependency.

Are nonprofit organizations capable of promoting the form of evidence-based practice that we advance it here? Yes, we believe they are. However, this conclusion is conditional. The ability of nonprofits to promote evidence-based practice depends on their own orientations and resource base. It also depends on the relationships they have with those organizations that support them and the expectations of the broader environment in which they operate. Those nonprofits most capable of promoting evidence-based practice may be the largest, most pragmatic, well-established, and well-funded ones with the strongest record of performance and innovation. These organizations may have the financial, technical, and political capital to assume the risks associated with evidence-based practice and to shape the environment so that it is more supportive of their work. We are less sanguine about the potential of smaller, more ideological, less well-established, and less well-funded nonprofits to do this work well.

K–12 Education and the Role of For-Profit Providers

Louis M. Gomez and Guilbert C. Hentschke

Having crossed the threshold into the postindustrial age, we are situated in a society and an economy where information, and our facility with it, matters significantly for our success and survival. In this chapter we focus on the current role and potential of for-profit enterprises in preparing students for the knowledge society of the twenty-first century. We explore the relationship between the products and services that schools buy and use and their ability to transform themselves and their students into effective participants in the postindustrial age. Interest in the role of for-profit providers is driven by a search for ideas to spur current schooling practices to a new level of productivity, capable of meeting twenty-first-century expectations.

AMBITIOUS TEACHING AND LEARNING

Before we turn our attention to the role that businesses might play in supporting schools and their transformation, it is important to take a brief look at the kind of instruction and schooling that the greater society is requesting of its schools. The popular press and current political commentary are replete with calls for schools to prepare learners to be productive members of the knowledge society. However, as Andy Hargreaves points out, the knowledge society, with its fast pace of new and changing information, should, more correctly, be referred to as the learning society.[1] Moreover, solutions to the problems students will face in their adult lives will not all be found in the present curriculum. What is really needed are people who are life-long learners and problem-solvers. Schools, then, must take as a fundamental charge the goal of providing the skills and habits of mind that encourage people to be critical and analytic consumers of new information and effective problem-solvers throughout their lives. So, what do schools that succeed at such ambitious goals and that motivate students to want to learn look like?

They look very different from most schools we see today. Currently, a hallmark of much of American schooling is a learning environment that is rife with rote learning activities and teaching that fails to link instruction to the world beyond school or to give students opportunities to engage in active problem-solving. It follows that to achieve the more ambitious goals of education in the 21st century, students need to work on consequential problems that are connected to real life, where they are not just focused on getting a correct answer but also on understanding how the skills and knowledge they are learning relate to a larger question.[2] In learning contexts like these, students must build deep repertoires of fundamental literacy and numeracy skills, but these are done in the explicit service of their utility in solving problems.

Consider as an example students studying the problem of groundwater contamination and its prevention. Learners might be required to become acquainted with domain-relevant textual information and quantitative information and to reason with these in ways authentic to the domain.[3] Students will also have to, among other things, make contact with the science, math, and other skills they have acquired in the past and apply them both in solitary reasoning and in the company of teachers and peers to bring intellectual order to this problem setting.

To meet ambitious learning goals, the adults in schools have to work together in coordinated and concerted ways. By and large adult work in schools today is typified by isolated islands of expertise, what has been described as the "loosely-coupled school."[4] For example, examining the groundwater contamination problem might require math teachers and science teachers to work together, much as environmental biologists, hydrologists, land use economists, and local zoning officials do. Further, it requires school leadership to change the structure of the school day to make all this possible.

The foregoing example suggests that ambitious teaching and learning requires well-planned and purposeful activity on a number of fronts. On the content side, it is clear that students need a range of materials, including texts from the specific technical domains and in some cases technologies for visualization and modeling. On the accountability side, we conjecture that ambitious instruction requires that students have new ways to demonstrate their learning and teachers have alternative ways to communicate with students about their learning. With respect to rhythm and pacing in the school day, instructional time may need to be reallocated to allow students and staff to work in new ways. Teachers need opportunities to learn to be effective and time to plan and collaborate with each other. Schools need new organizational, curricular, administrative, and clerical tools that support teachers' work.

Districts and schools rely substantially on the private sector to help them do their work. They face "buy versus make" decisions like all other organizations; and for some goods and services, it is more efficient and effective to buy them than it is to try to make them. Part of the reason schools rely on the goods and services created by firms is that they have no funds to invest in their own research and development (R&D). We refer to these firms as private sector intermediaries, whose aim is to make a profit by meeting the needs of their customers in a manner that is more distinctive and more cost effective than their competitors and more cost effective than their customers could produce in-house. In short, private sector intermediaries seek to innovate through the products they provide. The private sector, then, is in a strategic position to promote meaningful school reform. The reality is that although the products of these firms could be crucial in establishing ambitious instruction as routine in schools, by and large they do not play this role.

Research and the Supply of Ideas for "Ambitious Instruction"

Why haven't private intermediaries filled this void and provided a host of products that assist schools in this transformation? Economists proffer one answer. They claim that two conditions must be met for the private sector to respond to the education market with inventive new products. First there must be a ready "supply" of useful declarative knowledge from the relevant sciences and technical disciplines. And, second, there must be "demand" that promises profit from new products that transform the declarative knowledge into procedural knowledge that supports praxis leading to ambitious teaching and learning.[5]

From the standpoint of the supply-side of ideas, we need to ask whether the fields of cognitive and learning science know enough about how people learn to spur product inventiveness or, at a minimum, to imagine powerful new learning tools. According to some scholars, the sciences of the mind have made important and relatively rapid progress in understanding the cognitive and social underpinnings of human learning and the kind of instruction that promotes it. While acknowledging the conceptual progress in this domain, other social scientists conjecture that problems faced by teachers and students are sufficiently complex, ill-defined, and irregular that they defy solutions from today's state-of-the-art cognitive and learning sciences. The critique goes on to suggest that knowledge which comes from cognitive science is sufficiently imprecise to prescribe action at the level of schooling. By comparison to the physical sciences and some domains in the biological sciences, knowledge from the cognitive sciences lacks granularity. Richard Nelson suggests that robust scientific findings from learning science often lack enough precision to guide action. The argument goes on to suggest that the utility of cognitive science is highly conditioned by context. In short, what works in one setting will not necessarily work in another. Because our theories of context are weak, we can't be sure whether insights will remain stable across contexts. These conditions, it is argued, serve to slow the ability of cognitive and learning science to spur product innovation.[6]

We appreciate this critique, but we think the knowledge base in the cognitive and learning sciences and its relevance to practice are seriously underestimated. We agree that scientific and technical progress that leads to productive product-level innovation must rest on a base of results that are both cumulative and replicated. It is apparent to us, as it has been to others,[7] that the cognitive and learning sciences have some way to go in establishing a robust base of cumulative results that can shape practice. Nevertheless, we do not believe that the cognitive and learning sciences are inherently incapable of establishing a base of useful knowledge that leads to product-level innovation. As Nelson points out, productive innovation requires both strong "basic" science and strong "bridge" sciences that help to translate fundamental insights into useful information that can be taken up in product-level innovations.[8] We believe that *cognitive science* can serve education as a substrate and *learning science* is an example of a bridge to practical innovation.

We conjecture that for knowledge about human learning to become broadly useful in schools, it must be contextualized and made part of routine action in specific settings. We consider as an example how a well-established fact—that prior knowledge (or preconceptions) fundamentally influences future learning—can become practically usable. Hunt and Minstrell reasoned that students in physics classrooms faced with new problem-solving situations bring their prior experience to bear on physics. Sometimes what students know is useful; other times it is not and is even a distraction. To make physics prior knowledge concrete, Minstrell compiled a set of facets of physics knowledge that students might bring to a classroom. Minstrell also specified the facets necessary to understand and solve specific physics problems. Finally, Minstrell and colleagues built a software application called

Diagnoser, which helps teachers assess and diagnose their students' facets of understanding, and design instruction that addresses details of student misunderstandings.[9]

Here we see an example of knowledge about the effects of prior understandings on learning being used to develop a tool that assists teachers in the domain of physics. While the learning and cognitive sciences needs a large repertoire of examples like this, the one we cite is not an isolated case. We could have pointed to a number of other examples, including the construction of online communities to support teacher learning, that draw on, for the specifics of their design, knowledge about the construction and effective collaborative communities of practice.[10]

The point of our example is that the cognitive and learning sciences are, in principle, up to the challenge of informing innovation with technical supply-side input. Results such as these are possible because over the last three to four decades, core understanding in the cognitive and learning sciences has made steady progress in characterizing the nature of human learning and the kind of tools and instruction that promote it. During the same period, computer and software scientists have become skilled at designing tools and applications that are explicitly focused on supporting complex social interactions.[11] We are left with the question: If the supply side of ideas in education is capable of providing information at a granular level that can support innovation at the product level, why aren't these products more pervasive in schools?

The Expression of Demands for Goods and Services by American Schools

The goal of firms in the Pre-K–12 education marketplace is to produce innovative goods and services that help them survive and thrive. This goal is neither remarkable nor uniquely characteristic of these particular firms.[12] Firms need to know what will sell as well as what to produce. This section on what shapes the *effective demand*—what school people want *and* are willing to pay for—explains why innovative and potentially effective goods and services are only rarely available.

Schools and districts are bound to for-profit providers by a complex web of buying and selling relationships. This web of relationships is largely externally and governmentally generated and not directly about sellers meeting the day-to-day, practice-based needs of schools to create effective learning environments. State and federal agencies shape demand for goods and services through the regulations they write and the money they supply to schools and districts. While the actual buying and selling that takes place between for-profit providers and school people is highly localized, it is subject to and stylized by public-sector purchasing regulations.

Figure 6.1 illustrates our sense of the education market's demand chain. The chain has several key elements that range from policy to on-the-ground routines. We conjecture that the school marketplace is organized by a set of strong (designated by filled arrows) and weak (designated by unfilled arrows) relationships. In our conception, the federal and state policy sector exerts its influence on local finance and governance. Governance and finance shapes school and school district demands for products and services. This in turn shapes the kinds of products and services for-profit suppliers create. As we noted earlier, these products and services are the tools that create the day-to-day routines in schools that affect children's educational opportunities. In this view, products are strongly shaped by a top-down process involving high-level policymakers and only weakly shaped by bottom-up feedback.

In our view, federal and state governments have a key role in the kinds of goods and services schools buy, and, so far, they have not promoted the kind of instruction we believe is needed to prepare students in the twenty-first century. Large-scale innovations are also limited by the realities of firms having to sell them to a fragmented set of potential customers in fifty states, 15,000 school districts, and over 100,000 schools. Relatively few firms are large enough to staff a national sales force, and therefore even the best solutions from the largest firms are rarely marketed across the entire country. We discuss below the consequences that this remote relationship to practice and the fragmented market has on the creation of products and services that support ambitious learning.

One of the challenges of private-sector firms that has broad impact on their ability to market goods and services is the extensive intra- as well as interorganizational compartmentalization of school districts. For example, schools often have different buyers for basal texts, supplementary services, testing, data management services, teacher professional development services, leadership training, afterschool programming, and other goods and services. In addition to segmentation by item of purchase, buying authority is further segmented by funding sources attached to policy initiatives (e.g., Title I, e-rate, state categorical grants). Thus, providers face multiple, poorly labeled, shifting sets of buyers, each buying on average relatively small quantities. Indeed, whether a particular good or service "qualifies" for funding from a given source is often unclear and a matter of judgment. Despite these and other challenges, a sizeable industry has grown up, but this industry is not geared to create products that are shaped by practitioners' needs.

FIGURE 6.1   Idealized Characterization of the Education Marketplace Demand Chain

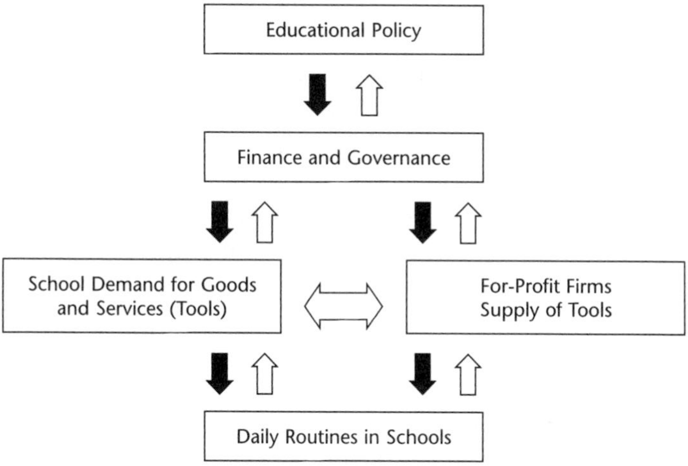

Note: The black arrows show strong systemic connectivity; the white convey weaker relations.

GOVERNANCE AND FINANCE

As agencies of state governments, most schools and districts are subject to oversight through two mechanisms: the rules imposed on schools and districts by higher levels of government (governance) and the amounts and conditions placed on money provided to schools (finance). As a consequence, changes in school governance and finance affect and are reflected in the goods and services that are sold to schools and school districts. In various combinations, rules and money shape demand.[13]

Governance

School practices depend substantially on decisions made at higher levels of government.[14] Superordinate bodies, such as state and federal agencies, provide three kinds of regulations: required ("you must"), permissive ("you may"), and prohibitive ("you can't"), or some combination of these. State textbook adoption policies, for example, usually stipulate a list of approved texts from which schools and districts can choose. (They are either prohibited from purchasing texts not on the lists or do not receive financial support if they purchase them.) Requirements in the federal No Child Left Behind (NCLB) Act have significantly increased demand for student information systems, assessment and testing services, basal materials in reading and math that are linked to standards, and supplementary services for low-performing students.

Textbooks at the state level and NCLB at the federal level are just two examples of how markets are shaped by policies related to finance and governance. Education research that provides ideas for more effective instruction plays an indirect and minor role in most school purchases. Regardless of whether textbook adoption policies, testing policies, or other policies foster ambitious instruction, it appears to us that the ideas from research must impact the policy environment before they can shape school and district demand for goods and services.

Finance

The money that enables schools and districts to enter the marketplace reaches them though a large number of separate "buckets" that differ from each other in at least three respects: (1) the amount (which may vary significantly from year to year); (2) the degree to which the money can only be spent on prespecified goods and/or services (categorical vs. general operating and/or block grants); and (3) the degree to which all possible recipients are to receive like amounts (entitlements versus competitive grants). Categorical money is not fungible; controlled amounts are aimed at limited categories of purchases. In contrast, the general operating budget of school districts and schools is usually locally generated and has relatively few restrictions. Even general operating funds are not protected from "encroachment" of new requirements from higher levels of government and must be used to pay for them. Because the school people operate within generally fixed (zero sum) budget constraints, new regulations change the shape of demand curves for all goods and services sold to them. While increasing demand for some goods and services, NCLB has simultaneously softened demand for others (e.g., supplementary materials, but not supplementary services), and noncore subject matter curricular materials and other goods and services typically purchased from the general operating budget.

Categorical funds have targeted requirements, "strings," attached by higher levels of government to increase the likelihood that their preferences and priorities are receiving support. For many years the federal government has provided about 8 percent of the education budget, much of it for categorical programs that supplement or complement those also funded by the states. State categorical funding has tended to grow over time, reducing local discretion. Earmarked money for education in California, for example, increased steadily from about 25 percent in state education funds in 1981–82 to nearly 40 percent in 1996–97. In 2001 California had fifty separate categorical programs covering more than 100 spending "categories." A recent study of the finance system in California concluded that the system has grown out of control and is now one of the most complex and bureaucratic states in the nation, lacking in both equity and effectiveness.[15]

Because of the absence of an integrated structure, the system of earmarked funding is extremely complex due to the many different purposes and various funding and accountability schemes. School people (and the for-profit firms selling to schools) are placed in the role of deciphering constraints placed on appropriations to them rather than evaluating goods and services that, in their judgment, best address their problems.

To assist in this process, a cottage industry of firms has emerged to provide innovative services for deciphering funding regulations. School people take advantage of these services because they offer real, tangible benefits for their schools and districts. Rather than scanning research for ideas that might foster effective instruction, school people are scanning the regulations to see what they are allowed to buy and in order to make the best choices they can among the available options. Certainly educators at the school and district levels have opinions about the relative value among purchasing options, and most likely those opinions are formed in no small part by what they consider to be "best practice." Nonetheless, those buying choices are significantly constrained by top-down policy pressures and perhaps, to a suboptimal extent, by the bottom-up realities of on-the-ground practice. When seen through the lens of our demand chain model, practice-centered relationships between school-level actors and for-profit actors are shaped by finance and governance arrangements.

EXAMINING THE IMPACT OF GOVERNANCE AND FINANCE IN THE EDUCATION MARKETPLACE

In schools and districts, the rules of governance and the options created by finance systems influence purchasing behavior, including how much can be spent, on what, for whom, and for what use. We argue that the education goods and services produced by private-sector firms reflect the confluence of these finance and governance rules and, later, suggest changes in these rules that would increase the likelihood of supporting more ambitious teaching and learning. As an illustration, consider the current bundle of goods and services being purchased to order to examine the forces that shape demand for them. Table 6.1 arrays for each of the segments in the Pre-K–12 marketplace their proportionate share of the market ($48.8 billion in 2002) as well as the annual growth rates (3 years actual, 1 year estimated, and 4 year average). The sizes of the nine separate market segments varies widely (28% to 2%), as do the year-to-year and four-year-average growth rates (13.8% to –2%). These variations reflect the interplay of the finance and governance variables.

High-Growth Market Segments: K–12 Delivery, Testing, Tutoring

First consider the three segments with the highest year-over-year annual growth: K–12 delivery, testing, and tutoring. Growth in K–12 delivery has been driven by continuing growth in charter schools, which have been legalized through permissive legislation now in more than forty states within the last fifteen years (about 60% of the business in this segment), as well as in contract management services with school districts. Permissive charter legislation is similar in impact (but larger in scale) to the growth in permissive legislation for homeschooling. Over the last three decades homeschooling first "flipped" from being banned in about two-thirds of the states to being a legal option in all states. Coupled with charter legislation, the regulatory environment was altered to pave the way for the introduction of commercial homeschooling services as well as virtual charter schools.

Proprietary schools, moreover, have benefited from the 2002 U.S. Supreme Court ruling allowing vouchers for attending private schools. Various states and municipalities have sought to formalize this option, including providing vouchers to students in continually low-performing schools. Virtual schooling options have also been used to solve several "traditional" schooling challenges, such as creating equal opportunities for all students, addressing shortfalls in credentialed/certified educators, maximizing limited financial resources, and promoting more individualized instruction opportunities.[16]

The second high-growth segment—testing—owes much of its growth to the testing requirements incorporated in the most recent reauthorization of the Elementary and Secondary Education Act (NCLB), including provisions that all states must test students in grades 3–8 in reading and math by the beginning of the 2005–6 school year and in grades 3–5, 6–9, and 10–12 by the 2007–8 school year. Simultaneously, many states have been implementing exit exams.

The pressures reflected in the testing mandates in the Elementary and Secondary Education Act (ESEA) are also increasing the demand for test preparation services. The traditional "business-to-consumer" (B2C) market for these

TABLE 6.1   Pre-K–12 Market Segments

	Relative Size %	2000	2001	2002	2003 est.	Average
Delivery						
Pre-K Education & Childcare	28	3.9	4.0	(1.0)	0.0	1.7 Low
K–12 Education	15	11.7	9.3	7.1	7.8	9.0 High
Publishing	17	14.8	11.0	(3.0)	1.0	6.0 Med
Infrastructure						
Computing Hardware	9	5.0	(4.0)	(5.0)	(4.0)	(2.0) Low
Enterprise Software & Services	3	6.4	6.4	6.8	6.9	6.6 Med
Services						
Testing	2	9.4	13.6	10.7	11.4	11.3 High
Tutoring	7	13.0	13.9	14.0	14.2	13.8 High
Professional Development	3	14.0	7.0	6.0	5.0	8.0 Med
Procurement	16	6.1	4.5	(1.0)	1.0	2.7 Low
TOTAL	100	8.1	6.1	1.0	2.7	—

services (parents paying for tutoring services for their kids) is now being increasingly added to by a "business-to-business" (B2B) market, as schools, districts, and even states increasingly allocate resources for test preparation resources for mandated state-specific exams. In Massachusetts, for example, the Department of Education contracted with *The Princeton Review* to provide students with free online access to practice tests for the statewide Massachusetts Comprehensive Assessment System (MCAS) exam.

Increased demand for tutoring services, the third among the high-growth market segments, has been driven by requirements of the 2001 reauthorization of ESEA, similar to its demand-inducing effects on testing and test prep. On the consumer retail, or B2C, side, increased testing requirements for schools and the high stakes associated with these assessments is placing considerable performance pressure on students.[17] For families with sufficient financial resources, supplementary tutoring services that augment classroom instruction continue to be a staple of students' academic experience. On the B2B side, Title I funding available for tutoring services to students in underperforming schools is driving up demand by schools for outsourced tutoring services to close their achievement gaps. Institutional providers include Sylvan Education Solutions and Kaplan's K12 Learning Services.

In all three high-growth market segments, increased demand was fueled by legislative changes which either permitted initiatives that fostered growing demand (e.g., charter schools) or imposed requirements that fostered increased demand (e.g., testing) for services.

Medium-Growth Market Segments: Publishing, Supplementary Materials and Software, and Professional Development

Growth in these middle three segments has been affected both positively and negatively by the interaction of finance and governance influences on school districts and schools. Publishing is generally funded out of general operating revenues to districts and schools, so state budget shortfalls translate into fewer resources for school districts to spend on instructional materials. "More than 30 states were forced to revise their budgets during 2002, with cuts in education spending a frequent result. Moreover, a number of states are considering postponing textbook adoptions."[18]

Countering this downward pressure to a degree are the mandates of ESEA requiring districts and publishers to demonstrate the educational efficacy of their offerings. Basal readers, the largest publishing segment, are possibly the biggest losers in this segment, due largely to recent state budget shortfalls. Supplementary materials providers, however, that provide products they claim to be research based and that focus on reading, math, and assessment are doing better. This emphasis carries over into reference materials as well, which also benefits from federal library-related (not school-related) funding initiatives.

Similar to publishing, enterprise software and services has been experiencing both downward and upward pressure and for similar reasons: state budget reductions (downward) and ESEA requirements (upward). In particular, the major reporting demands embedded within the ESEA are driving districts (and states) to invest in new software solutions. Schools try to pull from a variety of funding sources to support technology development, including the E-rate program, grants and donations, bonds, and state and federal appropriations. But to the extent that districts see technology as discretionary, demand will slide further.

The countervailing pressures facing the professional development are slightly different from those facing publishing and enterprise software. To be sure, the regulatory stimulus of ESEA on states to raise the number of teachers who are "highly qualified" coupled with several billion dollars in new (categorical) funding to meet these new standards has fostered the growth of the professional development segment. Countering these upward pressures, however, have been reductions in state funding of schools and districts. In addition, districts and schools are outsourcing a declining share of their professional development work, seeking to save money, grow internal capacity, and better align services to priorities.

Slow-Growth Market Segments: Pre-K Delivery, Hardware, Procurement

Those segments that have grown and are likely to grow the least—pre-K delivery, computing hardware, and procurement—share two characteristics: They are financially supported largely by noncategorical funds, and they are not specifically required on a large scale. Pre-K Education and childcare is perhaps the most obvious of the segments. The largely B2C focus on both the few large and many (about 116,000) small firms ties demand for these services to the overall domestic economy. Coupled with this, for-profit providers are facing increasing competition from public schools seeking to respond to community calls for universal pre-K services. These services are provided at no cost, and, in conjunction with a growing number of nonprofit providers offering similar services at heavily discounted prices, they are soaking up the pool of potential children. In addition, firms in this particular segment have had to deal with issues of teacher quality and high turnover, further reducing the incentives for firms to expand in this segment.

The markets in computing hardware are driven directly by funding and only indirectly by the regulatory environment, such as ESEA. Although federal categorical funding (E-rate) has spurred some demand for hardware, it has been more than countered by cutbacks in state and local spending. Moreover, some states (e.g., Texas and California) have cut their categorical programs in technology, cuts that cascade down to districts and schools, where upgrades and replacements are being postponed. Cost pressures are carried over to firms in this area, forcing them to come up with solutions that shrink overall costs of ownership. Growth in wireless networks is beginning to take place, due in part of lower costs and ease of implementation.

The procurement segment of the education marketplace is among the slowest growing segments for reasons similar to pre-K delivery and computing hardware because of dependence on the general operating budget rather than categorical funds and a lack of a regulatory driver stimulating demand. It labors under the additional disadvantage of its fragmented structure. Firms in this segment are composed of small, regional, family-owned businesses with less than $20 million in annual revenues. Besides facing diminishing school budgets, they are facing increasing pressure from large-scale retail office supply stores, which often provide competitive pricing, rapid delivery options, single-source supply, automated inventory, and electronic ordering. These same factors are forcing consolidation of firms within this segment.

In this section we have examined how changes in policies (reflected in changes in governance and finance) appear to influence demands for goods and services. The pursuit of profitability by firms selling to education, including their ability to produce innovative goods and services, is governed as much by their access to investment capital as it is to demands from schools. For-profit businesses seek, but don't always get, the investment capital they need to grow. Being "attractive" to investors is as important for these firms as being "attractive" to school and district buyers, and it is important to understand this motivation if we are to identify under what conditions these firms might produce tools for more ambitious instruction in the future.

For-Profit Firms' Response to Demand and Access to Investment Capital

Firms in the education industry are, for the most part, typical of most profit-seeking businesses in basic structure, motivation, and the metrics that matter. Risk takers are required to finance the production of innovative goods and services.

For-profit firms need "free cash" beyond that generated by sales. They must incur startup expenses, such as for their own research and development, to first make their product or service ready for sale to customers and, later, to expand capacity in response to growth opportunities. Operating expenses, including marketing, typically must be paid before the cash income from sale of the product or service will be received. As the business grows, the need for cash is often the greatest because the investment necessary to achieve growth usually occurs before the generation of sufficient revenue from new sales. Risk capital seeks the highest possible risk-adjusted return on investment (ROI), thereby imposing a high degree of market discipline on innovators. In short, capital flows to the innovations with the greatest risk-adjusted potential ROI.[19] In today's world of education providers, successful innovation (resulting in penetration of and growth in the marketplace) is made possible by venture investors. Profitability is a function of profit margins and scale, and margins are a function of differences between sales prices and costs of production. Tools for ambitious instruction will be produced when demand can be met profitably, when there is a realistic chance for a firm to realize appropriate margins and scale.

The for-profit investor is primarily seeking return on investment and relying on similar incentives for senior management to pursue returns on investment through scale and related efficiencies as well as growing market share. The for-profit investor picks and chooses among the organizations in which to invest, typically looking for potential profitability and scalability. Attributes of a provider that are relevant to investors include: the business models it employs; its track record of top-line and bottom-line financial performance; earnings before interest, taxes, depreciation, and amortization (EBITDA); organic growth rates; record of acquisitions; history as a technical innovator; array of services; competition it faces; and the overall attractiveness of the industry.

In the ten-year period from 1991 through 2000, private equity investors invested nearly $9 billion in education and training companies, with roughly $5.5 billion of that invested in 1999 and 2000 alone. Investments in for-profit firms selling into the K–12 marketplace increased steadily and dramatically from $98 million in 1997 to $723 million in 2000.[20] Each of these dollars is "profit-seeking." (Investment slowed dramatically in 2001 and 2002, reflecting trends in the broader economic environment.) Education businesses have to compete against *all* other businesses for investment capital. Tools for ambitious instruction are interesting to investors only to the extent that they grow out of a compelling business model. The likelihood of an individual firm succeeding or failing over the long run is greatly influenced by its attractiveness (or lack thereof) to investors.[21]

The flow of investment capital to K–12 providers can be attributed both to "attracting" factors and "repelling" factors. Poor performance of existing education providers, (e.g., Education Alternatives Inc., Edison Schools, and Nobel Learning Communities) sends repelling signals to the investor. Some provider services are inherently more difficult to sell to practitioners because they more visibly compete with practitioners and could replace practitioner jobs. Some of the battles over for-profit education management organizations (EMOs) and private school vouchers reflect this perspective, mitigating the business potential of provider services, regardless of their merit. Professional development, for example, is among those services that many practitioners would prefer to provide in-house rather than to outsource. Public school districts allocate about 3 percent of their total expenditures to professional development (about $3 billion) but outsource only a tiny fraction of this amount.[22] To invest in a firm selling professional development to schools and districts, the investor would have to be convinced that the firm will be successful despite the competition it faces not only from other firms but also from districts and schools themselves. The drive toward innovations by education businesses is partly motivated by the desire to create products and services that are not currently available elsewhere and also difficult to duplicate.

The factors that shape the market of educational products and services have heretofore not fostered teaching that we believe will prepare the nation's children for the kind of problem-solving and life-long learning that is required to be successful in the twenty-first century. Do any policy levers exist that might foster the demand for, and the supply of, tools for more ambitious instruction? We frame this question narrowly as one that focuses on the buying/selling relationships, because that characterizes most of the way in which these two types of organizations currently relate to each other.

FOSTERING THE SUPPLY OF GOODS AND SERVICES FOR AMBITIOUS INSTRUCTION

Our analysis suggests several generalizations. First, the largely governmental organizations that shape and exercise their demand for goods and services *and* the largely for-profit organizations that sell into that market are characterized by high levels of fragmentation and variability. There are many small schools, districts, and firms that make up the marketplace, but there are also a small number of very large organizations on both sides. Both sides are consolidating—schools through district consolidation and firms through mergers and acquisitions. Nonetheless, in comparison with other industry sectors, K–12 has a lot of public money but also many buyers, most of which can only make small purchases. On the demand side, fragmentation across the large number of states, districts, and schools is compounded by the fragmentation of categorical grants, uncertainty in annual appropriations, and accounting traditions that separate operating from capital expenditures.

It is at least plausible that if this fragmentation was lessened, and demand could be enhanced, the products and services available to teachers, administrators, and children might be improved. In retrospect, some of the more pronounced experiences that educationalists have with innovation can be seen through the problematic lens of fragmentation. For example, educational researchers often lament the effects of hothouse innovation.[23] In this case, researchers and practitioners see exciting innovations taken up for a time in a few ideal sites followed by a quiet oblivion. One might interpret effects like this as an inability of largely small, special-focus firms to sustain good (large, complex, ambitious) ideas and place them into an articulate value chain that leads to real products and services. In a similar vein, one can see fragmentary effects on the demand side. School reformers who work in large states and city environments sometimes lament the fact that among state and city cohorts there are a few schools that really understand the underlying principles of a reform and want to implement new products and practices, but these school organizations are often separate and diffuse and don't have easy ways to coalesce around some form of educated demand. The result is frequently a sporadic implementation of a set of new tools or services coupled to a reform that then fails to take hold. While we suspect that there is no silver bullet to address problems of fragmentation in the world of education, we will suggest four strategies that may serve to improve the current state of affairs that places schools, districts, and states (the demand side) in a market relationships with for-profit businesses (the supply side).

At the end of the day, fragmentation is a function of social relationships. When there exist forms of governance and streams of revenue that mitigate the collaborative intentions of people who should work together, those rules and regulations have created social relationships that are not productive for innovation. In a similar vein, when research innovations and initial trials show promise but funding streams are unavailable for continued development, social relationships that can create productive products possibly fail to form. We offer several proposals for discussion that could serve to create a climate that might help remedy some of this fragmentation and result in "raising the bar" on both the demand for and the supply of tools that promote ambitious instruction.

K–12 Technology Transfer

The general concept here is to create in U.S. K–12 schooling the beginnings of what has come to be known in higher education as "tech transfer." Characteristics of tech transfer include: externally funded R&D leading to commercialization of the resulting goods and services, usually achieved via partnerships between educational and for-profit organizations.[24] In this context, the suggestion would be to *create a competitive, multiyear "macro-block grant" to selected districts for product codevelopment with a consortium of firms. Through permissive legislation, create a relatively small (initially) number of opportunities for school districts to propose to codevelop, in partnership with a consortium of firms, ambitious, innovative teaching and learning products that are designed to be commercially viable.* The bulk of the costs of this effort would be borne through a "macro–block grant"—a unique bundle of state and federal categorical grants—supplemented with gifts, grants, and investment capital promised by the district and the firms. The particular categories of funding would be those most closely associated with the product being developed. Entrepreneurial districts and firms[25] would form consortiums; propose creation of new products and services; describe how targeted children would be served during the development phase, how the diverted categorical funds would be deployed in development, and how the resulting intellectual property would be commercialized after its development. Several major "grants" would then take on the additional function of "investments."

There are a number of variations on the K–12 tech transfer theme that can be considered, reflecting both more and less dramatic departures from current practices. A somewhat less ambitious proposal would be to *create competitive awards of a "macro-waiver" to enable a sole-source multiyear contract between a consortium of firms and districts for new product codevelopment based on phased upgrades as well as new product development.* In this variation, states permit districts in partnership with a consortium of firms to propose an innovative product supporting ambitious instruction and award to the winning districts the right to enter a long-term, sole-source relationship to codevelop the product and subsequently capture any licensing royalties that result from commercialization. The macro-waiver is different from the macro–block grant in several respects: (1) current funding streams are not altered but are assured at predetermined levels going forward; and (2) the usual bidding requirements are waived and substituted with regular oversight from the appropriate state or federal agency. All other elements (e.g., intellectual property and commercialization) are roughly the same. Just as is the case with tech transfer at research universities in higher education, K–12 tech transfer will have payoffs only over the long run as research capacity is grown and merged with expertise in commercialization.

Venture Philanthropy for Tool Development

Many philanthropic organizations identify K–12 schooling as a mission priority; many of those education foundations assert a keen interest in school improvement by influencing policy. With very few exceptions, these foundations employ the mechanism of "grants" as opposed to "program-related investments" or venture philanthropy. We suggest urging one or more leading education foundations to undertake a distinct initiative in venture philanthropy to support the joint development (schools and businesses) and ultimate commercialization of tools to support ambitious instruction. A central element of venture philanthropy is explicit encouragement of the grantee to pursue sustainability through commercialization, much like the way that the National Science Foundation encourages university grantees. This encouragement includes granting to the grantee districts the rights to the intellectual property resulting from development efforts.

The long-run outcome will be a tighter programmatic relationship among research, commerce, and practice. Some of the most productive innovations in education couple research and practice together early on. Too often, while researchers and policymakers often decry the naïve linear relationship between research insights and products, there are too few examples of more dynamic relationships and even fewer examples of funding strategies that couple research, practice, and commerce relatively early in the process of idea development and tool development. It is often naively assumed that commercial actors have venture resources to develop ideas early on, even if public school agencies don't. Venture money is often available only for proven ideas with a very promising ROI. We suggest the creation of funding streams, perhaps from foundations, that will provide the kind of venture resource that is more focused on having good ideas being jointly informed by research, practice, and commerce much earlier in development.

Open-Source Environments for Innovators

We suspect the continuation and acceleration of standards environments like Schools Interoperability Framework (SIF) will create opportunities for more innovators to get exciting products to the marketplace quicker. If, for example, an inventor or researcher creates an accountability tool to help teachers better communicate with parents, children, and central offices about performance in an environment of rich interoperability frameworks, the tool's marketability might be accelerated. Open-source environments could jointly encourage school districts and other demand-side agencies to expect comprehensive tool suites, while innovators could be assured that small, but valuable, components of these suites could be created and sold independently.

More Attention to Implementation

In the intellectual economy of education today, there is too little information available about the details of implementation, including the incorporation of products and services into the operation of schools, districts, and state education systems. What prescription exists is often declarative. Consider, for example, the emerging "What Works Clearinghouse."[26] This repository of "programs that work" may be valuable; however, it is a kind of declarative information. It is largely about "that the programs work" rather than providing much detail about how they work (or not) in practice and the program's developmental trajectory. Consequently, we believe that an important set of developments might be a common language and Web-based infrastructure for better documentation and communication of the details of program implementation as well as the details of programmatic change based on feedback from program implementation efforts. This would provide a more robust level of knowledge among educators as they purchase and incorporate goods and services into their operations and, at the same time, enhance the feedback from educators to education businesses about the practical merits of their products and services.

In closing, we return to a simple observation from the beginning of this chapter. Most of the tools and materials that schools use in the day-to-day conduct of instruction are bought from the for-profit sector. It follows that the structural, political, and financial relationships that govern the working arrangement between schools and for-profit providers should be optimized to get the best tools, materials, and services in practice.

While the potential is great for educators and for-profit businesses to jointly develop tools to support instruction and improve practice, these relationships have to be nurtured. In all likelihood the process of nurturing new relationship patterns will involve interventions at multiple levels in the system of instruction and its governance. The goal we pursued in this chapter was, first, to put the essential need and opportunity for a new set of relationships between education's supply and demand sides in sharper relief. Second we sought to start conversations about ways to get these partnerships under way. New partnerships that draw the supply side closer to the granular details of activity on the demand side are going to be part of the solution to make ambitious instruction more of an ongoing instructional reality in American schools.

APPENDIX 6.A

Forces Attracting Providers to the Education Market

In this chapter we dwell on the disincentives for investors to back the work of education providers. There are, however, thousands of education providers and investors who have committed resources into the education marketplace. The forces that are drawing these actors in are, in effect, "pushing against" the factors discussed in the chapter. To the extent that these forces grow (due in part to the growing private returns to schooling), they will attract more providers and investment capital.

New Sources of Revenue. Limits on tax revenues for funding public institutions have encouraged educational leaders to pursue new or nontraditional revenue sources. Among these new sources are tax appropriations to programs other than education but related to it: juvenile justice, health, early childhood development. Other sources include donations from nonprofit education philanthropists and "donations" from businesses in exchange for advertising or even access to student markets and investments from for-profit education businesses. As the relative share of nontax revenues for education has grown, so too have the share of nongovernment-run education businesses.

Greater Reliance on Outsourcing. Rather than providing goods and services within a school or college, educators are contracting with specialty firms who can provide a good or service at a better price because they specialize. These specialty firms—public, nonprofit, and for-profit organizations—provide direct services to students through contracts with public educational organizations or by charging private fees directly to students. Specialties range from music lessons to technology training to teaching services for children with learning disabilities.

Increasing Competition. Traditional geographic segmentation of educational services—what school one attends being determined solely by where one lives—is giving way to competition across these old boundaries. Since the 1980s charter schools, magnet schools, voucher programs, interdistrict transfer, and open enrollment policies have come into existence and grown up alongside the fixed attendance boundaries of neighborhood public schools. Distance-delivered programs for school age (homeschooling) and postsecondary students are delivered across the state boundaries in which they are chartered as well as across boundaries of regional accrediting agencies. As these political barriers to entry fall, new "virtual" education businesses providing online education such as K12 and Capella University are increasingly able to serve students across attendance area, district, state, and national boundaries.

Increasing Emphasis on Performance. In K–12 and community college systems especially, state governments are increasingly tying state funding to student academic performance while relaxing laws that require compliance with uniform procedures. California, for example, now provides financial rewards to schools that exceed their performance growth targets and intervenes in schools that are underperforming. Schools can now also request waivers from regulations governing how they must operate. As a consequence of these changes, new education businesses (and new programs created by existing education businesses) that promise increased student performance are more acceptable in the market than they were in the past.

Increasing Reliance on Technology. Rapid developments in technology are enabling the creation of new educating businesses, fundamentally altering the organization and service mix and reach of many education organizations. A number of new education firms have emerged in recent decades whose core mission entails some form of "e-learning," such as Riverdeep, K12, Cisco, and WebCT.

APPENDIX 6.B

Providers Selling to Households as Well as Practitioners
The Example of LeapFrog Enterprises, Inc.

Knowledge Universe and LeapFrog Enterprises, Inc., incorporated research on early literacy into the design, development, and marketing of its Leap-Frog SchoolHouse, LeapPad, and other products. LeapFrog Enterprises, Inc., designs, develops, and markets technology-based educational products and proprietary content. Its current offerings include more than twenty-five educational products and more than forty interactive books, in addition to six learning platforms focusing primarily on children from pre-K through eighth grade (and the company is expanding its product line to include high school). LeapFrog Enterprises has also established its LeapFrog SchoolHouse business, which publishes curriculum and assessment content for the pre-K–8 market. Founded in 1995, its early development and expansion was aided by investments from Knowledge Universe. It sold more than 700,000 LeapPads in its first year of operation, went public in 1999, and posted $314 million in revenues in 2001. Approximately 20 million LeapPads are in U.S. households today, representing a market penetration of as much as two-thirds of households with small children, depending on assumptions about numbers of pads per household.

LeapPads responded to a perceived demand in the market for instructional toys that would improve early literacy development in children, enabling them to improve their reading, language recognition, and early writing skills and, hence, performance in school. Building on research in early literacy development in particular, phonemic awareness, LeapPad/LeapFrog developers build products that directly link visual and sound recognition of letters, letter groupings, and words (basic skills). By utilizing available technology and multinational supply chains, their products could be produced at price points that were easily affordable to parents of young children as well as to professional educators. Leap products are marketed in large quantities principally through big-box chain stores such as WalMart and Target.

LeapFrog illustrates some of the defining characteristics of providers, only a few of which are explicit in the profile above, including the structure and incentives of for-profit enterprises and the relative importance of effective demand, innovation, access to capital, and time to market.

CHAPTER 7

Instructional Research and the Improvement of Practice

Alan H. Schoenfeld

This chapter addresses the current status of educational research and its relationship to educational practice. It focuses largely on instructional research, with an eye toward the production of ideas and materials that have the potential to improve instruction. It is written at a time of significant federal efforts to determine "what works," primarily by the use of randomized controlled trials as the "gold standard" of educational research. As noted independently by many authors in this volume,[1] these efforts draw needed attention to educational outcomes, but they also raise fundamental questions of what should count as valued learning outcomes and what kinds of methods are most appropriate for exploring them.

ROAD MAP

The narrative proceeds in three main sections addressing (1) the state and prospects of educational theory; (2) the preparation of educational researchers; (3) the research-practice divide. It concludes with a discussion of recommendations for change, some of which include:

- The field needs to identify (much more than it has in the past) a robust set of consensus findings that can serve as the bases for educational interventions.[2]
- Partly because we need to get our own methodological act(s) together and partly because of external attempts to restrict the methodological canon

to an inappropriately small subset of research methods, we need to devote significant attention to what it means to do rigorous and relevant empirical educational research. We need to codify rigorous research methods and practices and contextualize them appropriately, indicating when they are appropriate to use, what they can and cannot deliver, and what it takes to use them properly.

- There is a need for increased standardization of tools and methods and perhaps the creation of common databases. Such work must be done so that it enables researchers to build on previous work and provides enough detail for findings to be used reliably to inform practice.
- There is a need for increased capacity for research and development in education. This includes the creation of new institutional infrastructures that focus directly on overcoming the research-practice divide. It also means thinking creatively about mechanisms for attracting people into the field.
- There needs to be a shift toward research and development (R&D) that is much closer to practice (and potentially in, or in partnership with, practice) than is typically the case. This will require some major shifts in the current university value system for promotion and tenure. Equally important, it will require making practice more accessible as the site of research. Partnerships are a two-way street.

INTRODUCTION

To provide a personal backdrop for the issues discussed here, I begin this essay with some autobiographical information. My Ph.D. is in mathematics; I moved into educational research after a few years of producing theorems. Thanks to a postdoctoral appointment at Berkeley, I embarked on what is now thirty years of studying thinking, teaching, and learning. My formative educational research was as a cognitive scientist. In my early work, my goal was to adapt the tools and techniques of artificial intelligence in order to construct models of mathematical problem-solving and to use the insights gained to improve mathematics instruction. For the first decade of my educational career, I engaged in a deeply interactive set of laboratory studies and instructional design, refining the theory and practice of problem-solving instruction as I went along.

It is now thirty years later, and as Judy Collins might have said, "I've looked at schools from both sides now." I've volunteered in classrooms for many years. I've worked with teachers and districts on professional development. I've done classroom research for most of my professional life. I remain passionately committed to making things better, while I have a much better sense of the complexities involved in doing so. As a researcher, I've seen educational research make tremendous strides. However, I've also seen the field stumble, sometimes because of external pressures but equally often because we shoot ourselves in the foot. Specifically, I will argue that

- Educational research has made astounding progress in terms of both theory and method over the past thirty years. There is a long way to go, however, and there are serious cultural/institutional obstacles to making solid progress.
- The bases of professional preparation of educational researchers need serious attention.
- Significant changes are necessary if education is to build solid bridges between research and practice, rather than falling into the chasm between them.
- New models of research-and-practice partnerships, and institutions to focus on melding research and practice, are needed if we are to make progress. This will require a substantial amount of money.

To further set the stage, let me invoke two definitions of "research." One, which I have used for some years and which has a long lineage, is that research is "disciplined inquiry" into some set of phenomena. A second definition, which may be useful in the current context, is that research entails the creation of descriptive-analytic models of well-defined classes of phenomena. I choose the word "model" because, in general, models are intended to explain how things work. Models represent claims of the type "in these circumstances, these things happen for the following reasons." Analytic models are data driven and are accountable to data. They also represent the type of theoretical commitments that say, "I choose to represent this situation with these objects and relations, which are sanctioned by the underlying theory."[3] My personal view is that rigorous, evidence-based characterizations of "what things are and how they work" are essential for progress in educational R&D.[4] This view applies across the board, from fine-grained studies of individual students working problems to large-scale studies of how schools and districts function in providing educational opportunities for their students.[5] My point is that a fundamental purpose of research is to figure out *how and why things work (including their contextual constraints)* not simply "what works." This contrasts with assumptions of others (e.g., from the What Works Clearinghouse [WWC]).

THE STATE OF THEORY AND METHOD

By way of context, it should be noted that educational researchers have traveled a bumpy road for much of their history. As documented by Powell and Lagemann, among others, educational research flirted with "science" off and on through the twentieth century, and it continues to do so.[6] This has caused problems, both because the result was (and is!) scientism as often as science, and because it has resulted in significant tensions between the research- and professionally oriented aspects of schools of education.

Early in the twentieth century, behaviorism (and, concomitantly, attempts to apply it to education) represented an attempt to banish "mentalism" and other "unscientific" approaches from psychology and its applications, thereby placing the field on a supposedly scientific footing. In the years following the Second World War, the appeal of science resulted in the social sciences (so called, said one cynic, because of "physics envy") having a very heavy dependence on statistical and experimental methods. This was not all for the good; by the 1970s there were the beginnings of a rebellion. In 1978, for example, Jeremy Kilpatrick wrote that the search for a particular kind of rigor had come close to producing rigor mortis and that the highly unrigorous and unscientific "teaching studies" conducted in the Soviet Union—studies in which researchers developed teaching ideas, tried them with a few students, and characterized the results in anecdotal form—were much richer in ideas than the sterile but rigorous studies conducted in the United States.[7]

Given the insistence on rigor in the social sciences, it was an uphill battle in the 1970s and 1980s for educational researchers to legitimize the study of mental phenomena. It is interesting, for example, to read Flavell on metacognition, where he rejoices that researchers can once again pay attention to phenomena that matter in people's lives and get this work published as "rigorous research."[8] Similarly, it is worth recalling the paradigmatic battles in the 1970s and 1980s over whether anything aside from observable behaviors could count as data. No less a figure than Nobel Prize winner Herbert Simon had to argue forcefully, for years, that people's verbal reports of their problem-solving efforts could be treated as legitimate data.[9] Even today there are large numbers of funders and researchers who do not understand that there are many ways of conducting rigorous, high-quality research in education, and that appropriately used statistical methods are only one category of such work.

Despite this background—or perhaps because of it, since there was so much to overcome—it can be argued that educational research has made phenomenal strides over the past few decades, in both theory and methods.

I will outline the story using my home field, mathematics education, as an example. To varying degrees, analogous substories can be told in other areas of education.

Changes in Research on Mathematics Learning

When I entered mathematics education in 1975, it was firmly in the grip of "social-scientism," the field having only recently coalesced into existence. The first International Congress on Mathematics Education was held in 1969, and the *Journal for Research in Mathematics Education* (as well as various international journals) had just begun to be published. If you leaf through the first few editions of *JRME*, you will find that it was almost exclusively experimental/quantitative. If a researcher thought he or she had an instructional "treatment" that worked, the researcher designed an experiment and performed statistical analyses to show whether it did. Or the researcher performed "factor analyses" to determine which aspects of mathematical performance contributed to problem-solving success and to what degree.

Much of that work turned out to be theoretically and empirically sterile. For example, in many comparison studies the most significant (and unmeasured) variables turned out to be whether an experimental treatment was taught before or after lunch, whether the same teacher taught both treatments (in which case the time of instruction or the differential enthusiasm of the instructor could be a major factor in shaping outcomes), or different teachers taught both (in which case the "teacher variable" might be significant). Moreover, despite the trappings of science, the "variables" were often ill-defined. For example, a series of about 100 studies over more than a decade examined the impact of "advance organizers"—top-level summary introductions of the text to follow—on reading comprehension.[10] The results were mixed, with about half the studies showing statistically significant positive results, and half showing either no effect or negative results. Why? A close review of the studies revealed that "advance organizer" was an ill-defined construct, and different authors had constructed them differently.

As noted above, rigor was stifling the field. Specifically, it was regarded as a violation of the zeitgeist to look at real people doing real problem-solving. Moreover, in my field there existed no theoretical frame for looking at problem-solving behavior; most of the frameworks in use at that time came from trait psychology, which measured simple "abilities." The measures of problem-solving performance typically employed were straightforward tests of content mastery grounded at times in *Bloom's Taxonomy* (a list of types of knowledge in hierarchical order).[11] These measures were, however, grounded in little or no understanding of the processes of problem-solving. The under-lying epistemology considered knowledge as something to be acquired, accu-mulated. Notions of problem-solving strategies, metacognition, belief sys-tems, and sociocultural practices were nowhere to be seen.

Advances in Theory

The cognitive revolution of the late twentieth century brought tremendous change.[12] For various reasons, the study of thinking and problem-solving became legitimized and a completely new view of thinking and learning took place. Problem-solving strategies, previously viewed as suspicious "mental-istic" phenomena, became the objects of study and became teachable. The topic of metacognition, which includes monitoring and self-regulation, was similarly studied and understood to be a major factor in problem-solving suc-cess.[13] So were beliefs. One well-known but powerful example is the problem that appeared on the 1983 National Assessment of Educational Progress test: "An army bus holds 36 soldiers. If 1,128 soldiers are being bussed to their training site, how many buses are needed?" Amazingly, the most frequent answer given on the exam—by 29 percent of the students—was that the num-ber of *buses*(!) needed was "31 remainder 12." How could they say so?

Simply put, what the students demonstrated was rote behavior. While "problem-solving" may have been an instructional mantra in the early 1980s, in classrooms it often boiled down to solving straightforward and typically formulaic word problems. Students read a problem, identified the numbers in it, performed the relevant operation, and wrote down the answer, period. Problem contexts were not seen as realistic situations to be modeled; stu-dents quickly came to recognize them as "cover stories" for arithmetic com-putations. In consequence, returning to the context to see if the answer made sense was not typically necessary, and students didn't do it.[14]

This discussion shows why sociocultural theories became essential. Peo-ple's understanding of the mathematical enterprise is shaped by their experi-ences in (and out of) classrooms, and it is essential to understand the social processes by which such learning took place.[15]

ADVANCES IN PRACTICE

The advances in theory discussed above were mirrored, albeit slowly and unevenly, by advances in practice. In 1989 the National Council of Teachers of Mathematics issued *Curriculum and Evaluation Standards for School Math-ematics*.[16] This document, written for teachers but grounded in the research of the previous decades, called for significant changes in classroom goals and practices. In the early 1990s the National Science Foundation (NSF) issued a request for proposals for the development of reform-oriented curricula in line with the *Standards*. Over the decade that followed, a number of such curricula were developed. These became highly controversial—ground zero for the math wars (which, like the reading wars, pitted traditionalists against reformers in the battle for control over curricular materials). But the new, standards-based curricula also experienced some success. Evidence suggests that the presence of the factors noted below leads to improvements in students' mathematical performance and to the reduction of some performance gaps between groups of people:

- A mathematically rich and rigorous set of standards
- Curricula aligned with those standards
- Assessment aligned with those standards
- Professional development aligned with those standards
- Enough stability in the system for all of the above to take hold[17]

Even under conditions that do not include all of these factors, preliminary evidence indicates that reform curricula are roughly equal to traditional curricula when it comes to student performance on skill-related tasks but that students in reform curricula do much better on measures of problem-solving and conceptual understanding.[18]

We are now in quite a different situation than we were thirty years ago. Robust theories of thinking and problem-solving exist.[19] Scientific (often laboratory-based) methods and rich, thick anthropological/sociological perspectives and tools, which once seemed to exist in separate universes, have grown and comingled to the point where it is possible to construct descriptive–analytic models of real-world phenomena such as classroom events.[20] Indeed, the argument has been made that there is now the capacity to carry on basic educational research previously conducted in the laboratory in applied settings such as schools and classrooms—that is, educational research in "Pasteur's Quadrant," contributing simultaneously to basic theory and to the solution of important problems.[21]

CONSTRAINTS ON RESEARCH PROGRESS

If these are the best of times, they are also the worst of times. Educational research is once again under attack. Consider this statement from the U.S. Department of Education's Strategic Plan for 2002–7: "Unlike medicine, agriculture and industrial production, the field of education operates largely on the basis of ideology and professional consensus. As such, it is subject to fads and is incapable of the cumulative progress that follows from the application of the scientific method and from the systematic collection and use of objective information in policy making. We will change education to make it an evidence-based field."[22] Or watch the video recordings or read the proceedings of the forum "Rigorous Evidence: The Key to Progress in Education?" held by U.S. Secretary of Education Rod Paige in November 2002.[23] At the forum, Reid Lyon, head of the Child Development and Behavior Branch at the National Institute of Health, discussed the need for "rigorous" research. In his introductory comments regarding the methodological sophistication found in schools of education, Lyon said, "You know, if there was any piece of legislation that I could pass, it would be to blow up colleges of education." Neither the panel nor the audience demurs in any way, and his comments overall are met with loud applause. Of course this disdain for educational research is hardly new.[24] As noted in the chapter 1 of this volume, one of the reasons for this book is to help different groups of stakeholders develop deeper understanding of how to collaborate in ways that allow us as a nation to create more fruitful theoretical and empirical coherence in our field.

CONSTRAINTS CREATED BY OUR BEHAVIORS AS RESEARCHERS

While it is true that (1) educational research has been dramatically underfunded; (2) the multidisciplinary character of educational research—especially applied educational research—makes it excruciatingly difficult to conduct such research well (it's much harder to do robust and meaningful research in education than, for example, in mathematics); and (3) the political context and/or the conditions of schools and school districts can often make it nearly impossible for even the best research to have practical impact, the sad fact is that we as educational researchers are in large measure responsible for the low regard in which educational research is held. As a community, we have not gotten our methodological or theoretical houses in order. Moreover, academic reward structures are organized in ways that make it counterproductive for individuals who try to do so.[25]

As a community, educational researchers are a highly disputatious lot who seem to have little stake in distilling what is known, for themselves and others, in clear and compelling ways. It is telling, for example, that there is no widely accepted core of readings or practices across graduate schools in education. While, as noted, the multidisciplinary nature of educational research makes it more difficult to settle on central findings and methods than might be the case in other fields, that is not the sole difficulty. One problem is that battles for theoretical dominance (e.g., behaviorsists versus gestaltists, situativity theorists versus cognitivists) lead to exaggerated claims of importance, both at the individual and collective levels. We pay a price for such disputes. From the outside (and the inside as well), it looks as though the foundations of the field are completely unsettled.[26]

Indeed, a lack of attention to consensus and foundations leaves educational researchers not only vulnerable to attack but unprepared with a strong defense. In broad political terms, one can view the National Research Council's *Scientific Research in Education* as a defensive reaction to the polemic in the U.S. Department of Education's 2002–07 Strategic Plan quoted above.[27] That is, *Scientific Research in Education* can be seen as a hastily constructed attempt to show that there *are* scientific ways of conducting educational research other than the "gold standard" of randomized controlled studies that is advocated by some as the only truly rigorous work in education. Yet within the educational community this document seemed as much a Rorschach test as it did a statement for the defense. Reaction papers in the November 2002 special issue of *Educational Researcher* ranged from attempts to explain that it's really, really hard to do good work in education (as opposed to science, which is easy in comparison) to attempts to dismiss science altogether.

The framing of individual studies is often problematic as well. In "Research Methods in (Mathematics) Education," I discuss a series of criteria by which research studies in education might be judged: descriptive power, explanatory power, scope, predictive power, rigor and specificity, falsifiability, replicability, generality, trustworthiness, and multiple sources of evidence (triangulation). These are intrinsic aspects of a study that can be judged. There is also the placing of a study relative to the field and the consideration of the contribution that the study makes. In that regard, I argue that it is worth considering studies along three dimensions.

- *Generality, or Scope.* The *claimed generality* of a study is the set of circumstances in which the author(s) of a study claims that the findings of the study apply. The *potential generality* of a study is the set of circumstances in which the results of the study (if trustworthy) might reasonably be expected to apply.
- *Trustworthiness.* How well-substantiated is the claimed generality of the study? How solid are the warrants for the claims? Do they truly apply in the circumstances in which the authors assert that the results hold?

- *Importance.* To put things bluntly, how much should readers care about the results?[28]

Burkhardt and I noted the following:

Generally speaking, papers (and even bodies of literature) tend to score well on one of these dimensions and poorly on the others. Many individual studies, for example, score reasonably well on *trustworthiness*, presenting specific findings that are reasonably well warranted by the evidence given. Often it is claimed that those findings are representative of a broad class of phenomena, which implies their *importance* and *generality*. But, a rigorous evidentiary warrant for these claims is rarely included with the research reported. Thus importance and generality remain hypothetical. . . . Such studies . . . tend not to provide adequate information to allow for replication and extension; they tend not to make the substantive (rather than suggested) case for generality.[29]

A case can be made that the current academic value system contributes in significant ways to the difficulties discussed above. At the grand theoretical level, fads and fashions tend to come and go. In education as everywhere else, being current is attractive to many; seeming to be on the cutting edge can result in publications (new things can be seen as more exciting than work in established traditions) and a personal reputation for innovation. There are, however, serious downsides to academicisms. One is that, in paradigmatic or theoretical battles, differences tend to be emphasized more than commonalities. A second is that areas that could be fleshed out are abandoned as researchers move on to the next "big thing." For example, much of the theoretical work on understanding problem-solving was completed by the mid-1980s, but twenty years later much of the relevant empirical work has not.[30] For robust implementation in practice, one needs a good idea of how much detail and how much practice are needed for students to develop mastery of various problem-solving strategies. Likewise, one needs to know which kinds of classroom practices will best support the development of metacognitive skills. Answers to these questions are necessary for the improvement of instruction. They are, however, seen by many academic researchers as engineering issues rather than theoretical issues and hence of relatively little interest and prestige. As a result, important work for these and other practical applications tends to be skipped over.

Many other factors shape the choice and execution of researchers' work with similar impact. Consider the following:

- Collaboration tends to limit one's visibility and is thus seen as bad for one's career. (Being second or third author, or part of an "et al.," is not helpful for purposes of name recognition. Applied projects generally call for teams of researchers, thus burying all but a few names.)
- Using tools developed by others may not be optimal (fine-tuning or changing the tools may make them slightly better for present purposes) and may also be seen as derivative. Hence, there is a strong tendency to develop one's own tools and measures, which are thus not directly comparable with others in the literature.
- The replication and extension of work done by others tends to be seen as a derivative rather than a creative act. It is often better, careerwise, to be seen as setting oneself apart than as building directly on the work of others. As noted above, this means that topics that have been worked through theoretically tend to be abandoned before their applications to practice have been developed.
- With some exceptions, working on consensus panels or working to distill trends in the literature also tends to be seen as derivative (with the same consequences).

The result, then, is a set of disincentives for collaborative or applied work and strong incentives for individualistic work that is hard to compare directly with that of others. It is not easy to build a cumulative knowledge base for a field under these conditions. It is worth noting that some collectives, such as the Rational Number Project, the early Algebra Project, and Cognitively Guided Instruction did manage to sustain collaborative inquiry over long periods of time. But, generally speaking, these are the exceptions that probe the rule.

Consider fields such as automotive engineering. Everyone knows Henry Ford's name. However, Ford Motor Company is huge, with countless anonymous engineers responsible for making sure that the company's products are continually improved. In academia, everyone aspires to be Henry Ford. It is time, I believe, to consider new forms of educational R&D enterprises, with newly defined roles and rewards for those who participate in the creation and examination of educational contexts and materials.

I also note, with some dismay, that the field has been astoundingly casual in considering and codifying research tools and methods—embarrassingly so. Where is our collection of handbooks of research methods? It should be possible to create a series of detailed research manuals describing, with precision, the ways in which various research techniques can and should be used, the contexts in which those methods are likely to be useful, what the methods can reveal and what they cannot. On the positive side, the American Educational Research Association (AERA) has produced a *Handbook of Complementary Methods in Education Research.*[31] This much-needed volume introduces graduate students to more than two dozen research techniques. However, each chapter is essentially an introduction to a research method, lacking the information that would enable researchers to use the method effectively. Each chapter could, in essence, serve as the introduction to a full volume devoted to explicating that particular research method. Where is the impetus to create such things?

In 1999 AERA was nearly fifty years old. AERA has had standing committees on various issues—half a dozen on equity, for example. However, the Association has had no mechanism for reflecting on the quality of educational research itself and for trying to improve the state of the art. I did succeed in having the Research Advisory Committee created during my AERA presidential term. Yet getting the committee to have an impact—to stimulate the Association to reflect on how educational researchers go about their business, with an eye toward improvement—has been an uphill battle. Neither the Association nor the field seems to view this as a high-priority issue. Individually, we do our research and get published. So what's the problem? As I see it, lack of respect and lack of impact are two major problems—and reasons to get serious.

THE PREPARATION OF EDUCATIONAL RESEARCHERS

As David Labaree points out, there is often a mismatch between the experiences and (emergent) goals of those preparing to become educational researchers.[32] A significant proportion of those who want to become researchers have been teachers. They have honed their skills at living in the moment, in seeing the very particulars of the specific teaching situation that need to be addressed (*this* child needs help with *this* topic in *this* way now!). In contrast, researchers look for generalizations and abstractions; the issue isn't necessarily what's happening right here but what issues the "here and now" illuminates. This tension between an action orientation and a predilection for reflection and abstraction is a serious issue and one of many the field confronts as it contemplates the preparation of researchers.[33]

A second issue is the absence of a robust knowledge base for the discipline—if it *is* a discipline. As Denis Phillips notes, the term "educational researcher" is uncommonly broad in what it encompasses; a multiplicity of paradigms and perspectives contribute to educational research. This makes it difficult to define high-quality research in a simple way. Phillips notes that in conducting rigorous research, "the main business at hand . . . is this: *Has the overall case . . . been established to a degree that warrants tentative acceptance of the theoretical or empirical claims being made?*"[34] Claims about what? Using what methods? Just how, in a heterogeneous, multidisciplinary field, do we converge on the standards for "evidence beyond a reasonable doubt?" The field needs to work on this.

As an antidote to "methodolatry"—rigorous adherence to sanctioned methods—Phillips notes the "refreshing remark" of Nobel Laureate Percy Bridgman that "the scientist has no other method than doing his damnedest."[35] But most scientists are grounded in a body of knowledge and method and then do their damnedest to transcend it. At present there is neither core nor canon in education. This may not necessarily be a problem.[36] In Kuhnian terms, education is not in a period of "normal science." Hence, the most important research skills to learn may be those of problem formulation and how to recover from one's (inevitable) mistakes. In any case, there are very few models for the successful preparation of graduate students as researchers, either with regard to what they should know or what set of experiences they should have. The NSF's new Science of Learning Centers are trying to help solve this problem by making the study of learning in diverse settings and with diverse methods (e.g., ethnography that accompanies experimental designs) a model for a new generation of researchers and practitioners who can collaborate.[37]

A third and related issue is the talent pool available and the money to support it. As a "soft," applied field with little prestige, education does not have the overt attractiveness of the sciences to those who want to work on crisply defined and obviously difficult problems; it tends to attract those who have strong social as well as intellectual aims. The irony is that problems in education are more complex than those in the hard sciences and require at least as much analytic thought for their solutions.[38]

This issue plays out in a number of ways. To some, problems in education lack the pristine attractiveness of those in the sciences and are perceived as being easier; yet making progress on them often requires more knowledge. If you are to study learning of a particular discipline, for example, you should understand the discipline *and* what learning is all about. Unlike the hard sciences, context is a variable in most of what we do. A major question is how

we can attract those people who have both humanistic and scientific inclinations into the field or compose teams that combine the strengths necessary to make progress on difficult problems. Another major question is how
to fund such people both during their training and during their careers. Here
money makes a difference.

THE RESEARCH-PRACTICE DIVIDE

If you read any history of educational research or any disquisition on the
state of the art, at least one of these two themes will emerge: the tension
between the professional and academic roles of schools of education and the
failure of educational research to have a positive impact on educational practice.[39] These are longstanding problems, and they must be addressed if educational research is to live up to its promise.

Burkhardt and I argue that

> the research-based development of tools and processes for use by practitio-
> ners, common in other applied fields, is largely missing in education. Such
> "engineering research" is essential to building strong linkages between
> research-based insights and improved practice. . . . Realigning the system
> to make it more educationally powerful will require significant changes in
> work patterns. There must be much closer coordination of effort between
> research, design, development, policy and practice. Equally important, a
> conscious change in the academic value system will be required to induce
> the necessary number of educational researchers to develop the relevant
> skills to engage in such work.[40]

We argue that there are commonalities in successful research-based fields
such as medicine and the design of consumer electronics, commonalities
that would help in education as well.

A Reasonably Stable Theoretical Base, Both at Global and Local Levels

As noted above, education has a good deal of "sorting out" to do theoretically—a main issue being not which theory is better but which theory applies
to which phenomena in which circumstances. For example, a version of constructivism is gaining acceptance in the field even though the concept is
often misunderstood. As noted elsewhere, constructivism is a theory a knowing, not a theory of pedagogy. The basic idea is that people construct new
interpretations based on what they already know. Even listening to lectures

involves a constructive process, and the same lecture can be effective or ineffective depending on the knowledge and beliefs of the listeners.[41] Constructivism has important implications for pedagogy, but it does not assert that the best learning is discovery learning. An example of constructivist implications for teaching is that actively working to find answers to interesting problems can create a "time for telling" that leads to much better learning and transfer from a lecture than simply hearing it as a class presentation with no previous inquiry.[42] Cognitive science, with its notion of active comprehension based on existing mental models, scores points at the grand theoretical level when it enables researchers to make predictions about the incorrect answers that students will obtain to problems before they work the problems.[43] These would seem to box behaviorism into a pretty small corner. However, if you're interested in the most efficient way to master and reinforce a particular skill, behaviorist research may offer some clues that neither of the other traditions do.

In the sciences, mixes of global theory (Newton's laws) and local theory (the specifics of aerodynamics) work hand in hand during the engineering process. Local or context-specific theories are developed to deal with specific classes of events and prove much more useful than the global theories for designing a particular object with particular properties. In the sciences, theories are carefully specified according to their conditions of application: "Under these circumstances, the following things happen." Education could use more of the same. It is worth noting that design experiments, when properly conceived, are very much a move in that direction.[44]

A Consistent Set of Standards and Tools for Comparing Findings and Building on Them in Straightforward Ways

The key word here is "cumulativity"—the notion that work should be done in ways that build on previous work by adopting some of the same tools (including measurement devices) and techniques and that provides enough information for replication and extension. As noted above, almost nothing in education research is standardized. The time has come for some standardization.

Taking Ideas from the Laboratory into "Engineering Design" and Then into Marketing

The current emphasis on the "gold standard" of randomized controlled trials to determine the effectiveness of educational or other "treatments" has distorted the research-into-practice (R-into-P) process in that researchers have rushed to "treatment A versus treatment B" comparisons without an adequate basis of contextual studies to precede the rigorous comparisons. Under ordinary circumstances, controlled studies are the *last* phase of development, when a well-researched and piloted study is finally ready for large-scale testing. But a lot comes before that. In mature R&D fields such as engineering or pharmacology, things progress more systematically. If laboratory studies (a-level or Stage I Clinical development) generate an idea or product that looks promising, a series of field trials (b-level or Stage II Clinical development) is used to explore the conditions under which it seems to work, what unintended or side effects might be, etc. The product is refined on the basis of information gleaned from these studies, and only then is it tested on a large scale (g-level or Stage III Clinical development) for effectiveness.

Educational analogs for these three levels of testing exist.[45] Preliminary studies, including laboratory experiments and initial ethnographic analyses can be considered as parallel to pre-clinical studies in medicine. That is, instructional designers get ideas from where they can—sometimes intuition, sometimes by putting themselves in settings that might help them notice new phenomena, sometimes prior small-scale studies. At some point, materials and the ideas that underlie them are ready for a more serious tryout. One research-based way in which to try out such materials is in design experiments where researchers collaborate in a theoretically based educational intervention and document its effects, in essence a-level/Stage I development studies. The product of a design experiment (or of many, since the process is cyclical) is typically an approach to instruction that has been thoroughly vetted in one context. It is important to note that design experiments are as much about theory development and testing as they are about testing materials.[46] Design experiments that are theory-based often create surprises that lead to newly refined ideas.

In the current political context, there is pressure to take potentially valuable and proven instructional materials (essentially a-level or Stage I clinically tested materials) and subject them to randomized controlled trials (g-level/Stage III studies) to validate their worth. However, this skips several steps. One is the need to support the kinds of work that lead to theoretical innovations. A second is to provide careful field studies of important conditions under which innovations do and do not work and find ways to increase their effectiveness and reduce harmful effects. For example, consider a medicine that has been shown to have beneficial effects under carefully controlled circumstances (Stage I). Does it matter whether that medicine is taken before, during, or after eating? Does it have a differential impact on men and women, on people with other medical conditions? Does it interact with other medicines or other things (e.g., some medicines are to be taken with food but not with grapefruit juice)?

In educational R&D, early versions of instructional materials—whether created by design experiments or by skilled designers—tend, like Stage I treatments, to have been tested under safe and controlled conditions. But anyone who has spent any time in schools knows that the same curricular materials will require different support structures and will typically produce different results, in inner-city schools, suburban schools, schools with large English as a Second Language (ESL) populations. The purpose of b-level or Stage II studies with regard to curricula would be to test such materials out in these circumstances and then provide information about the kinds of adaptations that make them successful in different contexts. Concerns about context raise a number of questions. What kind of curriculum support is necessary for English-language learners? How important is the mathematics background of the teachers? For example, is additional support necessary in schools where the percentage of credentialed teachers is low, and, if so, what kind of support enables the curriculum to "work"? Which demographic or administrative variables (e.g., class size, block schedules, common teacher prep, departmental coherence) seem to affect implementation in what ways? Late–Stage II studies would seek to codify some of these results and develop methodological tools that support Stage III work—simple measures of the variables that have been shown to be important in the early Stage II studies and straightforward measures of the competencies deemed important.

Central to this work is the need to employ meaningful and appropriately broad standardized outcome measures. At present this is a serious problem. Because the widely available standardized tests tend to focus on skills and not on conceptual understanding and problem-solving, a significant proportion of curriculum experimentation has made use of locally developed assessment measures. This affects credibility (were they "teaching to the test"?) and makes it difficult to compare the impact of different curricula. Hence, assessment development is a major issue for the field.

Once contextual studies of an instructional intervention have been conducted, the intervention would then be ready for g-level/Stage III studies. Here, randomized controlled trials are entirely meaningful and appropriate. They can also be used to document contextual effects as well. After randomization, one could document the impact of the curriculum across the board (i.e., on a random sample of the whole population of interest) *and* on sub-populations of interest, such as urban schools, schools with high proportions of ESL learners, low or high proportions of credentialed teachers, and so on. After all, the information that a superintendent or a principal *really* wants is "are these materials right for my district or school?" A good example is recent research by Jeremy Roschelle and colleagues that looked at large-scale outcomes of experimental and comparison groups for a mathematics innovation but also carefully modeled when, for whom, and why these interventions help. Several chapters in this volume refer to the Tennessee class size study as an example of problems that occur when these kinds of questions about context are not asked.[47]

The observational and testing technologies for gathering rigorous context-sensitive data are known. Studies of context sensitivity would improve products. They should be a major component of "educational engineering." So why haven't they been done? One reason is economic. Doing such studies is expensive and, until educational consumers start demanding results, not necessary. If, as is common practice, publishers can discover what pleases their audience by holding focus groups, and if instructional materials produced in line with the focus groups' comments will sell, why would any for-profit business go to the trouble and expense of conducting contextual studies? Compare the vetting of education products with that of consumer products. If you are a consumer electronics manufacturer and produce a barely functional cell phone, any number of consumers' magazines will call you on it. When your product is compared side-by-side with its competitors in consumer magazines, potential purchasers have access to evidence that may cause them to choose a competitor's product. Hence, you take pains to make sure your product is adequate in engineering terms. At this point, the educational marketplace has no stable analog to this vetting process.[48]

If the commercial sector will not take on such tasks, what about academia? The fact is that academia as currently constituted is ill-suited to take on such tasks. Contextual studies take time and a large workforce. They typically call for working on someone else's materials rather than one's own. Unlike design experiments, which are currently cutting edge and have an aura of excitement about them, commercial production processes typically are (or at least become) more or less routine; they call for refinement of ideas, using more or less standardized tools. Given the highly individualistic culture of academia, pursuing this path is at best unglamorous; at worst, given the current criteria for promotion and tenure, it represents potential academic suicide. This is, as one reviewer of this article has noted, good reason for the existence of independent R&D institutions. Such institutions—which include, for example, AIR, BBN, SRI, and TERC—have made notable contributions, but they also face challenges in that they must be continually entrepreneurial, bringing in funding for ongoing efforts. This mitigates against long-term programmatic continuity.

Teams of Adequate Size to Deal with the Phenomena at Hand over the Time Scale Required

It is worth noting that in the early 1990s the National Science Foundation believed that it was necessary to provide funding on the order of tens of millions of dollars to catalyze the development of standards-based instructional materials in mathematics. Producing a new text series in mathematics is a very expensive enterprise and, in the case of radically new curricula, very risky as a commercial endeavor. Commercial publishers wouldn't produce such materials until they were seen to be commercially viable. And academia? With the exception of a very small number of innovative academic centers around the world,[49] universities wouldn't think of keeping designers on academic staff lines. (After all, what such people produce is not research.) Thus, the academic sector is unlikely, at present, to be hospitable to employing the collection of people necessary to produce and test high-quality educational materials over the time frame required to do the work well.

A second kind of large-scale work that universities could undertake, but rarely do, is a research partnership with policymakers to study change as it happens in real-time in important educational contexts. One positive example of this type is the High Performance Learning Communities (HPLC) project, a collaboration among the University of Pittsburgh's Learning Research and Development Center, Harvard University, and New York City Community School District No. 2.

> HPLC was created to investigate the continuous improvement of District #2, an urban schooling success story, where a commitment to instructional improvement through content-driven reform has had notable results. The broader goals of our research include investigating how district leadership has implemented various multiple subject-matter initiatives, what structures are in place to support those initiatives, and what mechanisms have been adopted for continuous improvement. Specific focuses of HPLC research include:

- Examining District #2's Theory of Action
- Examining District #2's leadership
- Investigating the specific subject-matter initiatives and their impacts on instruction
- Exploring the subject-matter initiatives and their relationships with Standards
- Investigating the results of district-wide reform on student achievement[50]

Such work is rare, in that (1) a school district administrator made his district's operations permeable to a team of highly qualified researchers in a relatively unprecedented way, and (2) the researchers committed themselves to being the analysts of someone else's actions. As Lauren Resnick noted, the researchers could not be decision makers in this context; the administrators had the responsibility for making change on a "real-time" basis.[51] The research team was committed to exploring what took place and to providing feedback on it. In this case the approach, the findings, and the opportunity for crafting new tools in situ were significant enough to lure a team of top-notch researchers into the collaboration. That too is rare, although some recent collaborations between the National Research Council and school districts in Boston and San Francisco seem promising.[52]

As Tony Bryk observed, one might hope for even more access and depth in such collaborations.

> [In District 2] the reforms were well developed before the documentation effort began. The HPLC group helped to elaborate in collaboration with their clinical partners a detailed theory of action for the "mature reform." They did not however elaborate a theory of change (i.e. where practices began and the specific changes necessary to effect over time) because these had already happened by the time they came on the scene. Absent such a theory of change, the problems associated with moving to scale were under-conceptualized.[53]

In sum, there is a great deal more that can be accomplished in research-in-practice implementation partnerships.

Sustained Funding at Realistic Levels

I will not review the state of educational funding in general but will instead quote from the 1998 U.S. House Committee on Science report: "Currently, the U.S. spends approximately $300 billion a year on education and less than $30 million, 0.01 percent of the overall education budget, on education research. . . . This minuscule investment suggests a feeble long-term commitment to improving our educational system."[54]

"Feeble" is an understatement. Mattel, Inc., a toy company, reinvests about 5 percent of its annual fiscal intake on R&D. Pharmaceutical companies may invest as much as 20 percent of their annual intake in R&D, with a quarter of that, 5 percent, going to basic research. Indeed, while our government invested $30 million in basic research on children's learning in 1998, a major pharmaceutical company spent $200 million performing basic research on dogs and cats.[55]

In short, the field is financially starved. For this reason, some of the problems I have discussed are not surprising. At the same time, the advances over the past forty years have been substantial, and increased investment, combined with the improvements suggested below, could yield substantial dividends in the years to come.

TAKING STOCK

The preceding conditions—a stable theoretical base, at local and global levels; standardization of tools, measurement devices, and data collection; the existence of robust R-into-P mechanisms; conditions that support the existence of large-scale teams; and sustained funding for large-scale enterprises—are the commonalities of fields that have successfully linked research and practice. Where does education stand with regard to these?

There is much to be done with regard to theory, but I believe the field is capable of getting its house in order. The same can be said in regard to standardization. Efforts have not been undertaken, but they could be. In both cases, part of what is at issue is the academic value system. Limiting one's theoretical claims to what is warranted by the evidence and using others' tools are hallmarks of academic integrity. They are also, however, ways to turn the academic spotlight away from oneself. That is a dangerous thing to do in the current entrepreneurial and individualistic academic culture. Value systems are an issue with regard to building close connections between research and practice: Unless and until testing others' ideas and making better products is considered an act of merit, few academics will dare take that path. As noted above, academic institutions are not hospitable to the stable employment of large teams if what they produce is not peer-reviewed research (not "just" materials that work well). Money of the scale required does not seem to be in the offing.

PRACTICAL ISSUES

Up to this point, I have focused on problems with the research half of the research-and-practice relationship but one could be equally critical about the practice side. I noted that one can see significant improvements in student performance and reductions in racial performance gaps in a context where there are high standards and goals, where curricula, assessment and professional development are aligned with them, and where there is enough stability for gradual evolution and improvement.

Such locations exist, but they are the exceptions that probe the rule. We live in a nation where teachers are not treated like professionals. Typically, after a year or two of training they are declared competent and sent off to teach, often without further support or opportunity to develop in meaningful ways. Dan Lortie's "egg crate" metaphor of teachers working in isolation from each other is as applicable now as it was when it was written.[56] Most teachers live in rather capricious environments that tend to have changing and/or inconsistent standards. They tend to have changing curricula, which may or may not correspond to the standards currently in place, and radically changing and inconsistent assessments.[57] Districts that offer reliable and robust professional development are few and far between. Stability is an even rarer commodity.

All this matters a great deal—not only for current teaching but for the potential of research-practice partnerships. In a world where teachers may or may not be well prepared, where they have few resources, where the presence of researchers may be seen as just another burden, and where there is little stability to support the development of any practice (including educational interventions), good research ideas may never have a chance. Here is one example. In a school district in which I have spent a substantial amount of time working with teachers, there are three middle schools. Up until 2004 there were two very different curricula in place in sixth grade: one a California-sanctioned "traditional" text, one a standards-based text that deals with the sixth grade curriculum in a different way and in a different order. Toward the end of the 2004 school year, the sixth-grade teachers at one of the schools decided that they were going to use a third text. They made this decision on their own and purchased the texts with funds the school had available. (This meant that there were now three incommensurate curricula being used in three schools—a curriculum and professional-development nightmare.) Later in the year I complained to the district official responsible for curricula that the teachers' action had caused a significant degree of chaos. (In addition to the problems coordinating content at grade 6, it turns out that students use a traditional text in grades K–5 and a different standards-based text in grades 7 and 8.) His response was, "They did what?" He had had no idea. The principal at the school in question was under the false impression that the teachers had made the curriculum choice because of a suggestion from our R&D project. The teachers went ahead and did as they wished.[58] Under conditions of curricular anarchy, one can hardly expect researchers to be effective in facilitating improvement.

Despite this somewhat pessimistic summary—and the fact that the problems we wish to solve, to have a real impact on practice, are extremely difficult—I believe there is room for optimism and progress.

POSSIBLE ACTIONS

Theory and Method

It is possible for us to get our house in order. First, it would be very useful to hold an extended series of conferences and/or consensus panels to define the state of the art with regard to theory, methods, and results. This would not only serve to lay out and strengthen the foundations of the field, it would begin to change external perceptions of the research community as a collection of researchers who can't agree on anything (and thus can be safely ignored). I note that there have been some successful attempts in this direction—for example the National Research Council's report *Preventing Reading Difficulties in Young Children* and its related popular guide, *Starting Out Right*[59]—but these are only a small part of what is needed (and these focus on results, not methods). The goal, at some level, should be the educational equivalent of the *Physician's Desk Reference,* a body of knowledge that evolves with time but is taken to represent the field's best understandings at the moment. We need to show that the field *does* know something and must provide more solid foundations for applications. Efforts such as *Scientific Research in Education* were too little too late in response to attacks on educational research.[60] We need to be proactive so that our foundations are firmer; our methodological canon is much better codified, useful, and powerful; and, in consequence, we are less subject to attack and more able to respond when we are attacked.

Along the same lines, and with full recognition that some surrender of autonomy is involved, it is time for the field to converge on mechanisms that foster cumulativity and sustainability (i.e., the standardization of tools and measures). Once high-quality tools and measures are developed, they should be the default option for researchers. If one chooses to use something different, one should have to explain why there is value added that compensates for the loss of the direct ability to compare results with and build on other studies.

Within the context of this assertion, I should address the prospects and problems of the one major attempt at standardization, the What Works Clearinghouse.[61]As its name suggests, the Clearinghouse is devoted to documenting what works, which interventions make a difference: "On an ongoing basis, the WWC gathers studies of the effectiveness of educational interventions (programs, products, practices, and policies). We review the studies that have the strongest design, and report on the strengths and weaknesses of those studies against the WWC Evidence Standards so that you know what the best scientific evidence has to say."[62]

The WWC modus operandi is purely statistical: WWC staff vets the quality of individual studies and plans to aggregate findings over those studies that pass muster. There is a very detailed (78 pages) protocol for evaluating research studies in mathematics education. To begin, only randomized experiments, quasi-experiments that use equating procedures, and studies that use the regression discontinuity design are even eligible for the WWC seal of approval. If a study falls into one of these categories, WWC staff examines it to see if it meets a wide range of technical criteria. Studies are rated as meeting WWC standards, meeting WWC standards "with reservations," or not meeting the standards. That decision is made on purely technical grounds.

However, the technical considerations can obscure some fundamental questions.[63] While WWC does ask whether a curriculum and the assessment used to evaluate it are aligned, it does not vet the assessment for content. One of the first WWC studies, for example, used a statewide "high stakes" assessment as its dependent measure. Reliability and validity data for the assessment were available, so the study received high marks for its outcome measures.

But there are serious problems here. Just what is one measuring with such an assessment? States across the United States vary widely with regard to what they assess; some focus on conceptual understanding and problem-solving while others focus on skills. This is a fundamental issue that undermines the meaningfulness of WWC approval. If one state certifies using the former and another the latter, how can you say what "certification" means?

Simply put, all tests are not created equal. There is evidence that scoring well on a skills-oriented test can yield false positives in the following sense:

a significant percentage of those who are certified "proficient" on a skills-oriented test will be deemed "not proficient" on a conceptually oriented test that covers the same subject matter.[64] Moreover, if the test used focuses only on basic skills, it cannot distinguish between a curriculum that teaches basic skills only and a curriculum from which students learn basic skills *and* conceptual understanding *and* problem-solving skills. The result is that WWC study reports, no matter how correct they are in statistical terms, can be seriously misleading if WWC does not conduct content analyses of the tests used in the studies. I brought this issue to WWC's attention, and they declined to act on it.

At present, then, the nation's most ambitious effort to review the literature using randomized controlled trials (RCTs) is seriously flawed. But that should not detract from attempts to use RCTs wisely—as noted above, they *are* an appropriate mechanism for evaluating large-scale curriculum use.

So, what's the problem? And why the fuss in the educational community over WWC's self-conscious use of randomized controlled trials? The problem comes when RCTs are considered to be the *only* legitimate way to arrive at definitive research findings—when the "gold standard" of RCTs becomes the *only* standard. In medicine and engineering, RCTs come at the end of a long R&D process. The prior work—discovery, theory refinement, product development, contextual studies—is all understood to be a fundamental part of research. More broadly, in a multidisciplinary field such as education, there are myriad ways to arrive at conclusions that are well warranted by data. *All* such methods should be available to researchers to be used when appropriate. *All* such work can be done rigorously. The relevant issues are: What does it take to do the work well? What evidence serves as warrants for claims, in what circumstances? What are the limits of the claims?

With all due respect, I would argue that when the only tool in your toolkit is a sledgehammer (i.e., randomized trials), you're in deep trouble. As a matter of survival (especially since funding agencies are increasingly demanding experimental designs for grant proposals), the field of educational research needs to refine and defend other methods. It also needs to get better at what it does and impose higher standards for publication. One of the reasons we've been vulnerable to attack is that a fair percentage of the work has not met the standards it should. Shoddy studies make us easy targets.

In addition to developing a more standardized set of tools and norms for reporting data, it might be worth considering the development of common databases and perhaps the requirement that data pertaining to published papers be entered into such databases. At minimum, researchers can publish data and methodological supplements to journal papers on their (or perhaps journal-sponsored) websites. Doing so is cheap and doesn't incur journal production costs.

A relatively small investment with a fairly large payoff is the creation of theme-based collaboratives: national networks of researchers who are all working on the same topic or who are linked in ways that support both their professional growth and the development of the field. Research-oriented networks might take on de facto responsibility for the ongoing monitoring of theory, methods, tools, and measures in their research areas. There is also a desperate need for increased human capacity for R&D in education. Efforts are needed to lure larger numbers of talented people into the profession, to provide better graduate preparation, and to provide better ongoing support for knowledge development and collaboration. This takes money—but it is worth remembering that a well-trained researcher is the gift that keeps on giving throughout a career.

The Research-Practice Divide

I echo the call in the National Academy of Education's *Recommendations Regarding Research Priorities* for increased attention to work in Pasteur's quadrant.[65] There are at least three major categories of studies that could be underwritten.

Partnerships in which researchers explore "real time" principled attempts at change in school districts that make themselves permeable to the researchers in exchange for help in understanding the impact of their policies. (The HPLC project discussed above is an example of such a partnership). It would be useful, for example, to conduct detailed research studies of what happens in various implementation attempts (such as systemic initiatives or the NSF's Math/Science Partnerships). Right now, major implementation attempts get *evaluated*—the question being "are they working?" What should happen is that any major intervention, as a condition of funding, has to make itself permeable to an independent team of researchers. That way we can find what happens *and why*; we can examine which factors seem to affect success or failure and how they operate. This kind of formative research is much more important than simply certifying that something has an impact (though that is important too).

It should be mentioned that R&D partnerships between researchers and school districts must involve some guarantees on the part of the districts regarding their part of the bargain, some degree of commitment to stability and coherence with regard to goals, curricula, assessment, and professional development. Interventions that get subverted by the environment to the point where they cannot be effectively implemented do nobody any good.[66] This is important, because we need some test cases. If there are good ideas that are ready for large-scale testing, we need to construct environments that are stable enough for the ideas to get a fair shot. Such environments will need an infusion of funds and commitments to stability on the part of researchers and practitioners. (As noted above, this might well involve firm commitments from both researchers and partner schools to surrender some autonomy in the interests of collaboration.) The funding and construction of such environments, with the right constraints, would be a noble experiment for a funding agency.

Developing the "engineering" or clinical model for educational R&D. A group might be funded for the extended design of much-needed educational materials and the refinement of the process by which they are produced. In addition to useful materials, this might provide a set of guidelines to be followed by other design groups.

As noted above, in the rush to move to randomized controlled trials (g-level/Stage III studies), the field has given short shrift to the kind of theoretical developmental work conducted in design experiments (a-level/Stage I studies) and has omitted the essential investment in studies of educational materials in different contexts (contextual or b-level/Stage II studies). There is some progress along this latter dimension. In a series of conferences held by the Research, Evaluation, and Communication Division of the NSF in 2003, each of three independent panels rated the use of contextual studies as being of the highest priority. Following this, the NSF Program Solicitation NSF 04-553, for the Interagency Education Research Initiative, explicitly offered funding for contextual studies.[67] Once again, the goal is to deepen our understanding of how and why things work in order to put us in a better position to make them work. To be sure, the goal of conducting experimental studies can serve as a strong motivation to engineer materials that work well in a range of contexts. The point is to be sensitive to contextual and main effects.

Funding the development of one or two model institutions designed to take on some of the large-scale projects discussed above. Such institutions might be the home for the development of new types of educational researcher-designers. And, if they provide "existence proofs" of the creation of materials that succeed in the marketplace, such institutions could prove that funding educational research is not necessarily a zero-sum game. Just as consumer electronics created the demand for new products, high-quality educational R&D can create products with the potential to change the dynamics of the marketplace. Once there is clear evidence that some products do work, other producers may feel the need to shift away from focus groups and start to produce rigorous evidence themselves.

Indeed, there is an opportunity for an adventurous funding agency to jump start a new kind of educational enterprise, one with new roles for researcher/designers, designer/teachers, and others who could contribute productively to the R&D enterprise without suffering from the negative incentive systems of current universities.

Given the long history of failure of educational research to have a significant positive impact on practice, one would be foolhardy to think that the suggestions made here will result in rapid improvements. At the same time, the state of the field is such that if the field begins to take some of these suggestions seriously, cautious optimism is justified.

Sincere thanks are due to the MacArthur Research Network on Teaching and Learning for providing me the opportunity to reflect on and write about the issues discussed in this paper and also for lively discussions of the paper's contents. I very much appreciate formative reviews of an earlier draft by Patricia Albjerg Graham and Tony Bryk and ongoing comments made by Tony Bryk as the manuscript has evolved. John Bransford gave the penultimate version of the manuscript a thorough going-over, much to the good, and pointed comments by Jeremy Roschelle resulted in a rethinking and rewriting of points large and small. Thanks also to the "refining fire" of the functions group at UC Berkeley, specifically to Indigo Esmonde, Vicki Hand, Mara Landers, Katie Lewis, and Ann Ryu. Many of the ideas discussed here come from reflections on my long-term professional partnership with Hugh Burkhardt and from my work as senior adviser to the Education and Human Resources Directorate of the National Science Foundation.

CHAPTER 8

How Craft Knowledge of Teaching Is Generated and Disseminated in Japan

Hidenori Fujita

apanese students repeatedly outperform American students, especially in math and science (e.g., OECD/PISA since 2000 and IEA/TIMSS since 1964).[1] This chapter examines features of the organization of schooling and teaching in Japan and strategies for connecting research and practice that most likely contribute to the relatively high performance of Japanese students. The larger policy context is also discussed, because it no doubt has supported the effectiveness of the educational practices described.

Three features of Japanese education are relevant to the use of systematic evidence in the practice of education. First, education is highly centralized in Japan, with the central government playing a critical role in curriculum reform, teacher education and professional development, and, to some degree, the involvement of research and researchers in reforms. Second, teachers enjoy greater prestige and higher pay relative to occupations requiring similar levels of education than in the United States. Greater investment is also made in their training and continued professional development, and teachers play a more central role in school management. Third, in Japan there are many institutionalized mechanisms for practitioners and researchers to interact in all aspects of education reform and improvement. In many respects, distinctions between practitioners' and researchers' roles are more blurred in Japan than in the United States and most Western countries, with teachers being encouraged and given opportunities to codify craft knowledge through lesson study and school-based research and development (R&D) programs. Japanese teachers' deep and productive involvement in research and development is made possible by their high level of training and the time and opportunities they are given outside of their classroom teaching.

The chapter begins with a brief overview of how evidence on effective practices is generated and disseminated. The chapter then elaborates on the special qualities of Japanese education mentioned above—centralization, teachers training and roles, and institutionalized connections between practitioners and researchers. Finally, methods for dissemination on a broad scale are described.

MECHANISMS FOR DEVELOPING AND DISSEMINATING KNOWLEDGE ON EFFECTIVE PRACTICES: AN OVERVIEW

The development and dissemination of knowledge about effective practices involves four major processes in Japan, referred to here as: (1) top-down regulation, (2) bottom-up construction, (3) trickle-down generative, and (4) normative diffusion.

Top-down regulation. The Ministry of Education (MEXT) creates policies and guidelines for school management, curriculum, pedagogy, and student guidance, yielding considerable influences through its top-down regulation processes. For example, every ten years the MEXT revises the National Course of Study based on a report by the Central Council of Education.

Education scholars who conduct research or are familiar with research findings usually serve as advisers or consultants, providing ideas, evidence, and reasoning for new policies, measures, and guidelines. Since there are many scholars involved in the advisory committee, decisions usually involve the negotiation of varying opinions. Through this process, research-based suggestions can become simplified and occasionally distorted.

Bottom-up construction. Craft knowledge is also developed, assessed, modified, and codified in the daily practice of teachers working at the school level. During this process, teachers introduce new approaches or material for teaching, assess them, fine-tune them, and share them with teachers in other schools. Their efforts are often inspired by research conducted or ideas disseminated by university professors, education commentators, experienced teachers, and educational researchers.

In the bottom-up construction process, education scholars usually serve as advisers or action research leaders who provide ideas, evidence, and theoretical bases for new practices. Some scholars are affiliated with a particular school or local education board for a period ranging from several months to several years. As advisers, they are often invited to school-based lesson studies and other events to comment or give a lecture. Although education researchers and scholars are involved in the bottom-up construction process, the initiative lies with schools and teachers, not university professors. Teachers, schools, and boards of education select and invite university professors to various lesson studies, R&D meetings, and teacher-training programs. Teachers are also centrally involved in this process as action researchers.

Trickle-down generative. Some innovations in teaching and management are based on reports of innovations developed in schools and shared through teacher-training programs, lesson studies, and various other meetings of teachers and principals, as well as through educational publications, school practice reports, and school-based action research reports, the latter two of which are produced by teachers who have been involved in school-based R&D programs.

Education scholars usually serve as mediators, interpreters, and advocates for new practices that were developed in schools and considered to be successful. In their commentaries they typically add their own interpretations and explanations for why the practices are successful and how they might be further improved. These analyses are disseminated in books, magazine articles, and lectures in teacher-training programs and other conferences for teachers.

Normative diffusion. Some innovations and new approaches are advocated by leading scholars in newspapers, magazines, and books as well as in MEXT publications. With time, a new idea may be adopted by enough teachers and schools that it becomes typical practice. New practices are more likely to become the norm when they are congruent with emergent or dominant ideas or reform trends.

The role of education scholars is similar to that of those in the trickle-down generative process. The difference between them lies in such factors as level of publicity and the perceived legitimacy of their proposals and arguments. If media attention is widespread, or if an advocate is widely known, the proposals tend to be taken more seriously, especially if the analysis is clear and compelling and consistent with emerging or dominant ideas or reform trends.

We turn now to the specific qualities of the education system in Japan that contribute to evidence-based practice and the political and social context that supports them.

CENTRALIZATION

The Ministry of Education has substantial influence over all aspects of education in Japan. For example, MEXT determines the requirements for teaching credentials and accredits teacher-training colleges and university departments to do teacher preparation. Prefectural boards of education (comparable to the state boards of education in the United States) issue credentials to students who meet the requirements of MEXT-certified teacher preparation programs.

MEXT is also responsible for revising the Course of Study about every ten years, which specifies the national curriculum and provides government guidelines for teaching and the contents of textbooks authorized by MEXT. When the new Course of Study is released (usually three years before its implementation), various educational publications carry articles written by ministry officials, university professors and other specialists, and local education boards. These articles describe and explain the changes so that schools and teachers can begin preparation for the transition.

MEXT is also deeply involved in teacher professional development. For example, it provides instruction on education policies, guidelines on school management, and the content of the revised national course of study to supervisors who are delegated from all prefectural boards of education. These supervisors then give lectures at training courses offered by prefectural and municipal boards of education.

Furthermore, MEXT subsidizes one-third of public school teachers' salaries (half until 2005), about one-third to one-half of the construction costs of public school buildings, and some other educational equipment, such as computers and LANs.

Centralization is supported by a system of laws (e.g., Fundamental Law of Education, School Education Law, Teacher Certificate Law) and ministerial ordinances as well as local regulations. For example, in 2007 a modification of the School Education Law requires schools to conduct and release the results of an external evaluation done according to MEXT guidelines

The centralization of education policies does not guarantee evidence-based practices. But it does provide a single "point of entry" for the adoption of practices that are well-supported by research. Thus, it is theoretically easier to implement innovative practices broadly. In contrast, in the United States, the fifty independent states and many relatively autonomous districts within states make the task of using educational research to inform practice more complex.

Japan is divided into forty-seven prefectures, primary local administration units that are comparable to the U.S. states. Under each prefecture there are cities, towns, and villages as secondary or tertiary administration units. An ordinance-designated city is a large city with a population of more than 500,000 and to which many administrative rights of the prefecture are delegated. They have the rights to appoint and to dismiss teachers and set teacher salaries. As of April 2008, there are seventeen cities of this status. A core city is one with a population greater than 300,000. These cities have the right to train the teachers appointed by the prefecture. As of April 2008, there are thirty-nine cities with this status.

PREPARATION, PROFESSIONAL DEVELOPMENT, AND ROLES OF TEACHERS

Recruitment, Placement and Retention

Teaching in Japan is a well-respected and a relatively well-paid profession. Teacher salaries are about 5 percent higher than that of the general public servant in Japan. According to the 2005 *OECD Education at a Glance,* the ratio of annual statutory teacher's salary (secondary school level) after fifteen years' experience to GDP per capita in 2003 was 1.60 (US$45,515) in Japan, while it was 1.17 (US$43,999) in the United States.[2] Because teaching jobs are highly competitive in Japan, there are private "cram schools" for teacher-selection examinations. For example, acceptance rate (applicants/intakes) of new teachers at the junior high school level was about 12 percent in the period from 2002 to 2005.[3]

The teacher-selection examination is composed of two parts. The first is a written examination and the second is an interview, both conducted by prefectural or ordinance-designated city boards of education. The newly hired teachers are assigned to particular schools and have to through a first-year training program. This first year is a probationary period, and after it is completed teachers are given tenure. The tenure rate is high (more than 95%) partly because the one-year probationary period was introduced more to provide in-service training than as a means for further screening.

All public school teachers are reassigned to schools within the same prefecture about every seven or eight years, according to individual teacher wishes, the principal's recommendation, and the teacher allocation scheme for each locality. The teacher rotation system in Japan is different from the system of many other countries, where each school selects its teachers, even though they are officially hired by the local board of education. The Japanese policy equalizes the quality of teaching among schools and makes it easier for each prefecture to adjust school size in accordance with demographic changes in student populations. Teachers who are assigned to schools in remote places are allowed to move to a school in a more desirable area after three years.

The salary of public school teachers is set higher than the rate for other civil servants, according to the Law for Securing Talented Teachers, and special stipends are paid for teaching at schools in remote places. Japanese teachers are paid their salary for twelve months, not nine, as in the United States. During the summer, teachers might advise students' clubs, attend various teacher-training programs, prepare school events such as field trips, and give supplementary lessons. All teachers are also expected to use the summer to improve their knowledge and capacity as teachers. Under the Japanese twelve-month system, teachers are able to concentrate on the job of teaching throughout the year and spend more time developing their teaching skills during the summer.

Partly due to intense training, both pre- and in-service, and the relatively high pay, the retention rate is high compared to most Western countries. The total number of teachers leaving teaching (elementary and secondary schools) in the 2003–04 school year was 30,519, compared to 26,647 entrants to teaching in the same school year. Resignations accounted for about 35 percent of all leaving.[4] The United States has much higher teacher turnover. According to the report of National Commission of Teaching and America's Future, the attrition rates of beginning teachers are 14 percent after one year, 33 percent after three years, and 46 percent after five years. Resignations account for about 72 percent of those leaving teaching.[5]

Training and Professional Development

Stevenson and Stigler identified two critical differences between teacher training in the United States and Japan.[6] First, in Japan teacher training takes place largely on the job, whereas in the United States it takes place primarily pre-service, in colleges and universities. Second, unlike the United States, where teachers spend most of their time isolated in their classrooms, in Japan teachers have ample time and opportunities to interact with each other to discuss teaching practices.

Pre-Service Training

Almost all Japanese teachers are educated at four-year colleges and universities. There are three levels of teacher certificates: advanced certificates (M.A. level), 1st-class certificates (B.A. level), and 2nd-class certificates (junior college level; a temporary certificate for older teachers). Each type of teacher certificate is divided into two categories: general school teachers and special school (i.e., for the disabled) teachers. There are also three types of teacher certificates: general certificates for elementary school teachers; special certificates such as music, art, and home economics for elementary and lower secondary school teachers; and subject-based certificates for secondary school teachers.

In order to get a first-class teacher certificate for junior high school level, all students have to take at least 67 credits in addition to the required credits for a B.A. degree at a university: 20 credits in a specified subject area; 31 credits on teaching occupation, including 12 credits on teaching methods, 6 credits on educational theory and child development, 4 credits on counseling and guidance, 5 credits (three weeks) of practice teaching at a junior high school, 2 credits on the significance of education, and 2 credits for a comprehensive seminar; 8 credits either in a subject area or on teaching profession; and 8 credits on the Japanese Constitution, physical education, information technology and foreign language communication. They also have to have more than seven days' practice at a caring and welfare facility. For a senior high school certificate, more credits in a specified subject area and fewer credits on teaching are required, while an elementary school teaching certificate requires 41 credits on teaching and only 8 credits in a specified subject area.

Professional Development

Figure 8.1 summarizes the extensive, continuous, and multilayered teacher-training and professional development scheme in Japan. There are five major levels of teacher training: (1) the national level, (2) the prefectural board of education level, (3) the municipal board of education level, (4) the school level, and (5) the voluntary educational association level. The extensive teacher training is discussed in some length because it is most likely critical to the success of practices that involve teachers directly in the development, assessment, and dissemination of effective educational practices.

National level. Training at the national level is largely classified into two categories: regular leader training and ad-hoc training for specific problems, such as information technologies, AIDS, or drug-abuse prevention. The regular leader training is further classified into three types. The first is general training courses for the middle-rank teachers and for principals and deputy principals who are delegates from prefectures. The second is the special training courses for the teacher-leaders who are delegates from prefectures. The third is the long-term overseas training program for young teachers and the short-term overseas program for experienced teachers. All courses except the overseas programs are offered by the national teachers training center. Travel expenses are subsidized by the local boards of education, and the expenses for the overseas programs are subsidized by MEXT. The participants in these training programs are expected to make reports to their schools, local boards of education, and other neighboring schools on various occasions and share what they learned with their peer teachers.

In these training courses and supervisors' meetings, lectures are given on recent education reforms and policies, including the revision of the National Course of Study. Most of these reforms and policies are proposed by the Central Council of Education, the advisory body for the Minister of Education. The Central Council and its upper-level subcommittees, which are composed of education professors, superintendents, mayors/governors, and business leaders, usually set the basic principles and frameworks, while lower-level subcommittees, which are composed largely of education professors, school principals, and superintendents, discuss and propose guidelines for specific issues. However, many participants, including education professors and school principals, are not necessarily specialists in the area of concern, and the reforms and policies proposed are not always coherent and rational in theory, system, and practice. The incoherence occurs partly because reforms are often influenced by the views of politicians and business leaders (especially since the 1990s) and the public. Accordingly, the task of making reforms and policies coherent among them and with the existing system is left to the MEXT officials and, later, to the local boards of education, schools and teachers, textbook publishing companies, and textbook authors. Essential to this process are the teacher-training programs provided by local boards of education and by various voluntary associations of teachers.

Local boards of education at the level of prefecture, ordinance-designated cities, and core municipalities. Boards of education in cities and prefectures have primary responsibility for offering a series of teacher-training courses every year that include: induction training for first-year teachers; training for all teachers with five, ten, or twenty years of service; training for curriculum managers, student guidance managers, deputy principals, and principals, with all newly appointed people in these positions obligated to attend; special trainings for

FIGURE 8.1   Teacher Training and Professional Development

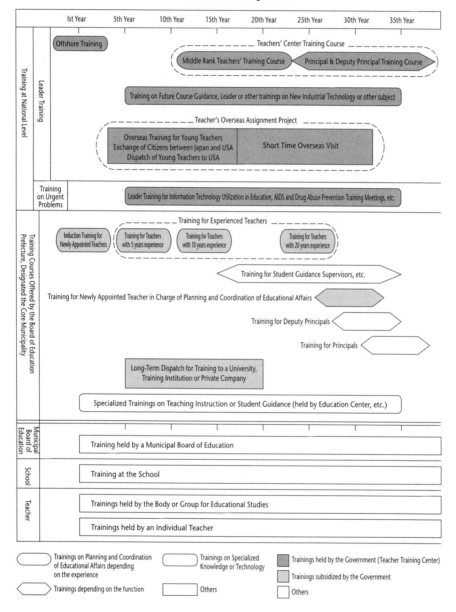

Educational Training Scheme

Source: "Formal Education," *Ministry of Education, Culture, Sports, Science, and Technology*, accessed August 27, 2008, from http://www.mext.go.jp/english/org/f_formal_16.htm.

subject instruction, student guidance, ICT utilization, etc. (attendance is voluntary, though at least one teacher from almost every school attends); and long-term (one- or two-year) programs for training in universities, research institutes, and private companies (more than ten teachers are selected every year from each prefecture and city).

Among the training programs, induction training and training for teachers with ten years of experiences are required by law, with attendance being obligatory. The others are not required by law, but all prefectures and cities institute rules and provide the programs following the suggestions by MEXT and various proposals of the Central Council. Most of the training, required or not, is in the form of lectures, seminars, and workshops at a teacher-training center. The length of voluntary training varies from locality to locality, with five days per year being the average.

Induction training takes place over the course of one year and is composed of two parts: training for more than sixty days at the teacher's school site and training for more than thirty days at a different site, with an additional five days in the teacher-training center of each locality. Under the guidance of an appointed mentor teacher, new teachers learn various skills related to classroom management, subject instruction, special school activities, and student guidance. Off-school training is composed of lectures, seminars, and workshops provided by and at the teacher-training center of the locality concerned and is complemented by visits to other types of schools and study through social activities.

Training for teachers with ten years' experience involves training for twenty days at the school site and twenty days of off-school training. For training at the school site, teachers undertake a series of lesson studies and a study of teaching materials. They conduct a self-assessment of their job performance and discuss it with the principal, the vice principal, and experienced teachers. Off-school training takes place at the teacher-training center of each locality and includes: basic training on school management and evaluation (one day); subject lessons through mock instruction and study of lesson materials in a small group (nine days); student guidance training (five days); and elective training on such areas as e-learning, environmental education, industrial education, moral education, education for the disabled, collaboration with other types of schools, nursing care, etc. (five days).

In lectures, seminars, and workshops of all types, education professors, an official of MEXT, supervisors of the local board of education, or other prominent figures are invited to give lectures and instruction. It is their role to make newly introduced changes concrete, appropriate, and coherent with the conventional practices and many other related parts of the system of teaching and schooling, as well as to offer ideas and explain the theoretical foundations behind them.

Teacher training offered by a municipal board of education varies among different municipalities and focuses on various educational issues and emerging tasks that each municipality recognizes as important for improving teachers' understanding of the issue and their capacity to cope with it. Recent themes have included information technology, counseling, adolescent problems and related intervention programs, and issues on education reform and sociocultural conditions. Most of the trainings are for a half-day, and are typically with a specialist, such as a university professor serving as a lecturer or instructor.

Schools and voluntary associations of teachers. There are four types of training at a school: (1) school-based lesson study; (2) training through a series of study activities of a designated R&D program; (3) training at the school site as a part of the officially ordained teacher training for newly appointed teachers and teachers with ten years' experience; and (4) training as an independent school-based program of lectures, seminars, or workshops on various educational issues and emerging tasks. In the first, second, and fourth cases, a specialist, such as a university professor, is usually invited as a lecturer or instructor, and trainings are often open to parents as well as teachers.

Teacher professional development is also organized by various volunteer groups or associations of teachers, including subject-based, region-based, and university-based organizations as well as teachers' unions and academic associations. For example, subject-based associations for each subject and for career guidance are organized at various localities and at the national level. They hold lesson studies and seminars at the local level every one or two months as well as at an annual national convention. Teachers' unions, which are divided into two major national unions and several regional unions, also hold seminars and workshops at each district level, at regional conventions, and at national conventions. Contrary to the study meetings of subject-based groups, the themes of union meetings usually cover a wide range of schooling and teaching concerns and tend to focus on emergent issues, such as revisions of the National Course of Study and policy issues. The number of attending teachers varies from meeting to meeting, ranging anywhere from twenty to thirty teachers to hundreds at local meetings and from several hundred to several thousand at regional meetings and national conventions.

In these meetings, specialists in the field (including university professors) are invited to give lectures and participate in symposia. Some professors spend about half of their summer vacations and once a week throughout the year giving lectures at such meetings.

Roles of Teachers

In part because of their extensive training, teachers are able to play significant roles in the management of schools. Leadership is more distributed in Japanese schools than in most Western countries, with teachers taking a variety of leadership roles as coordinators of the management of each grade, lesson studies, R&D projects, school events and ceremonies, and various committees. The distributed leadership necessitates and promotes collaboration among teachers and contributes to organizational learning.

Teachers lead collaborations to design the curriculum, evaluation schemes, and lesson studies. They develop strategies for career guidance and guidance for learning habits and healthy lifestyles. They also participate in various committees for school management, such as the disaster prevention committee, the R&D committee, the teaching materials selection committee, the school excursion committee, and the public relations committee. Collaboration occurs in formal settings, such as monthly staff meetings and various committee meetings, as well as informal settings. Japanese teachers often meet at bars or restaurants near the school to exchange ideas about student learning, teaching skills, and school management.

Similar organizational structures are found in almost all elementary and secondary schools in Japan, partly because it is ordered by the Operational Regulation of School Education Law, which requires schools to have a system in place that is designed to promote harmonious school management. It also requires that in each elementary school the principal appoints a grade manager, a curriculum manager, a health guidance manager, and other coordinators should the need arise. In addition to these managers, there must be managers of guidance counseling and student guidance in each junior and senior high school and subject division heads in each senior high school. These managers are in charge of coordinating and promoting the collaborative activities in each respective area. Though these managers are obliged to attend the respective training programs offered by the local board of education, their qualifications are no different from the other teachers'. All teachers are expected to take charge of some roles in the scheme of school affairs and to collaborate with others.

The Structure of Teaching

Teachers' involvement in school management and R&D activities requires a different structure for teaching than is found in most American schools. In Japan, average lesson periods per week are 18.5 for public elementary school teachers (with 71 percent of teachers teaching about 23 periods), 15.1 for junior high (with 48 percent teaching about 17 periods), and 13.6 for senior high school teachers (with 84 percent teaching about 16 periods).[7]

According to one survey comparing Japan and Great Britain, Japanese teachers spent about ten hours and twenty minutes per day at school and about fifty minutes at home on school matters, while British teachers spent about eight hours and forty minutes at school and about one hour and thirty minutes at home on school matters.[8] These survey results suggest that Japanese teachers tend to spend more time on their jobs and have more time at school out of the classroom to commit to the collegial and collaborative activities at the school than teachers in Great Britain do.

INSTITUTIONALIZED MECHANISMS FOR R&D

A major difference between Japan and the United States is the degree to which teachers are involved in research and development, primarily through the opportunities they are given to develop, assess, and codify craft knowledge. This occurs primarily through cooperative processes that are facilitated by the way school buildings are constructed and by institutionalized activities.[9]

Physical Space Designed to Promote Collaboration

The staff room arrangement illustrates the culture of collaboration that typifies Japanese schools. Figure 8.2 shows a typical teachers' staff room in a public junior high school in Tokyo. All teachers have their own desks where they spend most of their time between classes and after regular lesson hours. Short daily staff meetings are held in the staff room, and although principals have separate offices, they often come into the staff room to give instructions and interact with teachers.

The staff room is the institutional locus for various collaborative activities. The desk arrangement by grade promotes a collaborative culture. Teachers are responsible for the cooperative management of their grade and for taking care of all students in the grade to which they are assigned as well as the management of their own homeroom classes. Grade management includes developing the yearly schedule, providing guidelines for subject lessons and

FIGURE 8.2   Teachers' Staff Room Layout

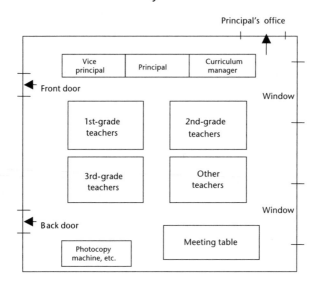

achievement targets, taking responsibility for student guidance, and managing many other school activities and events. Grade teachers collaborate on all of these activities.

Lesson Study

Lesson study is a unique form of collaboration, and it is the primary strategy for developing, assessing, documenting, and disseminating effective instructional practices in Japan.[10] It involves both teachers and researchers in different roles than are typically found in the United States School-based lesson study typically involves first formulating the student learning goals of the lesson and preparing the lesson and then implementing it, with one teacher doing the instruction and other participants observing and, finally, discussing the effectiveness of the lesson and possible improvements. The analysis is thorough, encompassing such aspects as the organization, content, and time allocation of the lesson; the materials used; the manner of the teacher's presentation, explanation, blackboard writing, raising of questions, and response to answers; interactions between the teacher and students and among students; the teacher's pacing of students' activities; students' involvement and enthusiasm; the level of students' learning and understanding; teacher's attitudes, behaviors, physical expressions, and enthusiasm; and the rhythm and tension of the lesson. Often staff gather informally after school at a bar or restaurant near the school to reward the teacher who conducted the research lesson for his or her efforts, to exchange further ideas about the particular lesson observed and instruction in general, and to promote friendships.

There are two types of school-based lesson study. One is closed within the school, and the other is open to the teachers from other schools, university professors, and other educators. In the former case, all teachers in the school are invited, occasionally with a university professor brought in as a guest commentator. In the latter case, many teachers from other schools attend, and a university professor or staff members of the local board of education are often invited as guest commentators.

Lesson study is practiced in almost all elementary and junior high schools and, to a lesser extent, in senior high schools. Although school-based lesson study is the most popular form, there are other forms of lesson study, one of which is subject-based lesson study conducted by a voluntary study group or association of teachers.

The lesson is a forty-five- or fifty-minute presentation—much like a symphony—that is basically organized into four sections. First, the theme, objective and/or task, of a particular lesson is introduced. Second, the major content related to the theme is presented, explained, and developed. Third, students are asked to engage in active exercises, experiments, or discussion. Finally, the teacher sums up the content, assesses what students have learned, and announces the theme of the next lesson.

Although this is the basic form, actual lessons take a variety of forms, often omitting either a development or practice/application section, repeating cycles of development and practice/application sections, or replacing an introductory explanation of the theme with an exercise such as a short test for confirming the mastery of content from previous lessons. Whatever its form, the success of a lesson depends on the well-designed, coherent organization of various activities and materials throughout the lesson period, with a rhythm and tone conducive to the harmony that results from a stimulating and enjoyable lesson. As a whole, a good lesson maintains a sufficiently high level of awareness and involvement of all students to make learning effective.

In the United States more emphasis is placed on the curriculum and choice of textbook or other curricular materials than the delivery of single lessons. Rarely do teachers have time to fine-tune a lesson in collaboration with other teachers. In Japan the curriculum is centrally determined, so the local focus can be on delivery. In the United States, best practices often travel through materials or teacher professional development programs, whereas in Japan open school-based lesson studies are a primary way to disseminate best practices.

The uniformity of lessons the lesson study approach engenders is criticized by some Japanese and Westerners for suppressing teachers' individuality and creativity and ignoring students' individual potential for development by forcing them to follow the teacher's instruction, direction, and pacing as well as the standardized curriculum. This criticism is unwarranted. Stevenson and Stigler point out that in Japanese classrooms all students are actors or players, while the teacher is a composer, a conductor, a facilitator, and a moderator.

> [Japanese] lessons are oriented toward problem-solving rather than rote mastery of facts and procedures, and make use of many different types of representational materials. The role assumed by the teacher is that of knowledgeable guide, rather than that of prime dispenser of information and arbiter of what is correct. There is frequent verbal interaction in the classroom as the teacher attempts to stimulate students to produce, explain, and evaluate solutions to problems.[11]

R&D Schools

Some schools in Japan are designated and supported financially as research and development schools by the local board of education or MEXT. They play a key role in the dissemination of the results of lesson studies. Their work can transcend particular lessons to include emerging educational topics such as environmental learning and international understanding as well as school management, education for the disabled, career guidance and internship programs, collaboration between elementary and secondary schools and among schools, localities, and businesses.

The selected schools, usually given a small R&D grant for two years, are proud of their selection and expend a great deal of effort to work on their theme. Teachers in the school work together on a project team that creates an R&D plan for the specified period, reviews various related materials, conducts research on the theme, and designs a series of lesson studies. University researchers are involved, but usually only in an advisory role.

The work usually culminates in a schoolwide lesson study and symposium attended by hundreds of teachers from other schools in the city. This event is carefully designed and well-prepared with the collaborative efforts of all the teachers and, in many cases, parents and local residents who have volunteered. After this event, and toward the end of the project period, teachers work collaboratively to include all the relevant outcomes in the R&D report. A typical program is composed of lesson studies in all classes in the morning and, in the afternoon, theme-based discussions among the participants divided into several groups and/or a lecture by a guest speaker, such as a university professor, a superintendent of the local board of education, or some other distinguished person.

ORGANIZATIONAL LEARNING AND KNOWLEDGE DISSEMINATION—"SCALING UP"

According to Argyris and Schon, organizational learning occurs in a situation in which members of the organization modify and restructure values and assumptions that are built into an organization's practice in response to changes inside or outside of the organization.[12] The collaborative culture of teaching in Japanese schools and its associated organizational and institutional arrangements promote an organizational learning community that adapts to changing contexts. Teachers, schools, and local boards of education all try to understand environmental conditions and their changes inside and outside schools, to modify and restructure their craft knowledge and daily practices, and to enhance teaching and learning as well as the school's management capability as an organizational entity. Organization learning is built in to the institutionalized collaborations at the school level and at the local and national levels. Lesson study plays an important role in the broad dissemination of educational practices that have been carefully analyzed and improved. There are, however, other mechanisms for knowledge development and dissemination.

Research, in the sense of systematic efforts to assess and codify effective practice, is conducted by university professors and researchers of public and private research institutes, as well as by government agencies, teachers and staff of teacher unions, teachers of voluntary study associations, and teachers who are involved in school-based R&D programs. Research findings are reported at annual conferences of academic associations and are published in academic journals and books. Findings rarely reach policymakers or practitioners at a broad level, however, unless the outcome is disseminated through the mass media or rewritten into a marketable book or education-related publication.

Popular Books and Monthly Publications

There are many Japanese educational publications that are published monthly by private publishers. An Internet search, for example, revealed 116 education-related monthly magazines (including special issues) published in August 2008 alone. These publications cover a wide variety of education topics based on subject-matter, level of education (from preschool to senior high school), specific aspects of schooling (e.g., school management, student guidance, child and adolescent psychology, curriculum evaluation), broader themes related to education, and policy (e.g., information and explanation of policies, measures, and activities of MEXT and local boards of education).

Many of these publications illustrate the integration of research and practice and the blurring of the practitioner and research roles. Unlike in the United States, where researchers and practitioners tend to publish in and read different books and journals, many Japanese educational publications include research-based articles written by university professors, education officials, education critics, and other prominent experts as well as practical cases of educational innovations written by teachers and principals. These publications also provide forums for communication among teachers, university professors, education officials, and other education specialists.

The Role of Education Experts

Educational researchers are directly involved in the dissemination of research findings largely through writing popular education books and articles for monthly education magazines as well as through the role they play in professional development activities. But much of the dissemination is done by mediators who interpret research findings and write essays and articles. Although they do not necessarily conduct research themselves, many mediators are recognized as experts among practitioners. Experienced teachers and officials of local boards of education and MEXT who are recognized as successful in the field also play a role in sharing research-based knowledge related to educational practice. Most Japanese teachers expect theory-based knowledge and research to inform their practice in addition to concrete advice and suggestions for improving their practices.

THE FUTURE FOR JAPAN

The mechanisms for the construction and dissemination of practical knowledge, as well as the teacher-training system and the culture of collaboration described in this chapter, have functioned fairly well for several decades in

Japan. Since the 1980s, however, the foundations of these features and their functioning have been challenged by various education reforms and by socio-cultural changes that are affecting teachers, schools, and public education.

A new tide of education reforms has emerged in Japan and other countries, and the policy discourse on public education is being reframed. Increasingly there is more emphasis on freedom than on equality; on quasi-public (or superficial) accountability than on the kind of accountability that demonstrates serious responsibility for children; on market efficiency than on intrinsic educational value; on direct managerial control than on professional expertise and autonomy; and on narrow, short-term measurable outcomes than on long-term, meaningful development. In this changing context, schools and teachers have been under attack from various stakeholders and have been forced to cope with the growing pressures of market efficiency and quasi-public accountability that are embodied in such rising trends as parental choice schemes, mindless accountability, and performance-based teacher evaluation and reward systems. These reform trends risk undermining the foundation of the collaborative culture and professional learning community that Japanese students have benefited from. The dominant reform discourse has furthermore cast a shadow over the tradition and utilization of research-based policies and practices. Regrettably, I see a trend toward policymakers and the mass media welcoming simple proposals and neglecting the underlying and complex context.

My hope is that Japan will not abandon the core strategies that have promoted continuous improvement by (1) involving teachers in the systematic development, evaluation, and codification of effective practices; (2) involving researchers and other educational experts in informing and disseminating research-based and craft knowledge; and (3) instantiating these sources of knowledge in national policies. It is because of the organizational structures and practices described in this chapter that Japan has been able to maintain an effective educational system that functions as a learning organization. It is not perfect, but it is important to maintain the qualities that make it work and to continue to serve as a useful model for integrating research and practice for other countries.

I wish to acknowledge the funding agencies without whom the work for this chapter would never have been possible: Japan Society for the Promotion of Science (JSPS) for my research (Grant No. 16330166 for the years 2004–07) and the MacArthur Foundation for the research, workshop, and book project. I am grateful to all who made this book project possible and especially those who made my chapter readable and appropriate for American readers: Deborah Stipek, John Bransford, Nancy Vye, Diana Lam, and Louis Gomez. And thanks, also, to and also to Catherine Lewis, who gave me valuable comments on the draft.

CHAPTER 9

Toward a Deeper Understanding of the Educational Elephant

Concluding Thoughts

Louis M. Gomez , Janet A. Weiss, Deborah J. Stipek,
and John D. Bransford

Meaningful school reform requires understanding the many parts of the educational system and aligning the various sectors affecting educational practice. Our goal in this final chapter is to highlight some of the insights in this collection about building bridges to create a coherent system of reform.

The authors of the chapters in this volume addressed the three central themes described in the introductory chapter. The *equity and excellence* theme emphasizes the goal of designing high-quality learning opportunities for all students (requiring continuous learning by many others, including teachers, parents, educational leaders, researchers, community members, and policymakers). The *elephants* theme reminds us that our educational system involves many sectors—including the federal and state governments, schools and districts, research organizations, and nonprofit and for-profit organizations—and that the perspectives of each must be considered in any reform effort. The *evidence* theme proposes that evidence of what works for whom and why is necessary to be effective and that the idea of using evidence-based practices (we prefer the term "evidence-informed practices" used by Hargreaves and Stone-Johnson) is more complex than it might appear at first glance.

In pursuit of the ambitious goal of strong academic performance for all students, we turn to the many valuable suggestions and recommendations made by the authors. As chapter 1 explains, we are especially interested in how to create tighter and more productive connections between knowledge and practice in order to improve student learning. Some of the suggestions lie in the domain of education policy, others in the practice of teaching and learning, and still others in the research, business, and nonprofit organizations that affect the quality of education.

INSIGHTS AND THEORIES FROM THE CHAPTERS

The chapters in this volume identify several patterns and characteristics in the U.S. educational ecosystem that make it difficult to develop productive connections between systematically developed knowledge and practice. One common theme is that the enterprise of education, while rich and varied, is carried out in overlapping but distinct institutional sectors. A number of the chapters make specific reference to the policy-practice divide. Policymakers at the federal, state, and local levels influence the quality of instruction, but each level operates in different spheres with different legal constraints, participants, and agendas. A policy created at one level often cancels the effectiveness of a policy made at another or, worse, causes harm. The active roles played by the thousands of nonprofit support and advocacy organizations and by the industry that produces educational products and services add more layers of complexity to the picture. There are few organizational structures, practices, and tools to bind education's various institutional sectors together into a system focused on improvement.

The weak link between research and practice in education is noteworthy, because in other arenas, such as medicine and agriculture, researchers' questions are more directly connected to the needs of "users." In contrast, educational researchers work in institutions largely disconnected from educational practice. Often research institutions have a culture of incentives resulting in findings and products that are not particularly useful or useable by educators and that are described in publications that are inaccessible or impenetrable to practitioners and policymakers. There are signs that educational research is becoming more relevant and useful.[1] Nevertheless, we have a long way to go.

A second observation made in several chapters is that the field of education lacks the strong theories or integrated conceptual models that exist in many other domains, such as medicine. Educational leaders tend to have relatively weak theories of their own practice. They have learned particular practices, but they may not understand the general principles explaining why they work or the circumstances required for them to work. This makes it difficult to choose appropriate adjustments when the situation or context changes. Although researchers have coherent, empirically supported theories about learning and understand a great deal about teaching, they are only beginning to develop robust theories about how to customize practice to the needs of particular students and teachers in local contexts and how to assess progress and prepare people for lifelong learning. Theories will need to be developed and tested if the field is going to provide research evidence that can guide effective intervention.[2]

A third common theme in this volume concerns the lack of agreement about the goals of educational practice and policy. Many of the authors have taken as a starting point the aspiration to provide "ambitious instruction" for all students. Definitions of "ambitious instruction" vary widely and are often reflected in debates about instruction and the best ways to assess student learning and skills. In addition, not all participants in the educational system embrace the general idea of ambitious instruction as their top priority. Practitioners, policymakers, parents, and outside organizations' interests in other important goals of schools—such as maintaining safety, supporting mental health, promoting moral and social development, preparing students for the world of work—cannot be dismissed. Diverse perspectives on the larger mission of education can have the effect of diffusing, if not confusing, the focus.

A fourth theme is the lack of agreement among educational researchers and evaluators about the value of the measures of performance that are available. Several authors in this volume discuss the pivotal roles played by commonly used standardized assessments of learning in defining "educational success." All of the authors agree on the need for measures of student outcomes, but many of us also emphasize the need to rethink and develop a deeper understanding of the measures we use.[3]

A recent *New York Times Magazine* piece offered a graphic illustration of how the preceding observations play out in the real world, in this case in the city of New Orleans. Among the many casualties of Hurricane Katrina was the New Orleans school district. If the education enterprise was a well-functioning ecology, there would be method and coherence to the process of rebuilding and reengineering the education infrastructure of New Orleans.[4] This has not been the case. Cadres of energetic, bright, and heroic people are attempting to reinvent education at the level of the central office and in individual schools. The development of organizational structures and schools is not guided by a set of empirically tested principles of effective organizations or schools. The theory that appears to be guiding action in New Orleans instead is "let a thousand flowers bloom"—or, in more Darwinian terms, mutation and selection. In large measure, the district office encourages the creation of new schools and will allow the successful ones to continue and close down the unsuccessful schools. Imagine building airplanes or developing pharmaceutical products on that basis. Imagine the damage that can be done by unsuccessful schools.

Our goal in this discussion is not to be critical of New Orleans but to make the point that efforts to build and reform schools and educational systems are based too much on trial and error and too little on a well-developed knowledge base. Education needs to be seen as a system of interconnected parts that have to be aligned, and it needs theories of effective organizations and practices to guide its development as well as a clear set of meaningful criteria and metrics to judge its performance. In short, education would benefit if a science of performance was deep in our cultural fiber.[5] If we had these theories and metrics, the work of rebuilding an entire urban school district after a tragedy would be better informed, more efficient, and, likely, more successful.

It is noteworthy that there is clarity about what defines a successful airplane but a lack of consensus on what defines a successful school and how we measure successes. If test scores go up, should schools be deemed better performing and hence encouraged? Would declining test scores mean that schools were not performing well and should be closed? As noted earlier, many people, including a number of authors in the volume, argue that typical standardized tests are weak measures of the effectiveness of a school and that a focus on them can even promote destructive practices. More multidimensional measures of performance would make it possible to assess schools in a more nuanced way and provide guidance for improving educational structures on more than one dimension. It is beyond the scope of this volume to discuss new ideas for assessments in any depth, but we emphasize the importance of having that discussion and moving forward with new ideas.

USING EVIDENCE WITHIN AND ACROSS INSTITUTIONAL BOUNDARIES

In the introduction, the editors liken our understanding of the educational ecology to that of a blind man trying to develop the concept of an elephant through exploration. This volume has, at the very least, offered us new tools to see and explore the "elephant" of education. But in addition to understanding the elephant as an integrated set of parts, we need multiple sources of data to understand all of the parts and their interconnections. Thus, another theme of this volume is the strong commitment to the use of evidence and research to guide educational improvement. This commitment is shared in many quarters of the policy domain, but the chapter authors observe that educational improvements are informed by evidence only weakly and intermittently or that uses of available evidence are over-romanticized (e.g., if Treatment X worked in System A, it will often work in System B). A fundamental aim of this volume is to identify ways to improve the connections between research and evidence on the one hand and the worlds of policy and practice on the other. Contributors to the volume have offered a number of recommendations.

We see from the chapters that evidence does make its way into the work of actors but in ways that vary by the segment of the educational ecology in which they work. The authors also point out that attention to evidence is not the same as the constructive use of evidence. Fortunately, they provide examples and suggestions for promoting better and more productive connections among research, policy, and practice that use evidence of effects as a binding force.

Mosher and Smith show that important findings from research in the academy can, and often do, spur the public policy and private foundation communities to action. For example, the Coleman Report, which graphically displayed the inequitable life opportunities for blacks and whites in the United States,[6] catalyzed far-reaching attempts to change the course of education. Both federal policymakers and national foundations have made investments in developing and funding education research that have the potential to guide intervention and improvement. In some cases, the laws, policies, and practices they have adopted have required school districts and schools to make use of data and evaluation as a condition of funding. Mosher and Smith suggest, however, that many forms of evaluation that qualify as "research" have proved inadequate to the needs of education policymakers. They follow Stephen Raudenbush in offering wise advice about productive directions for research on instruction that may be far more useful for helping practitioners improve student learning.[7]

The story at the state and local district level, as explained by Schwartz and Kardos and by Coburn, Honig, and Stein, also demonstrates sporadic and uneven definitions and uses of evidence. While some policymakers at these levels express strong interest in research and evidence, their own institutional practices often interfere with their capacity to use even the evidence that is available. Still, Coburn, Honig, and Stein provide informative examples of cases where effective collaborations between district officials and researchers have led to the generation of better evidence about students and learning. When evidence was generated with active involvement of researchers and practitioners, participants on both sides of the research-practice divide developed a better understanding about what the evidence meant and how it might be used.

Coburn, Honig, and Stein go on to discuss some promising structures within a school district that may be more likely to help it use evidence and make sense of the available research. The designation of a senior staff member to spearhead the search for evidence about the implementation and effectiveness of interventions can enable the entire district office to acquire a more systematic grasp of available data. Another promising practice is the design of structured protocols to search systematically for evidence about implementation or effectiveness of interventions. Districts that carry out such protocols have decision makers who are better informed about the success of instruction in their districts. With good leadership, this leads to effective strategies to improve.

At the level of schools and teachers, Hargreaves and Stone-Johnson analyze teaching practice through a variety of lenses that explain why teachers often struggle to find ways to use evidence productively in their work. Teachers have access to far more data than they can use, although not all of this data would be recognized by academics as systematic or scientific. Nevertheless, it falls to teachers themselves to sort through the streams of available data and figure out what is useful. When new data are simply layered onto existing systems, Hargreaves and Stone-Johnson note, teachers become overloaded, with few good results. They suggest promising solutions, however. For example, their research finds that incorporating new streams of evidence into an integrated system of data management in the school makes it possible for teachers to use data routinely as part of their regular instructional work. They emphasize that "it works best when it evolves into a routine way in which the school and teachers operate—so that whenever a problem is experienced, the school's first response is not 'what do we *do* about this?' but 'what do we *know* about this?'"

Discussions in this volume also explore the roles for the many public service entities that are part of our educational ecosystem. The literature on evidence use by these entities offers several key questions to pose as we search for those conditions that facilitate knowledge use. First, we must ask, what is the practice we wish to inform? Second, how does evidence make its way from research to practice? Third, who are the individuals who produce or consume evidence, and how do they interact with one another? And fourth, what vehicles and tools actually do the work of getting research evidence into use? Each of these questions is explored in more detail below.

What Is the Practice?

The practices of interest in this volume span several parts of the educational ecology. We discussed the practice of policymakers and the practice of teachers and education leaders. The factors that govern evidence utilization are often different for each of these groups, and the contextual factors that affect evidence use may vary widely.

The work of federal and state policymakers is highly politicized. The clash of values, the claims of multiple constituencies, competition for resources, and the need for electoral support all shape the way policymakers use evidence in their practice. For example, as Mosher and Smith note, the education programs that grew from LBJ's Great Society and the War on Poverty were set against the backdrop of JFK's assassination, the civil rights movement, and the Vietnam War. The arrival on the scene of the Coleman Report has to be understood in the context of competing ideas about why the country was experiencing such turbulence. The chapters by Hargreaves and Stone-Johnson and by Coburn, Honig, and Stein give examples of the importance of political factors in the interpretation of research and evidence by practitioners. But although politics is present, it is much less prominent in the practice of teachers. What is salient for teachers, and what creates a lens for interpreting evidence, is a teacher's passion for subject matter, moral commitments, ethical stances, and beliefs about who can learn and how to help all students.

These passions and beliefs explain why teachers' actual classroom practices are hard to influence with evidence. It is easier for evidence to guide the purchase of new computing equipment or software than to guide the design and use of this equipment, and it is even tougher for evidence to guide choices for a new reading curriculum. Curriculum decisions, like many others that teachers deal with, activate deeply held convictions and beliefs about what is taught, how it is taught, and how learning is assessed.

How Does Evidence Make Its Way to Practice?

The chapters identify a variety of paths by which knowledge and evidence may travel to the locus of practice. This is a highly complex process that is contingent on many factors. As Sandra Nutley and colleagues argue, the linear model that has predominated a great deal of thinking fails to describe the ways that research evidence makes its way into practice.[8] Among the flaws in the linear model is an unstated assumption that the users of research are passive receptacles for information. To the contrary, as mentioned above, the users of research, like the purveyors of research, have value systems, beliefs, and political contexts, all of which actively shape the acceptance and use of information. Furthermore, as a colleague who studies the travel of innovation, Bill Penuel, points out, diffusion of new products and practices itself requires innovation.[9] If knowledge about effective practices is to impact the practice of education, we need to develop new and creative strategies for moving findings, tools, and ideas into practice. The idea of diffusion *as* innovation represents an important addition to how issues of innovation and "travel" have been framed in the past.

Mosher and Smith's account of selected federal policy initiatives offers a glimpse of the problems with the linear model. Some provisions of the No Child Left Behind (NCLB) legislation mandate research on educational practices (e.g., the What Works Clearinghouse). The theory of action behind the Clearinghouse is that getting "what works" into the hands of teachers will improve their classroom practice. A problem, however, is that users of research in the world of educational practice—from policymakers to classroom teachers—all have well-formed belief systems they use to judge the credibility of information that comes to them from research or any other source. They may or may not accept findings as true or relevant. And for practitioners, knowing a method proven to be effective in research and implementing it in their local context are very different things. Even if they enthusiastically embraced findings, teachers often lack the skills or tools to implement "what works," or they find that what worked in a study located in one context does not necessarily work in their context.[10]

Schwartz and Kardos explain in their chapter why policymakers also do not immediately act on research findings, even when they are readily available. Citing work by Carol Weiss, they note that legislators appreciate and understand information that comes to them from professional advocacy organizations like teachers' unions in large part because they know how to appraise the interests and perspectives of the advocacy organization and make appropriate corrections. They are less certain about how to assess the credibility of information that comes to them from the academy because they are unsure of the personal agendas and values of the researchers.[11]

The paths between evidence and practice are complex, iterative, and constructed by multiple communities. Rather than waiting for information from researchers to flow to them, practitioners need and seek information from many sources. Sometimes the information that arrives from the research community is ill-suited to their needs and misaligned with their values and beliefs. Schoenfeld's chapter raises pointed criticism of the shortcomings of educational research and the research culture that minimizes its value for practice. But even when researchers have made extraordinary efforts to craft their work in constructive and accessible ways, practitioners' willingness and capacity to be informed by evidence is often limited by the constraints of their work and the competing claims on their attention and priorities.

As Schoenfeld suggests, a promising strategy for connecting research and practice more effectively, tried by some and touted by others, involves ongoing partnerships: researchers working collaboratively with teachers, school districts, students, and others, together identifying and defining problems to be solved and creating useful and usable research and practice. One way this kind of work can unfold is to document how researchers and practitioners who are attempting to work in these close collaborations do their business.

The MacArthur Teaching and Learning Network sponsored one such sustained partnership involving teachers, administrators, and researchers, the Information Infrastructure Systems (IIS) project. Because this kind of R&D collaboration is relatively new, the process itself was documented and analyzed so that what was learned in this experiment could be used to guide future efforts of this kind.[12] The IIS team studied the way teachers used videos in school-based professional development. Using this evidence, they designed a new computer-based system to support teacher learning with video. They are now assessing the effects of the video-based intervention using a random trial design. Collaborations like this are just beginning, and their promise is far from realized. Moreover, as Shoenfeld points out in his chapter, substantial changes in the academy and schools will be needed to support this kind of research that is embedded in practice—what might be referred to as research *in* rather than *on* practice.[13] We recommend further experimentation with this approach, along with careful documentation of the contextual factors that both supported and thwarted it.

Who Are the Individuals Who Produce or Consume Evidence?

In some of the chapters, the authors document the challenges of creating meaningful links between purveyors of evidence and consumers of evidence. They point out that these groups typically work in different professional communities that involve different kinds of expertise, norms, and perspectives. Those seeking solutions to these challenges point to the need to reduce the barriers between these different communities. They recommend bridging the research-practice and research-policy divide by encouraging better understanding and more mutually responsive relationships between researchers and policymakers and practitioners, including the kind of practitioner-researcher partnerships described above. For example, Schwartz and Kardos suggest that states create venues for policymakers and researchers to meet regularly to exchange information and ideas. They describe Policy Analysis for California Education (PACE) as a model of such a venue, in which researchers and analysts have developed the expertise to communicate effectively with state policymakers.

In the majority of the chapters (the chapter by Schoenfeld being a notable exception), the authors focus less on changing how the individuals on both sides do their work and more on designing systems and contexts for communication across the research-practice divide. But the focus on researchers getting evidence into the hands of practitioners and policymakers—indeed, the whole notion of "producers" and "consumers"—rests on the linear model of research moving to practice that has been found problematic. The problem is more complex than producers of research failing to communicate effectively or consumers failing to implement findings. The problem requires a systemic solution. For evidence to be used effectively by practitioners, daily routines and the organization of work need to be fundamentally changed to include analysis of evidence. Evidence needs to be built into the systems that guide educational practice.

The need for systems and changes in the organization of work—in both schools and universities—does not, of course, preclude individuals from taking productive steps to make their research useful and accessible. As noted earlier, more and more researchers are finding opportunities to work closely with practitioners. The many examples of these collaborations, and the quality and usefulness of the knowledge and tools they produce, demonstrate that the two communities can be merged, or at least allied. Collaborations can also lead to shared beliefs about the direction of reforms and the sorts of evidence that are valuable in guiding reform. But, as is clear in the chapters by Coburn, Honig, and Stein and Schoenfeld, the success of these collaborations depends on the support they receive and the time provided for sustained interactions. As mentioned above, if implemented on a large scale, such collaborations will require significant changes in the expectations and organization of work for both researchers and practitioners.

What Are the Vehicles That Promote Evidence-Based Practice?

The chapters identify a number of mechanisms for promoting evidence-based practices. Their success depends in part on the nature of the evidence and the practices they might inform. The National Academy of Science report "How People Learn: Bridging Research and Practice" identifies a set of pathways in which knowledge about learning can affect classroom practice: through educational materials, preservice and in-service education for teachers, policy, and mass media.[14]

In their chapter, Gomez and Hentschke explain why publishers rarely base the development of educational goods and services on research. Given their overriding imperative of profitable sales, publishers only look to research when there is substantial demand for research-based materials by school districts that might purchase them. And even then, much of what is viewed as research by publishers as well as the consumers is not likely to meet the standard that university researchers might demand.

Although Gomez and Hentschke are not optimistic that the market demand is large enough to stimulate the supply of many materials grounded in research, we hope that funders will heed Schoenfeld's call for them to make an "essential investment in studies of educational materials" that work well in a range of contexts. Perhaps if solid research-based materials were developed outside of the private sector, businesses, which are in the best position to disseminate materials on a broad scale, might pick them up. There are other strategies that could be used to increase the demand for critical evaluation and research-based materials and services. Preservice and in-service education for teachers provide opportunities for communicating the value of research and evidence to teachers. Pressure on schools to implement only evidence-based practices, and training in how to do that, could also create pressure on the private sector to provide credible evidence for the effectiveness of their goods and services. Specific policies can also raise the profile of research, such as requiring districts or schools to conduct evaluations or to use only programs that have been shown to be effective. The fourth vehicle for promoting research-based practice, noted also in Fujita's chapter on education in Japan, is public opinion. Although publication of research results through specialized outlets or through popular media can reach large numbers of readers, it seldom has direct impact on practice. But publications can affect public views and seed public pressure on policymakers and education decision makers.

Another strategy for promoting evidence-based practice is to focus on the kind of intermediary organizations Smylie and Corcoran describe in their chapter. These organizations work directly with schools and districts and influence policies and practices using many strategies, including coaching teachers and administrators. As in the for-profit sector, the survival of non-profit organizations depends on district decisions to purchase their services. They tend, therefore, to be conservative and avoid challenging the beliefs and expectations of senior district officials. Some of the same strategies suggested for the private sector might also be effective in promoting attention to evidence in the nonprofit sector.

Governments at all levels often develop processes explicitly designed to promote decisions informed by evidence. At the state and federal level, policy offices are often created within education agencies, with the mandate to collect data and provide analysis to illuminate decisions and directions. For example, this is the purpose of the National Center for Education Statistics and the National Assessment of Education Progress. Large districts often have offices for data collection and analyses, but on a much smaller scale. Legislatures also have well-developed mechanisms for bringing evidence to bear on legislative decisions, such as testimony before legislative committees and meetings with lobbyist. And budget offices and research services in many legislative contexts are designed to ensure that policymakers have access to relevant evidence as they make critical decisions.

Similar to what Fujita describes in Japan, some scholars and practitioners in the United States have accumulated the persuasiveness and the gravitas to play the role of opinion leaders in their communities. What they say may have a great impact on what evidence, and from what sources, gets taken seriously by policymakers and practitioners. Some research and policy analytic organizations have also developed track records of reliability and credibility as valued sources of information. Examples include such organizations as the RAND Corporation and the American Institutes for Research.

Overall, the foregoing discussion makes it clear that education, as an enterprise, lacks consensus on improvement. Without some broad agreements about what counts as evidence and how it makes its way from one sector to another, we will not be able to work cooperatively toward improvement.

CONSENSUS ABOUT THE PRIMACY OF INSTRUCTION

We have yet to achieve consensus on the goals of education in this country, and we probably never will. But as Mosher and Smith suggest, education reformers have slowly, perhaps even grudgingly, come to agree that instruction has to improve in order for student achievement to improve. An implication is that while funding, mandates, and structural interventions like accountability, vouchers, small schools, and charters may have value, they are productive only inasmuch as they lead to improvements in instruction.[15]

From this perspective, the central goal for education improvement is to create and support instructional regimes that produce improved outcomes for students, with "regimes" being "systematic approaches to instruction, in which the desired outcomes are specified and observed, and in which the intended outcomes are rationally related to consistent methods of producing those outcomes."[16] Instructional regimes involve the coherent arrangement of constituent resources of schooling, such as content material, incentives, and teacher and student actions, in order to reach specified goals. Appropriate assessments are needed to monitor and continue to improve those regimes that prepare students for our fast-changing world.

Instructional regimes unfold in complex school contexts and, in some cases, can be limited to one classroom or to a particular subject matter. In other cases instructional regimes apply to multiple classrooms and domains, as in whole school reform efforts, and some connect informal and formal learning.[17] Given the diversity of purpose in instructional regimes and the diversity of instructional settings, an important challenge for the entire educational enterprise is to recognize the particular affordances of any regime for improvement in specific content and context.

As noted earlier, fundamental to the selection and monitoring of effective instructional practices is the nature of the assessments used as metrics for success.[18] It has been noted throughout this volume that there is currently a great deal of productive debate about the "success metrics" used to ensure that all students are prepared for continued lifelong learning in our global, rapidly changing world. Current assessments measure specific facts, concepts, and skills that students have learned in the past, but they do a poor job of assessing the degree to which students have been prepared for lifelong learning—which includes the ability to analyze or evaluate new information, solve new problems, tolerate ambiguity, actively seek feedback to improve, and engage in other behaviors that are not tapped by traditional assessments.[19] Researcher and practitioner partnerships are beginning to form to tackle issues such as these

Current strategies used to help teachers select, adopt, and adapt effective instructional strategies and practices vary greatly—from one- or two-day "professional development workshops" to texts that advance particular instructional strategies. In the chapters in this volume, the authors find that few such strategies are powerful enough to help teachers. A more promising alternative is a multipronged, long-term set of practices to create professional learning communities (PLCs) among teachers and school personnel. Hargreaves and Stone-Johnson suggest that PLCs are powerful organizational interventions to improve instruction, in part by bringing the consideration of evidence to instructional enactment. However, our authors remind us that professional learning communities do not by themselves necessarily lead in positive directions. Without constant feedback and refinement and environmental scans of emerging theories, tools, and evidence, educators within the same school and community can easily go in wrong directions, or subsets can go in different directions that ultimately conflict.

PLCs have gained traction for educators because there is information from multiple sources that they have value. For example, there is research evidence that student achievement is generally higher in schools characterized by a strong professional community.[20] A central component of an effective professional community is collegial trust, which has also been found by researchers to be associated with higher student achievement and a sense of work satisfaction among practitioners.[21] This kind of evidence has helped create momentum to invent organizational forums within schools that serve to make PLCs a reality.

Today, all over the United States, schools are implementing PLCs with varying degrees of success. Like any practice, *how* it is implemented is as important as *that* it is implemented. Hargreaves and Stone-Johnson note that communities of practice can actually lead to poor rather than strong practices. The chapter by Fujita describing Japanese lesson studies helps us envision the broader school system and cultural contexts that are required for learning communities to work effectively.

The Japanese example is instructive, but PLCs still need better specification. Answers to remaining questions could guide the development of effective PLCs: What should teachers in schools do to create PLCs? What should district and state level personnel do to sustain PLCs in schools? What kind of research on PLCs needs to be done to guide their development, not just demonstrate their value? The integrated understanding that flows from answers to questions like these is what is needed to align the various sectors of the educational ecology so as to promote the widespread implementation of a strategy that has worked well in some schools.

Instructional regimes, like all activities on the "job floor," are instantiated in and supported by regular work routines and tools that manage the coordination, cooperation, and communication of people. Organizational routines of various forms structure behavior in organizations.[22] PLCs, for example, shape the way teachers use common meeting time. The way in which an instructional regime is implemented in any particular place may be invisible to district-level decision makers or academic researchers, but the variations in implementation are enormously consequential. For routines to be leveraged for change, they have to be made visible, and people working at various levels in the institution have to understand them.[23]

ROUTINES, TOOLS, AND BOUNDARY OBJECTS

We are intrigued by the possibility that routines and tools can be designed and implemented to encourage the development of better evidence and to direct more attention to evidence by practitioners. If school or district routines were designed to improve communication across institutional lines, they might promote coherence of action within a school or district. Consider two strikingly different examples from this volume. Schoenfeld describes a school in which a group of middle school teachers decide to adopt a new math curriculum that differs from the two already in use within the district. In making this decision, they neither consulted nor informed the district curriculum office. Nor did they need to do so, since they had access to resources that allowed them to purchase the materials they needed. Obviously, the structure of decisionmaking in this district permitted curriculum decisions to be made in a highly decentralized way. By comparison, consider the Japanese schools described by Fujita. Teachers of mathematics work in close coordination with central curriculum experts; their curriculum decisions are tightly connected with decisions made by administrators and teachers about purchases of books and materials, daily lesson planning, professional development, and assessment of student learning. The differences in the routines of communication revealed by these two examples show how organizational settings can shape the ways in which teachers do their work. But more important for our purpose is that the differences in the routines of communication lead to significant differences in the ability of these two schools to use evidence to improve their ability to help students learn mathematics. A major problem is that many educational communities provide good piecemeal examples of instruction, but they fail to cohere in ways that create the learning trajectories that students need to develop deep expertise.

   Some routines for taking action and making decisions might be thought of as boundary objects, which Bowker and Star define as those objects that both inhabit several communities of practice and satisfy the informational requirements of each of them. Boundary objects are thus both plastic enough to adapt to local needs and constraints of the several parties employing them, yet robust enough to maintain a common identity across sites. They are weakly structured in common use and become strongly structured in individual-site use. These objects may be abstract or concrete. . . . Such objects have different meanings in different social worlds but their structure is common enough to more than one world to make them recognizable, a means of translation. The creation and management of boundary objects is a key process in developing and maintaining coherence across intersecting communities.[24]

In the world of schooling, important boundary objects could be tools like planning documents. Effective planning documents serve the needs of teachers in carefully articulating instructional objectives and plans and the needs of administrators in judging the coherence of things like instructional approaches within and across areas of study.[25]

Since boundary objects inhabit multiple communities of practice and are recognizable across them, they have the potential to be helpful in improving practice. One conjecture is that more attention to the design and implementation of boundary objects may lead to more effective practice for those communities that share the boundary. Shared understanding of key sources of evidence might help state and district policymakers understand better the issues each group may face. As Coburn, Honig, and Stein discuss, shared development of research and evaluation indicators may help academics and district staff learn a great deal about one another's challenges and priorities and work more effectively toward areas of common concern. Conversely, the absence of boundary objects may explain the mutual misunderstanding that characterizes many interactions between researchers and education practitioners. Such misunderstanding makes it more likely that research and evidence generated by academics or researchers in government agencies or think tanks will be overlooked or deemed irrelevant by policymakers and practitioners.

If routines are truly shared across boundaries, they may help dispel the lack of mutual understanding that often interferes with communication across the divides of research and policy, research and practice, or policy and practice. Michael Feuer and colleagues make a similar point that disparate members of the educational enterprise do not trust one another's conclusions because they do not understand one another's work in granular detail.[26] For example, researchers who conduct randomized field trials are trained not to rely on the value of teachers' knowledge based on years of professional experience. Conversely, teachers' perspective on the complexity inherent in instruction leads them to mistrust the knowledge generated by randomized field trials of instructional regimes. From our perspective, an important message that has emerged from this volume is that educational reform may benefit from an investment of more time and effort in creating tools and routines that encourage consensus among key stakeholders about methods and measures.

Such tools can rely on narrative or stories to build shared understanding. Julian Orr found that stories of practice are an important means to convey cross-organizational knowledge.[27] In his study of repairmen who work on photocopy equipment, the stories of repairmen proved to be useful within the community of repairmen to share ideas about successful repair practice and also helpful to the distinct community of product engineers and designers, whose work is to build better systems for repairmen. In a similar vein, teachers' stories about their experiences in professional learning communities are likely to be helpful to other teachers, of course, but also to those who design social arrangements for teachers and those who seek to study how professional communities are associated with valued educational outcomes. The National Writing Project offers a fascinating example of this kind of institutional practice that connects practitioners across institutional boundaries and connects them with evidence about the success of their practices. In the National Writing Project, groups of professional teachers gather to hone the craft of writing and writing instruction. But the ways they do this vary tremendously from location to location.[28] It would be valuable to capture stories about the Writing Project which are organized and distributed in ways that are keyed to successful practice so that emerging professional groups might adopt and learn from the experience of the Writing Project much faster. Our point with these examples is that there are untapped reservoirs of knowledge we might use to encourage connections within the education enterprise. Systematic ways to capture and share insights of those stories and narratives across classrooms, schools, and districts, as well as across institutional sectors to reach those in policy roles, for-profit, and nonprofit educational service organizations, might be especially helpful. And of course, this shared knowledge needs to be constantly vetted so that systems can continually improve.

One strategy for building shared understanding across institutional boundaries might make use of the power of information technology to share information. One fascinating prototype of what such systems could look like is Patients Like Me, an innovative idea to create communities of practice among patients, doctors, researchers, and organizations who are concerned with the treatment of well-known diseases.[29] By creating a forum on the web for patients to post information about their symptoms and treatment, Patients Like Me creates a vehicle for evidence about individual experiences of disease to become public. Access to this evidence may be useful to individuals who suffer from the same disease, clinical practitioners who treat it, and researchers who study it. While instructional regimes in education are very different from treatment regimes for diseases, they do have a common goal of improved experience for a heterogeneous group of individual clients. Instructional regimes aim to help students learn, and the success of individual students who are served by the instructional regime will vary. By examining the successes of individual students who experience different regimes, designers of core instructional regimes would learn more about the ways in which their regimes vary in practice, and this evidence might then improve their strategies. Such information could accelerate learning about how to set up professional learning communities, which would help instructional designers to follow the recommendations made here by Hargreaves and Stone-Johnson.

A FINAL WORD

As the authors of the chapters above have written so eloquently, the challenge of improving educational practice is immense. One cannot help but be impressed by the complexity and difficulty of achieving significant progress. But just as clear is the necessity of concerted efforts. The costs of the inadequate system of education we have now are just too great—for the students and for the society.

Much of this volume is a story of the large, well-developed silos through which the educational enterprise operates. The existence of silos often prevents opportunities for improvement. Lortie's egg crate model, meant to describe classrooms in schools, equally well describes the entire ecology of the education process.[30] The egg crate persists because we have failed to develop systematic and institutionalized processes that encourage communication, cooperation, and collaboration. These processes are essential if we are to ensure that all the parts of the education elephant fit together and function as a whole.

There is more to the solution than communication and collaboration, although these are essential. We must also address the shortcomings of the evidence provided by research. This volume helps us see that much of the knowledge gained from research is not usable in practice, even if it reaches practitioners. Improving education research will require a commitment on the part of funding agencies and a willingness on the part of the institutions where research is currently conducted to change in the many ways outlined in this book. Whether one looks at the policy and practice side of the street or at the research and evidence side, there is much work to be done.

Notes

PREFACE

1. Network Core members include Deborah Stipek (director), Tony Bryk, John Bransford, Cynthia Coburn, Tom Corcoran, Tom Glennan, Louis Gomez, Diana Lam, Fritz Mosher, Nancy Owen, Charla Rolland, Mary Kay Stein, and Janet Weiss.
2. Cynthia E. Coburn and Mary Kay Stein, eds., *Research and Practice in Education: Building Alliances, Bridging the Divide* (New York: Rowman and Littlefield, forthcoming); Cynthia E. Coburn, Judith Toure, and Mika Yamashita, "Evidence, Interpretation, and Persuasion: Instructional Decision Making in the District Central Office," *Teachers College Record*, forthcoming; Amanda Datnow and Vicki Park, "Research into Practice: A Case Study of How Success for All Builds Knowledge for School Improvement," in *Theory and Research in Educational Administration*, ed. Cecil Miskel and Wayne Hoy (Greenwich, CT: Information Age Publishing, 2006); Randi A. Engle, "Establishing Collaborations in Design-Based Research Projects: Insights from the Origins of the MMAP project," in *Proceedings of International Conference of the Learning Sciences 2008*, ed. P. A. Kirschner, F. Prins, V. Jonker, and G. Kanselaar (Atlanta: International Society of the Learning Sciences, forthcoming), 216–23.
3. Anthony Bryk and Louis M. Gomez, "Ruminations on Reinventing on R&D Capacity for Educational Improvements," in *The Future of Educational Entrepreneurship: Possibilities for School Reform*, ed. Frederick Hess (Cambridge, MA: Harvard Education Press, 2008); Louis M. Gomez, Philip Herman, and Kim Gomez, "Integrating Text in Content-Area Classes: Better Supports for Teachers and Students," *Voices in Urban Education* 14 (Winter 2007): 22–29.
4. Cynthia E. Coburn, Soung Bae, and Erica O. Turner, "Authority, Status, and the Dynamics of Insider-Outsider Partnerships at the District Level," *Peabody Journal of Education* 83, no. 3 (2008): 364–99; Cynthia E. Coburn and Joan E. Talbert, "Conceptions of Evidence-Based Practice in School Districts: Mapping the Terrain," *American Journal of Education* 112, no. 4 (2006): 469–95.

INTRODUCTION

1. John Godfrey Saxe, "The Blind Men and the Elephant," in *Poetry of America*, ed. William James Linton (London: George Bell & Sons, 1878), 151–52.
2. John D. Bransford, Mary Slowinski, Nancy Vye, and Susan Mosborg, "The Learning Sciences, Technology and Designs for Educational Systems: Some Thoughts About Change," in *Learners in a Changing Learning Landscape: Reflections from a Dialogue on New Roles and Expectations*, ed. Jan Visser and Muriel Visser-Valfrey (New York: Springer, 2008), 37–68, 38.

3. For example, National Academies, *Rising Above the Gathering Storm: Energizing and Employ-ing America for a Brighter Economic Future* (Washington, DC: National Academies Press, 2007); National Commission on Community Colleges, "Winning the Skills Race and Strengthening America's Middle Class: An Action Agenda for Community Colleges," accessed August 30, 2008, from http://professionals.collegeboard.com/profdownload/winning_the_skills_race.pdf; Patricia F. Mead, Rick Stephens, Michael Richey, John D. Bransford, and Baba Kofi Weusijana, *A Test of Leadership: Charting Engineering Educa-tion for 2020 and Beyond*, paper presented at the 48th AIAA/ASME/ASCE/AHS/ASC Struc-tures, Structural Dynamics, and Materials Conference, Honolulu, April 2007; National Academy of Engineering, *The Engineer of 2020: Visions of Engineering in the New Century* (Washington, DC: National Academies Press, 2004); John D. Bransford, "Preparing Peo-ple for Rapidly Changing Environments," *Journal of Engineering Education* 96 (January 2007): 1–3; and "Foundations for Success: The Final Report of the National Mathematics Advisory Panel" (Washington, DC: U.S. Department of Education, 2008).

4. For example, John Bridgeland, John Dilulio, and Karen B. Morison, "The Silent Epi-demic: Perspectives of High School Dropouts" (report by Civic Enterprises in association with Peter D. Hart Research Associates for the Bill & Melinda Gates Foundation, Wash-ington, DC, March 2006).

5. For example, Partners In Learning, *School Leader Development: Assessing 21st Century Learning* (Redmond, WA: Microsoft Corporation, 2006), CD-ROM.

6. Aaron Corvin, "Failure to Compute," *Washington CEO*, July 16, 2008, accessed July 16, 2008, from http://www.washingtonceo.com/home/story-display/article/204/failure-to-c.html.

7. Technology Access Foundation, accessed September 1, 2008, from www.techaccess.org; Trish Diziko, email message to authors, July 16, 2008.

8. Ellen C. Lagemann, "Contested Terrain: A History of Education Research in United States 1890–1990," *Educational Researcher* 26, no. 9 (1997): 5–17.

9. For example, see Karl E. Weick, "Educational Organizations as Loosely Coupled Sys-tems," *Administrative Science Quarterly* 21, no. 1 (1976): 1–19.

10. For example, see John D. Bransford, Nancy J. Vye, Reed Stevens, Patricia Kuhl, Daniel Schwartz, Philip Bell, Andrew Meltzoff, Brigid Barron, Roy Pea, Byron Reeves, Jeremy Roschelle, and Nora Sabelli, "Learning Theories and Education: Toward a Decade of Syn-ergy," in *Handbook of Educational Psychology*, vol. 2, ed. Patricia A. Alexander and Philip H. Winne (Mahwah, NJ: Erlbaum, 2006), 209–44.

11. Grover J. Whitehurst, *The Institute of Education Sciences: New Wine, New Bottles*, address at the American Educational Research Association Meeting, San Francisco, April 2003.

12. See also Marc Prensky, "Escape from Planet Jar-Gon: or, What Video Games Have to Teach Academics About Teaching and Writing: A Review of What Video Games Have to Teach Us About Learning and Literacy," *On the Horizon* 11, no. 3 (2003): 1–15.

13. Whitehurst, *The Institute of Education Sciences*, 5.

14. Ibid.

15. Department of Education, "What Works Clearinghouse," accessed August 28, 2008, from http://ies.ed.gov/ncee/wwc/.

16. What Works Clearinghouse.

17. James J. Jenkins, "Four Points to Remember: A Tetrahedral Model of Memory Experi-ments," in *Levels of Processing and Human Memory*, ed. Laird S. Cermak and Fergus I. M. Craik (Hillsdale, NJ: Erlbaum, 1978), 429–46.

18. Helen V. Bateman, John D. Bransford, Susan R. Goldman, and John R. Newbrough, *Sense of Community in the Classroom: Relationship to Students' Academic Goals,* paper presented at the annual meeting of the American Educational Research Association, New Orleans, 2000; Xiaodong Lin and John D. Bransford, "Impact of Personal Background Knowledge on Cross-Cultural Understanding" (manuscript under review); and Anthony S. Bryk and Barbara L. Schneider, *Trust in Schools: A Core Resource for Improvement* (New York: Russell Sage Foundation, 2004).

19. Jeremy D. Finn and Charles M. Achilles, "Answers about Questions about Class Size: A Statewide Experiment," *American Educational Research Journal* 27, no. 3 (1990): 557–77; Jeremy D. Finn and Charles M. Achilles, "Tennessee's Class Size Study: Findings, Implications, Misconceptions," *Educational Evaluation and Policy Analysis* 21, no. 2, (1999): 97–109.

20. For example, Jeremy Roschelle, Deborah Tatar, and James Kaput, "Getting to Scale with Innovations That Deeply Restructure How Students Come to Know Mathematics," in *Handbook of Design Research Methods in Education,* ed., Anthony Kelly, Richard Lesh, and John Y. Baek (New York: Routledge, 2008), 369–95.

21. Jeremy Roschelle et al., *Extending the SimCalc Approach to Grade 8 Mathematics (No. 2)* (Menlo Park, CA: SRI International, 2007); Jeremy Roschelle et al., *Can Technology-Enhanced Curriculum Improve Student Learning of Important Mathematics? Results from 7th Grade, Year 1 (No. 1)* (Menlo Park, CA: SRI, 2007)

22. Jeremy Roschelle, personal communication to authors, August 28, 2008.

23. David L. Sackett, William M. C. Rosenberg, J. A. Muir Gray, R. Brian Haynes, and W. Scott Richardson, "Evidence Based Medicine: What It Is and What It Isn't," *British Medical Journal* 312 (1996): 71–72, 71.

24. David H. Hargreaves, "In Defense of Research for Evidence-Based Teaching: A Rejoinder to Martyn Hammersley," *British Educational Research Journal,* 23, no. 4 (1997): 405–19, 408–9.

25. Michael Fullan, *Leading in a Culture of Change* (San Francisco: Jossey-Bass, 2001).

26. John D. Bransford and Daniel Schwartz, "It Takes Expertise to Make Expertise: Some Thoughts on Why and How," in *The Measurement and Development of Professional Expertise: Toward Measurement of Expert Performance and Design of Optimal Learning Environments,* ed. K. Anders Ericsson (Cambridge, England: Cambridge University Press, forthcoming).

27. John D. Bransford, Linda Darling-Hammond, and Pamela LePage, "Introduction," in Darling-Hammond and Bransford, *Preparing Teachers for a Changing World,* 21.

28. Ibid., 22.

29. Daniel Schwartz, John D. Bransford, and David Sears, "Efficiency and Innovation in Transfer," in *Transfer of Learning: Research and Perspectives,* ed. Jose P. Maestre (Greenwich, CT: Information Age Pubishing, 2005), 1–51; John D. Bransford, Sharon Derry, David Berliner, Karen Hammerness, and Kelly Lyn Beckett, "Theories of Learning and Their Roles in Teaching," in Darling-Hammond and Bransford, *Preparing Teachers for a Changing World,* 40–87.

30. John D. Bransford, Drue Gawel, Rachel Phillips, Vanessa Svihla, Nancy Vye, and Megan Brown, *New Approaches to 21st Century Schooling: Preparation for Future Learning Assessments and Their Instructional Implications,* paper presented at Center for the Assessment and Evaluation of Student Learning International Conference on Learning in Science, San Francisco, October 2008.

31. Michael Cohen, "Meeting the Information Needs of State Education Policymakers: Report of a Survey of State Policymakers" (No. 400-83-0051; Washington, DC: State Education Policy Consortium, National Association of State Boards of Education, 1985).

CHAPTER 1: THE ROLE OF RESEARCH IN EDUCATION REFORM FROM THE PERSPECTIVE OF FEDERAL POLICYMAKERS AND FOUNDATION GRANTMAKERS

1. See "About the Contributors" for biographical information on the authors.
2. John D. Rockefeller, *Random Reminiscences of Men and Events* (Tarrytown, NY: Sleepy Hollow Press, 1984), 112.
3. Christopher T. Cross, *Political Education: National Policy Comes of Age* (New York: Teachers College Press, 2004).
4. *No Child Left Behind Act of 2001*, Public Law 107-110 (January 8, 2002); Susan H. Fuhrman, Margaret E. Goertz, and Elliot H. Weinbaum, "Educational Governance in the United States: Where Are We? How Did We Get Here? Why Should We Care?" in *The State of Education Policy Research,* eds. Susan H. Fuhrman, David K. Cohen, and Fritz Mosher, (Mahwah, NJ: Erlbaum, 2007), 41–61.
5. James S. Coleman, Ernest Q. Campbell, Carol J. Hobson, James McPartland, Alexander M. Mood, Frederic D. Weinfeld, and Robert L. York, *Equality of Educational Opportunity* (Washington, DC: Government Printing Office, 1966).
6. James B. Conant, "Social Dynamite in Our Large Cities," *Crime and Delinquency* 8, no. 2 (1962): 103–15.
7. Ellen C. Lagemann, *The Politics of Knowledge: The Carnegie Corporation, Philanthropy, and Public Policy* (Middletown, CT: Wesleyan University Press, 1989).
8. Coleman, *Equality of Educational Opportunity.*
9. Christopher Jencks, Marshall Smith, Henry Acland, Mary Jo Bane, David Cohen, Herbert Gintis, Barbara Heyns, and Stephan Michelson, *Inequality: A Reassessment of the Effect of Family and Schooling in America* (New York: Basic Books, 1972).
10. Marshall S. Smith, "Equality of Educational Opportunity: The Basic Findings Reconsidered," in *On Equality of Educational Opportunity,* ed. Frederick Mosteller and Daniel P. Moynihan (New York: Random House, 1972), 316.
11. National Research Council, *Improving Student Learning: A Strategic Plan for Educational Research and Its Utilization* (Washington, DC: National Academies Press, 1999); David K. Cohen and Carol A. Barnes, "Research and the Purposes of Education," in *Issues in Education Research: Problems and Possibilities,* ed. Ellen Lagemann and Lee S. Shulman (San Francisco: Jossey-Bass, 1999), 17–42; Brian Rowan, Richard Correnti, and Robert Miller, "What Large-Scale, Survey Research Tells Us About Teacher Effects on Student Achievement: Insights from the Prospects Study," *Teachers College Record* 104, no. 8 (2002): 1525–67; David K. Cohen, Stephen W. Raudenbush, and Deborah B. Ball, "Resources, Instruction, and Research," *Educational Evaluation and Policy Analysis* 25, no. 2 (2003): 119–42; Brian Rowan, Eric Camburn, and Carol Barnes, "Benefitting from Comprehensive School Reform: A Review of Research on CSR Implementation," in *Putting the Pieces Together: Lessons from Comprehensive School Reform Research,* ed. Christopher Cross (Washington, DC: National Clearing House for Comprehensive School Reform, 2004), 1–52; and Stephen W. Raudenbush, *Schooling, Statistics, and Poverty: Can We Measure School Improvement?* 9th Annual William H. Angoff Memorial Lecture, Educational Testing Service, Princeton, NJ, April 1, 2004.

12. Cross, "Political Education: National Policy Comes of Age," 80–81.

13. Paul Berman and Milbrey W. McLaughlin, *Federal Programs Supporting Educational Change* (Santa Monica, CA: RAND, 1975).

14. Cohen, Raudenbush, and Ball, "Resources, Instruction, and Research," 135–38.

15. National Commission on Excellence in Education, *A Nation at Risk: The Imperative for Educational Reform* (Washington, DC: Government Printing Office, 1983).

16. Ronald Edmonds, "Effective Schools for the Urban Poor," *Educational Leadership* 37, no. 1 (1979): 15–27.

17. Michael J. Dunkin and Bruce J. Biddle, *The Study of Teaching* (New York: Holt, Reinhart, and Winston, 1974); William W. Cooley and Gaea Leinhardt, *The Instructional Dimensions Study: The Search for Effective Classroom Processes* (Pittsburgh, PA: University of Pittsburgh Learning and Research Development Center, 1978); and Jere E. Brophy and Thomas L. Good, "Teacher Behavior and Student Achievement," in *Handbook of Research on Teaching*, 3rd ed., ed. Merlin C. Wittrock (Washington, DC: American Educational Research Association, 1986).

18. William L. Sanders and June C. Rivers, "Cumulative and Residual Effects of Teachers on Future Student Academic Achievement" (Knoxville: University of Tennessee Value-Added Research an Assessment Center, 1996).

19. This concern was raised early on by Jencks in his long appendix on the quality of the SEEO data. Christopher S. Jencks, "The Quality of the Data Collected by the Equality of Educational Opportunity Survey," in Mosteller and Moynihan, *On Equality of Educational Opportunity*, 230–342.

20. Rowan, Camburn, and Barnes, "Benefitting from Comprehensive School Reform."

21. Catherine E. Snow, *Reading for Understanding: Toward an R&D Program on Reading Comprehension* (Santa Monica, CA: RAND, 2002); and RAND Mathematics Study Group, *Mathematical Proficiency for All Students: Toward a Strategic Research and Development Program in Mathematics Education* (Santa Monica, CA: RAND, 2003).

22. John D. Bransford, Ann L. Brown, and Rodney R. Cocking, eds., *How People Learn: Brain, Mind, Experience, and School* (Washington, DC: National Academies Press, 1999).

23. Catherine Snow, M. Susan Burns, and Peg Griffin, eds., *Preventing Reading Difficulties in Young Children* (Washington, DC: National Academies Press, 1998); and National Institute of Child Health and Human Development, Report of the National Reading Panel, "Teaching Children to Read: An Evidence-Based Assessment of the Scientific Research Literature on Reading and its Implications for Reading Instruction" (NIH Publication No. 00-4769; Washington, DC: U.S. Government Printing Office, 2000).

24. Sharon Griffin and Robbie Case, "Re-Thinking the Primary School Math Curriculum: An Approach Based on Cognitive Science," *Issues in Education* 3 (1997): 1–65; Thomas P. Carpenter et al., *Children's Mathematics: Cognitively Guided Instruction* (Portsmouth, NH: Heinemann, 1998); Karen C. Fuson, *Children's Counting and Concepts of Number* (New York: Springer-Verlag, 1988); and Alan Schoenfeld, "Instructional Research and the Improvement of Practice" (this volume).

25. Suzanne Donovan and John Bransford, eds., *How Students Learn: History, Mathematics, and Science in the Classroom* (Washington, DC: National Academies Press, 2005); and Richard A. Duschl, Heidi A. Schweingruber, and Andrew W. Shouse, eds., *Taking Science to School: Learning and Teaching Science in Grades K–8* (Washington, DC: National Academies Press, 2007).

26. Roschelle et al., *Scaling up SimCalc* ; Roschelle et al., *Extending the SimCalc Approach to Grade 8 Mathematics* ; Roschelle et al., *Can Technology-Enhanced Curriculum Improve Student Learning of Important Mathematics?* ; Pamela Grossman and Alan Schoenfeld, with Carol Lee, "Teaching Subject Matter," in Darling-Hammond and Bransford, *Preparing Teachers for a Changing World*, 201–31 ; and Schoenfeld, "Instructional Research and the Improvement of Practice."_

27. For a notable exception see Roschelle et al., *Scaling up SimCalc;* Roschelle et al., *Extending the SimCalc Approach to Grade 8 Mathematics (No. 2)*; and Roschelle et al., *Can Technology-Enhanced Curriculum Improve Student Learning of Important Mathematics?*

28. Banks et al., *Learning In and Out of School in Diverse Environments*; and John Bransford et al., "Learning Theories and Education," 209–44.

29. This idea of adaptive instruction is rooted in a distinction made in the 1970s by Robert Glaser between the prevalent function of schooling that serves to select students according to their abilities and provide them expectations and opportunities to learn accordingly and an alternative that would try to adapt instruction according to what each student might need to enable him or her to progress and succeed. One reference to Glaser's thinking on this is Robert Glaser, *Adaptive Education: Individual Diversity and Learning* (New York: Holt, 1977). For Mosher this distinction was first made clear in conversations with Lauren Resnick, Glaser's colleague at the University of Pittsburgh Learning Research and Development Center, who has played a central role in trying to find ways to make adaptive instruction the norm in American schools.

30. Cohen, Raudenbush, and Ball, "Resources, Instruction, and Research."

31. Stephen W. Raudenbush, "Advancing Educational Policy by Advancing Research in Education," *American Educational Research Journal* 45, no. 1 (2008): 5–6.

32. Cohen, Raudenbush, and Ball, "Resources, Instruction, and Research."

33. Richard J. Murnane and Richard R. Nelson, "Improving the Performance of the Education Sector: The Valuable, Challenging, and Limited Role of Random Assignment Evaluations," *Economics of Innovation and New Technology* 16, no. 5 (2007): 307–22; and Michael Fullan, Peter Hill, and Carmel Crevola, *Breakthrough* (Thousand Oaks, CA: Corwin Press, 2006). See also Thomas D. Cook, "Generalization in the Social Sciences," in *The Encyclopedia of the Social and Behavioral Sciences*, ed. Neil Smelser and Paul Baltes (Oxford, England: Elsevier, 2002).

34. Thomas Corcoran and Fritz Mosher, "The Role of Assessment in Improving Instruction" (draft paper for the Center on the Continuous Improvement of Instruction of the Consortium for Policy Research in Education, 2007, available at http://www.cpre.org/ccii/images/stories/ccii_pdfs/role%20of%20assessment_fm%26tc.pdf); and Margaret Heritage, "Learning Progressions: Supporting Instruction and Formative Assessment" (policy paper for the Formative Assessment for Student and Teachers, State Collaborative on Assessment and Student Standards (FAST/SCASS) of the Council of Chief State School Officers, 2007).

35. Richard Elmore, *School Reform from the Inside Out* (Cambridge, MA: Harvard University Press, 2004).

36. David K. Cohen, Susan L. Moffitt, and Simona Goldin, "Policy and Practice," in *The State of Education Policy Research*, ed. Susan Fuhrman, David K. Cohen, and Fritz Mosher (Mahwah, NJ: Erlbaum, 2007).

37. As Richard Elmore has pointed out, the "long-run" gap between gaining the benefits of announcing the reform and public understanding that the reform has failed or had negative side can indeed be quite long—long enough for those who initiated the policy to have reaped the political benefits and moved on before the chickens come home to roost. If that is the purpose, however, he says it is a risky gamble in the case of performance-based accountability, since the evidence of its success or failure is built into the reform itself. See Elmore, *School Reform from the Inside Out*, 223–25.

38. Marshall S. Smith and Jennifer A. O'Day, "Systemic School Reform," in *The Politics of Curriculum and Testing: Politics of Education Association Yearbook*, ed. Susan H. Fuhrman and Betty Malen (London: Taylor and Francis, 1991), 233–67; and Jennifer A. O'Day and Marshall S. Smith, "Systemic School Reform and Educational Opportunity," in *Designing Coherent Education Policy: Improving the System*, ed. Susan Fuhrman (San Francisco: Jossey-Bass, 1993), 250–312.

39. Smith and O'Day, "Systemic School Reform," 238.

40. Daniel L. Schwartz and John D. Bransford, "A Time for Telling," *Cognition and Instruction* 16, no. 4 (1998): 475–522.

41. In *Breakthrough* Fullan and his colleagues make the distinction between "scripted" approaches to instruction and what they call "precise" ones. By this they mean that scripting tends to be used to deliver common content to all students, while precision refers to pedagogical responses that are directly responsive to information about the particular needs of particular students and that have been warranted in research and/or by the shared experiences of other teachers in the same situation. As in the conception of dynamic treatment regimes, the teacher may be responding in quite different ways to many students in the class at one time, though the particular responses should precisely fit the particular students and, where the appropriate knowledge exists, should be based on that knowledge. They argue that this notion of precision is much closer to what is meant by evidence-based professional practice in other fields, that it can be learned, but that it should not be seen as deskilling in the way that many view scripting.

The detailed conceptions of the paths students are likely to follow or the stages they go through as they acquire knowledge and skill in a subject, and of the kinds of misconceptions and difficulties they may face, that are needed to support these precise responses we would call "learning progressions." (For more information, see also Margaret Heritage, *Learning Progressions*.) This concept needs further development, and that development should rely on a combination of the work of cognitive scientists and learning and development researchers, on the logic of each academic discipline or school subject, and on the accumulated and codified experience of teachers in the subjects, as should the ideas about how to respond to students at particular stages or who have particular problems. But we think learning progressions have promise as an alternative to the roles that standards and curriculum frameworks were expected to play in systemic reform. Their advantage over standards is that they can describe progress in pedagogically meaningful terms that encompass the complexity of the relationship between content knowledge and disciplinary skills and practices as they grow over time (of course, standards can still be set simply by choosing a desired point in the scale of progress). They might be indistinguishable from good curriculum frameworks, but again they are likely to be less content- and grade-/time-bound than many frameworks turn out to be.

They are meant to adapt to and to make clear the fact that students proceed through these progressions at quite different rates but that in expecting them to keep proceeding until they reach significant levels, we could escape the "soft bigotry of low expectations" even as we accommodate individual differences. Progressions also would provide a much more powerful and interpretable basis for designing assessments, whether for summative or formative purposes. Developing these themes and helping to encourage and test instructional regimes and supports designed to implement them in practice is the mission of the Hewlett Foundation–supported Center on Continuous Instructional Improvement (http://www.cpre.org/ccii/).

42. RAND Mathematics Study Group, *Mathematical Proficiency for All Students*; Hugh Burkhardt and Alan H. Schoenfeld, "Improving Educational Research: Toward a More Useful, More Influential, and Better-Funded Enterprise," *Educational Researcher* 32, no. 9 (2003): 3–14; Schoenfeld, "Instructional Research and the Improvement of Practice"; Fullan, Hill, and Crevola, *Breakthrough*; and Bryk and Gomez, "Ruminations on Reinventing an R&D Capacity for Educational Improvement."

43. Bryk and Gomez, "Ruminations on Reinventing an R&D Capacity for Educational Improvement."

CHAPTER 2: RESEARCH-BASED EVIDENCE AND STATE POLICY

1. Michael Cohen, "Meeting the Information Needs of State Education Policymakers: Report of a Survey of State Policymakers" (No. 400-83-0051; Washington, DC: State Education Policy Consortium, National Association of State Boards of Education, 1985).

2. Timothy A. Hacsi, *Children as Pawns: The Politics of Educational Reform* (Cambridge, MA: Harvard University Press, 2002).

3. Edward Word, J. Johnston, Helen Pate-Bain, B. D. Fulton, Jayne Boyd-Zaharias, Charles M. Achilles, et al., "The State of Tennessee's Student/Teacher Achievement Ratio (STAR) Project" (Technical Report 1985–90; Nashville, TN: State Department of Education, 1994).

4. M. Cohen, "Meeting the Information Needs," 3.

5. Carol H. Weiss, "Congressional Committees as Users of Analysis," *Journal of Policy Analysis and Management* 8, no. 3 (1989): 420.

6. M. Cohen, "Meeting the Information Needs," 1.

7. Rudolf Flesch, *Why Johnny Can't Read* (New York: Harper and Row, 1955).

8. Alan H. Schoenfeld, "What Doesn't Work: The Challenge and Failure of the What Works Clearinghouse to Conduct Meaningful Reviews of Studies of Mathematics Curricula," *Educational Researcher* 35, no. 2 (2006): 13–21.

9. This is not to suggest that the only support for school choice comes from the Right. Like the standards movement, the school choice movement draws support from across the political spectrum. In Michael Mintrom's intriguing study *Policy Entrepreneurs and School Choice* (Washington, DC: Georgetown University Press, 2000), his entrepreneurs are mostly people who would define their politics as liberal.

10. Hacsi, *Children as Pawns*, 211.

11. James S. Coleman, "Equality of Educational Opportunity" (Washington, DC: Government Printing Office, 1965).

12. Hacsi, *Children as Pawns*, 214.

13. Word, Johnston, et al., "Tennessee's Student/Teacher Achievement Ratio (STAR) Project."

14. Frederick Mosteller, Richard J. Light, and Jason A. Sachs, "Sustained Inquiry in Education: Lessons from Skill Grouping and Class Size," *Harvard Educational Review* 66, no. 4 (1996): 797–828; AERA Research Points, "Class Size: Counting Students Can Count," *American Educational Research Association* 1, no. 2 (2003): 1–4.

15. Hacsi, *Children as Pawns.*

16. AERA Research Points, "Class Size"; Hacsi, *Children as Pawns.*

17. Mosteller, Light, and Sachs, "Sustained Inquiry in Education." *821.*

18. Hacsi, *Children as Pawns.*

19. Barbara Nye, Charles M. Achilles, Jayne Boyd-Zaharias, B. D. Fulton, and M. P. Wallenhorst, "Small Is Far Better: A Report on Three Class-Size Initiatives: Tennessee's Student Teacher Achievement Ratio (STAR) Project (8/85-8/89), Lasting Benefits Study (LBS: 9/89-7/92), and Project CHALLENGE (7/89-792) as a Policy Application: Preliminary Results" (Center of Excellence for Research in Basic Skills, Tennessee State University, Nashville, 1992); Donna Walker James, Sonia Jurich, and Steve Estes, "Raising Minority Academic Achievement: A Compendium of Education Programs and Practices" (Washington, DC: American Youth Policy Forum, 2001).

20. George W. Bohrnstedt and Brian M. Stecher, eds., "What We Have Learned About Class Size Reduction in California: Capstone Report" (Palo Alto, CA: American Institutes for Research, 2002).

21. Hacsi, *Children as Pawns,* 131–32.

22. Ibid., 123.

23. Community Training and Assistance Center, "Myths and Realities: The Impact of State Takeover on Students and Schools in Newark" (Boston, MA: CTAC, 2000); Kenneth K. Wong and Francis X. Shen, "City and State Takeover as a School Reform Strategy," *ERIC Digest 2003,* accessed August 21, 2008, from http://www.ericdigests.org/2003-2/city.html; Ronald C. Brady, "Can Failing Schools Be Fixed?" (Washington, DC: The Thomas B. Fordham Foundation, 2003); Wendy Togneri, "Islands of Excellence: What Districts Can Do to Improve Instruction and Achievement in All Schools—A Leadership Brief" (Washington, DC: Learning First Alliance, 2003).

24. K. Finnegan and J. O'Day, *External Support to Schools on Probation: Getting a Leg Up?* (Philadelphia, PA: Consortium for Policy Research in Education, 2003).

25. Interestingly, the problem districts in Massachusetts are as likely to be in small, isolated rural or working-class communities as in urban centers.

26. For a full listing of Richard Ingersoll's publications, see http://www.gse.upenn.edu/faculty/ingersoll.html. For more on the Project on the Next Generation of Teachers at the Harvard Graduate School of Education, directed by Susan Moore Johnson, go to www.gse.harvard.edu/~ngt.

27. Susan Fuhrman, *Education Policy: What Role for Research?* paper presented at the Annual Meeting of the American Educational Research Association, New Orleans, April 2000.

28. More on the Consortium for Policy Research in Education available at www.cpre.org.

29. More on Policy Analysis for California Education available at www.pace.berkeley.edu.

30. Michael W. Kirst, "Bridging Education Research and Education Policymaking," *Oxford Review of Education* 26, no. 3 (2000): 379–91.

31. For a textbook example of California's educational policymaking, see Lorraine McDonnell's fascinating examination of the rise and fall of CLAS, the state's innovative student assessment system. Lorraine McDonnell, *Politics, Persuasion, and Educational Testing* (Cambridge, MA: Harvard University Press, 2004).

CHAPTER 3: WHAT'S THE EVIDENCE ON DISTRICTS' USE OF EVIDENCE?

1. *No Child Left Behind Act of 2001*, Public Law 107-110 (January 8, 2002).

2. More specifically, we searched the ERIC database by combining the search terms *central office*, *district*, and *superintendent* with *data-based, data-driven, decision maker, data management, decision making, knowledge utilization, policy making, research utilization, policy making, research, research-based,* and *working knowledge.* We also searched ERIC for names of researchers known for addressing evidence use and decisionmaking in school district central offices and other public bureaucracies. Our initial searches located 3,689 documents. We reviewed abstracts for all of these documents and ultimately selected 120 articles and books that were related to evidence use in district central offices. From the reference lists of these works, we identified an additional twenty-two articles, books, and dissertations. We then searched the program of the AERA conferences for 2004 and 2005 to ensure that we captured the most recent research in this area. This search netted seven additional articles, bringing the grand total of pieces to review to 149. A significant percentage of these pieces were either advocacy pieces (arguing why districts should use research or data) or "how-to" pieces (providing step-by-step instructions for using research or data). While important, these pieces did not promise to help us understand the empirical base on how district central offices may actually use evidence. After excluding those pieces, we ended up with the fifty-two pieces that form the basis of this review.

3. Meredith I. Honig and Cynthia E. Coburn, "Evidence-Based Decision Making in School District Central Offices: Toward a Research Agenda," *Educational Policy* 22, no. 4 (2008): 578–608.

4. Mary Beth Celio and James Harvey, *Buried Treasure: Developing a Management Guide from Mountains of School Data* (Seattle, WA: Center on Reinventing Public Education, 2005).

5. Tom Corcoran, Susan H. Fuhrman, and Catherine L. Belcher, "The District Role in Instructional Improvement," *Phi Delta Kappan* 83, no. 1 (2001): 78–84; Jane L. David, "Local Uses of Title I Evaluations," *Educational Evaluation and Policy Analysis* 3, no. 1 (1981): 27–39; Jane M. E. Roberts and Shirley C. Smith, *Instructional Improvement: A System-Wide Approach* (Philadelphia: Research for Better Schools, 1982); and Russell F. West and Cheryl Rhoton, "School District Administrators' Perceptions of Educational Research and Barriers to Research Utilization," *ERS Spectrum* 12, no. 1 (1994): 23–30.

6. Corcoran, Fuhrman, and Belcher, "The District Role"; Michael Fullan, *The Role of Human Agents Internal to School Districts in Knowledge Utilization* (Toronto, Canada: Ontario Institute for Studies in Education, 1980); Diane Massell and Margaret E. Goertz, "District Strategies for Building Instructional Capacity," in *School Districts and Instructional Renewal*, ed. Amy M. Hightower, Michael S. Knapp, Julie A. Marsh, and Milbrey W. McLaughlin (New York: Teachers College Press, 2002), 43–60; West and Rhoton, "School District Administrators' Perceptions"; Michael H. Kean, "Research and Evaluation in Urban Educational Policy" (No. 67, ERIC/CUE Diversity Series, 1980); and Michael H. Kean, "Translating Research and Evaluation into Educational Policy," *Urban Review* 15, no. 3 (1983): 187–200.

7. David, "Local Uses of Title I"; Corcoran, Fuhrman, and Belcher, "The District Role"; Kean, "Translating Research and Evaluation"; Massell and Goertz, "District Strategies"; William E. Bickel and William W. Cooley, "Decision-Oriented Educational Research in School Districts: The Role of Dissemination Processes," *Studies in Educational Evaluation*

11, no. 2 (1985): 183–203; Richard M. Englert, Michael H. Kean, and Jay D. Scribner, "Politics of Program Evaluation in Large City School Districts," *Education and Urban Society* 9, no. 4 (1977): 429–50; and Michael H. Kean, *Institutionalizing Educational Productivity,* paper presented at the annual meeting of the American Educational Research Association, Los Angeles, April 1981.

8. Corcoran, Fuhrman, and Belcher, "The District Role."

9. Patricia E. Burch and Claudia H. Thiem, "Private Organizations, School Districts, and the Enterprise of High Stakes Accountability" (unpublished manuscript, 2004); and Robert E. Reichardt, *The State's Role in Supporting Data-Driven Decision-Making: A View of Wyoming* (Aurora, CO: Mid-Continent Research for Education and Learning, 2000).

10. David, "Local Uses of Title I"; Mary M. Kennedy, "The Role of the In-House Evaluator," in *Working Knowledge and Other Essays,* ed. Mary M. Kennedy (Cambridge, MA: The Huron Institute, 1982), 127–64; Martha A. MacIver and Elizabeth Farley-Ripple, "Bringing the District Back In: The Role of the Central Office in Improving Instruction and Student Achievement" (CRESPAR Report No. 65; Baltimore, MD: Johns Hopkins University, 2003).

11. Fullan, *The Role of Human Agents.*

12. Bickel and Cooley, "Decision-Oriented Educational Research"; Thomas B. Corcoran and Ullik Rouk, *Using Natural Channels for School Improvement: A Report on Four Years of the Urban Development Program* (Philadelphia, PA: Research for Better Schools, 1985); Meredith I. Honig, "District Central Office-Community Partnerships: From Contracts to Collaboration to Control," in *Educational Administration, Policy, and Reform: Research and Measurement,* ed. Wayne K. Hoy and Cecil G. Miskel (Greenwich, CT: Information Age Publishing, 2004), 59–90; Mary M. Kennedy, "Working Knowledge," in Kennedy, *Working Knowledge,* 1–28.

13. Kennedy, "Working Knowledge," 13.

14. Bickel and Cooley, "Decision-Oriented Educational Research"; David, "Local Uses of Title I"; West and Rhoton, "School District Administrators' Perceptions"; Kennedy, "Working Knowledge"; Jane Hannaway, *Managers Managing: The Workings of an Administrative System* (New York: Oxford University Press, 1989); James P. Spillane, "Cognition and Policy Implementation: District Policymakers and the Reform of Mathematics Education," *Cognition and Instruction* 18, no. 2 (2000): 141–79.

15. Meredith I. Honig, "Building Policy from Practice: Central Office Administrators' Roles and Capacity for Implementing Collaborative Education Policy," *Educational Administration Quarterly* 39, no. 3 (2003): 292–338.

16. James P. Spillane, Brian J. Reiser, and Todd Reimer, "Policy Implementation and Cognition: Reframing and Refocusing Implementation Research," *Review of Educational Research* 72, no. 3 (2002): 387–431.

17. Joseph F. Porac, Howard Thomas, and Charles Baden-Fuller, "Competitive Groups as Cognitive Communities: The Case of Scottish Knitwear Manufacturers," *Journal of Management Studies* 26, no. 4 (1989): 397–416; and Karl E. Weick, *Sensemaking in Organizations* (Thousand Oaks, CA: Sage Publications, 1995).

18. Kennedy, "Working Knowledge," 1–2.

19. Ibid.

20. David, "Local Uses of Title I"; Bickel and Cooley, "Decision-Oriented Educational Research"; Sarah Birkeland, Erin Murphy-Graham, and Carol H. Weiss, "Good Rea-

sons for Ignoring Good Evaluation: The Case of the Drug Abuse Resistance Education (D.A.R.E.) Program," *Evaluation and Program Planning* 28, no. 3 (2005): 247–56; Cynthia E. Coburn and Joan E. Talbert, "Conceptions of Evidence-Based Practice in School Districts: Mapping the Terrain," *American Journal of Education* 112, no. 4 (2006): 469–95; Mary M. Kennedy, "Evidence and Decision," in Kennedy, *Working Knowledge,* 59–103.

21. Hannaway, *Managers Managing;* Honig, "Building Policy from Practice"; Spillane, "Cognition and Policy Implementation."

22. Hannaway, *Managers Managing;* Honig, "Building Policy from Practice." See also James G. March, *A Primer on Decision Making* (New York: Free Press, 1994).

23. Hannaway, *Managers Managing.*

24. Meredith I. Honig, "Street-Level Bureaucracy Revisited: Frontline District Central Office Administrators as Boundary Spanners in Education Policy Implementation," *Educational Evaluation and Policy Analysis* 28, no. 4 (2006): 357–83.

25. Hannaway, *Managers Managing;* Kennedy, "Working Knowledge"; Kennedy, "Evidence and Decision"; Spillane, Reiser, and Reimer, "Reframing and Refocusing Implementation Research."

26. Coburn and Talbert, "Conceptions of Evidence Use"; Kennedy, "Evidence and Decision"; James P. Spillane, "State Policy and the Non-Monolithic Nature of the Local School District: Organizational and Professional Considerations," *American Educational Research Journal* 35, no.1 (1998): 33–63.

27. Coburn and Talbert, "Conceptions of Evidence Use."

28. It is possible to imagine ways that political pressures could influence the interpretation process as well. For example, some voices would carry more weight in the social processes by which interpretation unfolds in groups. However, while there is evidence that political processes shape interpretation at the school level, there is no research that investigates or illuminates this issue at the district central office level. For more about the political processes that shape interpretation at the school level, see Cynthia E. Coburn, "Framing the Problem of Reading Instruction: Using Frame Analysis to Uncover the Micro Processes of Policy Implementation in Schools," *American Educational Research Journal* 43, no. 3 (2006): 343–79.

29. Englert, Kean, and Scribner, "Politics of Program Evaluation"; Jane Hannaway, "Political Pressure and Decentralization in Institutional Organizations: The Case of School Districts," *Sociology of Education* 66, no. 3 (1993): 147–63.

30. Englert, Kean, and Scribner, "Politics of Program Evaluation."

31. Kennedy, "Evidence and Decision."

32. See Bickel and Cooley, "Decision-Oriented Educational Research"; Carol H. Weiss and Michael J. Bucuvalas, *Social Science Research and Decision-Making* (New York: Columbia University Press, 1980); Carol H. Weiss, Erin Murphy-Graham, and Sarah Birkeland, "An Alternate Route to Policy Influence: How Evaluations Affect D.A.R.E.," *American Journal of Evaluation* 26, no. 1 (2005): 12–30.

33. Weiss, Murphy-Graham, and Birkeland, "An Alternate Route." Weiss and colleagues put forth a new category of evidence use, which they term *imposed use*. However, in this paper we are focusing on different roles of evidence in the decisionmaking process rather than categories of use. The role of evidence in imposed use appears to be sanctioning the programs that district administrators are required to adopt. Thus, we use the term *sanctioning* rather than *imposed use*.

34. Honig and Coburn, "Evidence-Based Decision-Making"; Weiss, Murphy-Graham, and Birkeland, "An Alternate Route"; Carol H. Weiss, "Knowledge Creep and Decision Accretion," *Knowledge: Creation, Diffusion, Utilization* 1, no. 3 (1980): 381–404.
35. Weiss, "Knowledge Creep," 11–12.
36. Kennedy, "Evidence and Decision."
37. David, "Local Uses of Title I."
38. Birkeland, Murphy-Graham, and Weiss, "Good Reasons"; and Weiss, Murphy-Graham, and Birkeland, "An Alternate Route."
39. Corcoran, Fuhrman, and Belcher, "The District Role."
40. Kennedy, "Evidence and Decision," 96.
41. David, "Local Uses of Title I"; Weiss, Murphy-Graham, and Birkeland, "An Alternate Route."
42. Weiss, "Knowledge Creep"; Weiss, Murphy-Graham, and Birkeland, "An Alternate Route."
43. Rita M. Fillos and William J. Bailey, "Survey of Delaware Superintendents' KPU" (Newark: University of Delaware, 1978).
44. Edward A. Silver, "Contributions of Research to Practice: Applying Findings, Methods, and Perspectives," in *Teaching and Learning Mathematics in the 1990s*, ed. Thomas J. Cooney and Christian R. Hirsch (Reston, VA: National Council of Teachers of Mathematics, 1990), 1–11.
45. Weiss, "Knowledge Creep"; Weiss and Bucuvalas, *Social Science Research and Decision-Making*.
46. Weiss, "Knowledge Creep"; Weiss, Murphy-Graham, and Birkeland, "An Alternate Route."
47. David, "Local Uses of Title I"; Corcoran, Fuhrman, and Belcher, "The District Role"; Kennedy, "Evidence and Decision"; Weiss, Murphy-Graham, and Birkeland, "An Alternate Route"; R. Manheimer, "System Leaders Apply Research in Their Decision Making," *School Administrator* 52, no. 6 (1995): 17–18; Carol M. Robinson, "Improving Education through the Application of Measurement and Research: A Practitioner's Perspective," *Applied Measurement in Education* 1, no. 1 (1988): 53–65.
48. Robinson, "Improving Education"; Kennedy, "Evidence and Decision"; Weiss, Murphy-Graham, and Birkeland, "An Alternate Route"; Corcoran, Fuhrman, and Belcher, "The District Role," 80.
49. See, for example, Robinson, "Improving Education"; Manheimer, "System Leaders Apply Research."
50. Englert, Kean, and Scribner, "Politics of Program Evaluation"; Dianne Massell, "The Theory and Practice of Using Data to Build Capacity: State and Local Strategies and Their Effects," in *From the Capitol to the Classroom: Standards-Based Reform in the States: One Hundredth Yearbook of the National Society for the Study of Education*, ed. Susan H. Fuhrman (Chicago: National Society for the Study of Education, 2001), 148–69.
51. Massell and Goertz, "District Strategies."
52. Weiss, Murphy-Graham, and Birkeland, "An Alternate Route."
53. Districts may also use this approach with schools. That is, districts may create lists of programs that are approved for use on the basis of the strength of the evidence of their effectiveness. Here we focus mainly on how districts respond when higher levels of government create such lists, not how schools respond when districts use this approach.

54. Weiss, Murphy-Graham, and Birkeland, "An Alternate Route."
55. David, "Local Uses of Title I"; Birkeland, Murphy-Graham, and Weiss, "Good Reasons"; Corcoran, Fuhrman, and Belcher, "The District Role"; Kennedy, "Evidence and Decision"; Massell, "The Theory and Practice of Using Data."
56. David, "Local Uses of Title I."
57. Kennedy, "Evidence and Decision."
58. Birkeland, Murphy-Graham, and Weiss, "Good Reasons."
59. Corcoran, Fuhrman, and Belcher, "The District Role."
60. David, "Local Uses of Title I"; Corcoran, Fuhrman, and Belcher, "The District Role"; Massell and Goertz, "District Strategies."
61. Corcoran, Fuhrman, and Belcher, "The District Role"; Englert, Kean, and Scribner, "Politics of Program Evaluation"; Hannaway, *Managers Managing*; Kennedy, "Working Knowledge"; Kennedy, "Evidence and Decision"; Weiss, "Knowledge Creep"; Manheimer, "System Leaders Apply Research"; Robinson, "Improving Education."
62. Massell, "The Theory and Practice of Using Data"; Robert E. Slavin, "PET and the Pendulum: Faddism in Education and How to Stop It," *Phi Delta Kappan* 70, no. 10 (1989): 752–58.
63. David, "Local Uses of Title I"; Mac Iver and Farley-Ripple, "Bringing the District Back"; Corcoran, Fuhrman, and Belcher, "The District Role"; Reichardt, *The State's Role*; Burch and Thiem, "Private Organizations, School Districts"; Honig, "Building Policy from Practice."
64. Roberts and Smith, *Instructional Improvement*; Corcoran, Fuhrman, and Belcher, "The District Role"; Honig, "Building Policy from Practice"; Massell, "The Theory and Practice of Using Data."
65. Reichardt, *The State's Role*; Burch and Thiem, "Private Organizations, School Districts"; Massell, "The Theory and Practice of Using Data"; and Kerri A. Kerr, Julie A. Marsh, Gina. S. Ikemoto, Hilary Darilek, and Heather Barney, "Strategies to Promote Data Use for Instructional Improvement: Actions, Outcomes, and Lessons from Three Urban Districts," *American Journal of Education* 112, no. 4 (2006): 496–520; Weiss, Murphy-Graham, and Birkeland, "An Alternate Route"; and Amanda Datnow, Lea Hubbard, and Hugh Mehan, *Extending Educational Reform: From One School to Many* (London: Routledge Falmer, 2002).
66. David, "Local Uses of Title I"; Cynthia E. Coburn, Judith Toure, and Mika Yamashita, "Evidence, Interpretation, and Persuasion: Instructional Decision Making in the District Central Office," *Teachers College Record* 111, no. 4 (2009).
67. Kerr et al., "Strategies to Promote Data Use"; Massell, "The Theory and Practice of Using Data"; David, "Local Uses of Title I"; Coburn, Toure, and Yamashita, "Evidence, Interpretation, and Persuasion"; Honig, "Building Policy from Practice"; Honig, "Street-Level Bureaucracy Revisited."
68. Kerr et al., "Strategies to Promote Data Use"; Corcoran and Rouk, *Using Natural Channels*; and James P. Spillane and Charles L. Thompson, "Reconstructing Conceptions of Local Capacity: The Local Education Agency's Capacity for Ambitious Instructional Reform," *Educational Evaluation and Policy Analysis* 19, no. 2 (1997): 185–203.
69. Bickel and Cooley, "Decision-Oriented Educational Research"; Kean, "Research and Evaluation"; Kean, *Institutionalizing Educational Productivity*; Roberts and Smith, *Instructional Improvement*; Kean, "Translating Research and Evaluation."

70. Honig, "Building Policy from Practice"; Honig, "District Central Office-Community Partnerships"; and Meredith I. Honig, "The New Middle Management: Intermediary Organizations in Education Policy Implementation," *Educational Evaluation and Policy Analysis* 26, no. 1 (2004): 65–87.

71. Kerr et al., "Strategies to Promote Data Use"; and Julie A. Marsh, Kerri A. Kerr, Gina S. Ikemoto, Hilary Darilek, Marika Suttorp, Ron Zimmer, and Heather Barney, *The Role of Districts in Fostering Instructional Improvement: Lessons from Three Urban Districts Partnered with the Institute for Learning* (Santa Monica, CA: RAND, 2005).

72. Mary Kay Stein and Laura D'Amico, *Observations, Conversations and Negotiations: Administrator Support of Literacy Practices in New York Community School District #2*, paper presented at the annual meeting of the American Educational Research Association, Montreal, 1999.

73. Spillane and Thompson, "Reconstructing Conceptions of Local Capacity"; James P. Spillane, "External Reform Initiatives and Teachers' Efforts to Reconstruct Their Practice: The Mediating Role of Teachers' Zones of Enactment," *Journal of Curriculum Studies* 31, no. 2 (1999): 143–75.

74. Cynthia E. Coburn, "Collective Sensemaking about Reading: How Teachers Mediate Reading Policy in Their Professional Communities," *Educational Evaluation and Policy Analysis* 23, no. 2 (2001): 145–70.

75. Englert, Kean, and Scribner, "Politics of Program Evaluation."

76. Julie A. Marsh, *Democratic Dilemmas: Joint Work, Education Politics, and Community* (Albany: SUNY Press, 2007).

77. For example, Jason Snipes, Fred Doolittle, and Corinne Herlihy, *Foundations for Success: Case Studies of How Urban School Systems Improve Student Achievement* (Washington, DC: Council of Great City Schools, 2002).

78. Mary K. Stein and Barbara S. Nelson, "Leadership Content Knowledge," *Educational Evaluation and Policy Analysis* 25, no. 4 (2004): 423–48.

79. Philip Davies, *Is Evidence-Based Government Possible?* Jerry Lee Lecture, Campbell Collaboration Colloquium, Washington, DC, February 2004.

80. David Tyack and Larry Cuban, *Tinkering toward Utopia: A Century of Public School Reform* (Cambridge, MA: Harvard University Press, 1995).

CHAPTER 4: EVIDENCE-INFORMED CHANGE AND THE PRACTICE OF TEACHING

1. Seymour Sarason, *The Predictable Failure of Educational Reform: Can We Change Course Before It's Too Late?* (San Francisco: Jossey-Bass, 1990); Susan Florio-Ruane, "More Light: An Argument for Complexity in Studies of Teaching and Teacher Education," *Journal of Teacher Education* 53, no. 3 (2001): 205–15; Deborah Meier, *In Schools We Trust* (Boston: Beacon Press, 2002); Lawrence Ingvarson, *Educational Reform Through Restructuring Industrial Rewards: A Study of the Advanced Skills Teacher* (Melbourne, Australia: Melbourne University, 1992).

2. David K. Cohen, Stephen W. Raudenbush, and Deborah B. Ball, "Objecting to the Objections to Using Random Assignment in Educational Research," in *Evidence Matters: Randomized Trials in Education Research*, ed. Frederick Mosteller and Robert Boruch (Washington, DC: Brookings Institution, 2002); Jennifer Evans and Pauline Benefield, "Systematic Reviews of Educational Research: Does the Medical Model Fit?" *British Educational Research Journal* 25, no. 5 (2001): 527–41; David H. Hargreaves, "In Defence of

Research for Evidence-Based Teaching: A Rejoinder to Martyn Hammersley," *British Educational Research Journal* 23, no. 4 (1997): 405–19; Gary Burtless, "Randomized Field Trials for Policy Evaluation: Why Not in Education?" in Mosteller and Boruch, *Evidence Matters*, 179–97; Thomas D. Cook and Monique R. Payne, "Objecting to the Objections to Using Random Assignment in Educational Research," in Mosteller and Boruch, *Evidence Matters*, 150–78; Robert E. Slavin, "Does Rigorous Research Knowledge Provide a Better Base for Improving Student Achievement than Teachers' Craft Knowledge?" *Journal of Educational Change* 2, no. 4 (2001): 347–48.

3. Marilyn Cochran-Smith and Susan S. Lytle, "Relationships of Knowledge and Practice: Teacher Learning in Communities," *Review of Research in Education* 24 (1999): 249–305; John Elliott, "Making Evidence-Based Practice Educational," *British Educational Research Journal* 27, no. 5 (2001): 555–74; Peter Grimmett and Allan MacKinnon, "Craft Knowledge and the Education of Teachers," *Review of Research in Education* 18 (1992): 385–456; Glenn Hultman, "Does Rigorous Research Knowledge Provide a Better Base for Improving Student Achievement than Teachers' Craft Knowledge?" *Journal of Educational Change* 2, no. 4 (2001): 349–52; Meier, *In Schools We Trust;* Andy Hargreaves, *Teaching in the Knowledge Society* (New York: Teachers College Press, 2003); Milbrey Wallin McLaughlin and Joan E. Talbert, *Professional Communities and the Work of High School Teaching* (Chicago: University of Chicago Press, 2001).

4. Philip Jackson, "The Functions of Educational Research," *Educational Researcher* 19, no. 7 (1990): 3–9.

5. Michael Huberman, *The Lives of Teachers* (New York: Teachers College Press, 1993).

6. Robert Floden, "Research on Effects of Teaching: A Continuing Model for Research on Teaching," in *Handbook of Research on Teaching*, 4th ed., ed. Virginia Richardson (Washington, DC: American Educational Research Association, 2001); Florio-Ruane, "More Light"; Nathaniel L. Gage, *The Scientific Basis of the Art of Teaching* (New York: Teachers College Press, 1978); Mary Budd Rowe, "Wait Time and Rewards as Instructional Variables, Their Influence on Language, Logic, and Fate Control: Part One—Wait Time," *Journal of Research in Science Teaching* 11, no. 2 (1974): 81–94; Rebecca Barr and Robert Dreeban, *How Schools Work* (Chicago: University of Chicago Press: 1983); Michael J. Dunkin and Bruce J. Biddle, *The Study of Teaching* (New York: Holt, Rinehart, and Winston, 1974).

7. N. L. Gage, "The Paradigm Wars and Their Aftermath: A 'Historical' Sketch of Research on Teaching Since 1989," *Teachers College Record* 91, no. 2 (1989): 135–50; Michael Fullan, *The Meaning of Educational Change* (New York: Teachers College Press, 1982).

8. For example, Neville Bennett, *Teaching Styles and Pupil Progress* (London: Open Books, 1976); and Maurice Galton, Brian Simon, and Paul Croll, *Inside the Primary Classroom* (London: Routledge, 1980).

9. D. H. Hargreaves, "In Defence of Research"; and Suzanne Wilson, Robert Floden, and Joan Ferrini-Mundy, "Teacher Preparation Research: An Insider's View from the Outside," *Journal of Teacher Education* 53, no. 3 (2002): 190–204.

10. Burtless, "Randomized Field Trials"; Cook and Payne, "Objecting to the Objections"; and National Research Council (NRC), *Scientific Research in Education* (Washington, DC: National Academy Press, 2002).

11. In the United Kingdom, a similar move toward evidence-based policy and practice of the more technical kind has developed out of market-driven trends in medicine and education that have used "effectiveness" as a performance measure of success for schools and

hospitals and their ability to base practice on the evidence of "what works." Yet, while medicine has an accepted and established base from which to derive knowledge about practice, the argument goes, education does not. See Evans and Benefield, Systematic Reviews of Educational Research"; D. H. Hargreaves, "In Defence of Education"; and Slavin, "Does Rigorous Research Knowledge Provide a Better Base."

12. Cook and Payne, "Objecting to the Objections"; Evans and Benefield, "Systematic Reviews of Educational Research"; D. H. Hargreaves, "In Defence of Research"; and Ann Oakley, *Experiments in Knowing: Gender and Method in the Social Science* (Cambridge, MA: Polity Press, 2000).

13. D. H. Hargreaves, "In Defence of Research," 408–9.

14. Atul Gawande, *Complications: A Surgeon's Notes on an Imperfect Science* (New York: Picador, 2003); Daniel F. Chambliss, *Beyond Caring: Hospitals, Nurses, and the Social Organization of Ethics* (Chicago: University of Chicago Press, 1996); Eliot Friedson, *Professionalism Reborn: Theory, Prophecy, and Policy* (Chicago: University of Chicago Press, 1994); Jerome Groopman, *Second Opinions: Stories of Intuition and Choice in the Changing World of Medicine* (New York: Penguin, 2002); Jean Watson, ed., *Applying the Art and Science of Human Caring* (New York: National League for Nursing Press, 1994).

15. Brian Rowan and Charles Denk, "Management Succession, School Socioeconomic Context, and Basic Skills Achievement," *American Educational Research Journal* 21, no. 3 (1984): 517–37.

16. Rowan and Denk, "Management Succession"; Hilda Borko, Joan Cone, Nancy Atwood Russo, and Richard Shavelson, "Teachers' Decision Making," in *Research on Teaching: Concepts, Findings, and Implications*, ed. Penelope L. Peterson and Herbert J. Walberg (Berkeley, CA: McCutchan, 1979), 136–60; Christopher M. Clark and Penelope L. Peterson, "Teachers' Thought Processes," in *Handbook of Research on Teaching*, 3rd ed., ed. Merlin C. Wittrock (New York: Macmillan, 1986), 255–96; Lee. S. Shulman, "Knowledge and Teaching: Foundations of the New Reform," *Harvard Educational Review* 57, no. 1 (1987): 1–22; David. C. Berliner, "The Nature of Expertise in Teaching," in *Effective and Responsible Teaching: The New Synthesis*, ed. Fritz K. Oser, Andreas Dick, and Jean-Luc Patry (San Francisco: Jossey-Bass, 1992), 227–48.

17. Andy Hargreaves, Lorna Earl, Shawn Moore, and Susan Manning, *Learning to Change: Teaching Beyond Subjects and Standards* (San Francisco: Jossey-Bass, 2001).

18. Fullan, *Leading in a Culture of Change.*

19. Michael Fullan, *Change Forces: Probing the Depth of Educational Reform* (New York: Falmer Press, 1993); D. H. Hargreaves, *Education Epidemic: Transforming Secondary Schools Through Innovation Networks* (London: Demos, 2004); and Peter M. Senge, *The Fifth Discipline: The Art and Practice of the Learning Organization* (New York: Currency Doubleday, 1990); Gary Hoban, *Teacher Learning for Educational Change: A Systems Thinking Approach* (Buckingham, England: Open University Press, 2002); Bill Mulford, "Organisational Learning and Educational Change," in *International Handbook of Educational Change*, ed. Andy Hargreaves, Ann Lieberman, Michael Fullan, and David Hopkins (Norwell, MA: Kluwer, 1998); Louise Stoll, Dean Fink, and Lorna Earl, *It's about Learning (And It's about Time): What's in It for Schools?* (London: Routledge Falmer, 2003).

20. John F. Jennings, "Opportunity to Learn or Opportunity to Lose," *Education Week*, November 26, 1997, accessed November 6, 2005, from http://www.ctredpol.org/pubs/oppor.html.

21. Willard Waller, *The Sociology of Teaching* (New York: Wiley, 1932).
22. Cochran-Smith and Lytle, "Relationships of Knowledge and Practice"; Wilson, Floden, and Ferrini-Mundy, "Teacher Preparation Research."
23. Margret Buchmann and John Schwille, "Education: The Overcoming of Experience," *American Journal of Education* 92, no. 1 (1983): 30–51; A. Hargreaves, "Experience Counts, Theory Doesn't: How Teachers Talk about Their Work," *Sociology of Education* 57, no. 4 (1984): 244–54; Mary Beattie, "New Prospects for Teacher Education: Narrative Ways of Knowing Teaching and Teacher Learning," *Educational Research* 37, no. 1 (1995): 54–70; D. Jean Clandinin, *Classroom Practices: Teacher Images in Action* (London: Falmer Press, 1986); F. Michael Connelly and D. Jean Clandinin, *Teachers as Curriculum Planners: Narratives of Experience* (New York: Teachers College Press, 1988); Freema Elbaz, *Teacher Thinking: A Study of Practical Knowledge* (New York: Nichols, 1983); Madeleine Grumet, "The Politics of Personal Knowledge," *Curriculum Inquiry* 17, no. 3 (1987): 319–29; Sigrun Gudmundsdóttir, "Story-Maker, Story-Teller: Narrative Structures in Curriculum," *Journal of Curriculum Studies* 23, no. 3 (1991): 207–18; Deborah P. Britzman, *Practice Makes Practice: A Critical Study of Learning to Teach* (Albany: SUNY Press, 1991); Kathy Carter, "The Place of Story in the Study of Teaching and Teacher Education," *Educational Researcher* 22, no. 1 (1993): 5–12; F. Elbaz, "Research on Teacher Knowledge: The Evolution of a Discourse," *Journal of Curriculum Studies* 23, no. 1 (1991): 1–19; Ivor Goodson, *Studying Teachers' Lives* (New York: Teachers College Press, 1992); Connelly and Clandinin, *Teachers as Curriculum Planners*, 25; Sally Brown and Donald McIntyre, *Making Sense of Teaching* (Buckingham, England: Open University Press, 1993); Meier, *In Schools We Trust*; and McLaughlin and Talbert, *Professional Communities*.
24. Walter Doyle and Gerald A. Ponder, "The Practicality Ethic of Teaching Decision-Making," *Interchange* 8, no. 3 (1977): 1–12; Fullan, *The Meaning of Educational Change*; K. S. Louis, "Reconnecting Knowledge Utilization and School Improvement," in A. Hargreaves et al, *International Handbook of Educational Change*; and Carol H. Weiss and Michael J. Bucuvalas, *Social Science Research and Decision-Making* (New York: Columbia University Press, 1980).
25. A. Hargreaves, "Experience Counts, Theory Doesn't"; Philip Jackson, *Life in Classrooms* (New York: Holt, Rinehart, and Winston, 1968); Dan Lortie, *Schoolteacher: A Sociological Study* (Chicago: University of Chicago Press, 1975); D. P. Britzman, "Beyond Rolling Models: Gender and Multicultural Education," in *Gender and Education: Ninety-Second Yearbook of the National Society for the Study of Education*, ed. Sari Knopp Biklin and Diane Pollard (Chicago: University of Chicago Press, 1993). See for example, Bransford and Schwartz, "It Takes Expertise to Make Expertise: Some Thoughts on Why and How."
26. Jeannie Oakes, Karen Hunter Quartz, Steve Ryan, and Martin Lipton, *Becoming Good American Schools: The Struggle for Civic Virtue in Education Reform* (San Francisco: Jossey-Bass, 2000); A. Hargreaves, "Revisiting Voice," *Educational Researcher* 25, no. 1 (1996): 12–19. See for example, Darling-Hammond and Bransford, *Preparing Teachers for a Changing World*.
27. A. Hargreaves, "The Emotional Practice of Teaching," *Teaching and Teacher Education* 14, no. 8 (1998): 835–54; A. Hargreaves, "Teachers' Perceptions of Their Interactions with Students," *Teacher and Teacher Education* 16, no. 8 (2000): 811–26; A. Hargreaves, "The Emotional Geographies of Teachers' Relations with Their Colleagues," *International Journal of Educational Research* 35, no. 5 (2001): 503–27; A. Hargreaves, "The Emotional

Geographies of Teaching," *Teachers College Record* 103, no. 6 (2001): 1056–80; Norman Denzin, *On Understanding Emotion* (San Francisco: Jossey-Bass, 1984).

28. Robert L. Fried, *The Passionate Teacher: A Practical Guide* (Boston: Beacon Press, 1995). See also Christopher Day, *A Passion for Teaching* (London: Falmer Press, 2004); A. Hargreaves, "Mixed Emotions"; Denzin, *On Understanding Emotion*; A. Hargreaves, "Emotional Geographies of Teachers' Relations"; A. Hargreaves, "Emotional Geographies of Teaching."

29. Carol Gilligan, *In a Different Voice: Psychological Theory and Women's Development* (Cambridge, MA: Harvard University Press, 1982); and Nel Noddings, *The Challenge to Care in Schools* (New York: Teachers College Press, 1992); Anthony S. Bryk and Barbara Schneider, *Trust in Schools: A Core Resource for Improvement* (New York: Russell Sage Foundation, 2004); Jennifer Nias, *Primary Teachers Talking* (London: Routledge, 1989); Judith Warren Little, "The Emotional Contours and Career Trajectories of (Disappointed) Reform Enthusiasts," *Cambridge Journal of Education* 26, no. 3 (1996): 345–59; Andy Hargreaves, "Inclusive and Exclusive Educational Change: Emotional Responses of Teacher and Implications for Leadership," *School Leadership and Management* 25, no. 2 (2004): 287–309; Andy Hargreaves, *Changing Teachers, Changing Times: Teachers' Work and Culture in the Postmodern Age* (New York: Teachers College Press, 1994); Peter Woods and Bob Jeffrey, *Teachable Moments* (Buckingham, England: Open University Press, 1996); and Jill Blackmore, "Doing 'Emotional Labor' in the Education Market Place: Stories from the Field of Women in Management," *Discourse: Studies in the Cultural Politics of Education* 17, no. 3 (1996): 337–49.

30. Elizabeth Campbell, "Challenges in Fostering Ethical Knowledge as Professionalism Within Schools as Teaching Communities," *Journal of Educational Change* 6, no. 3 (2005): 207–26; Gary D. Fenstermacher, "Some Moral Considerations in Teaching as a Profession," in *Moral Dimensions of Teaching*, ed. John I. Goodlad, Roger Sodor, and Kenneth A. Sirotnik (San Francisco: Jossey-Bass, 1990), 132.

31. David T. Hansen, *Exploring the Moral Heart of Teaching: Toward a Teacher's Creed* (New York: Teachers College Press, 2001); Hugh Sockett, *The Moral Base for Teacher Professionalism* (New York: Teachers College Press, 1993); Robert J. Starratt, *Ethical Leadership* (San Francisco: Jossey-Bass, 2004); Kenneth Strike and P. Lance Ternasky, eds., *Ethics for Professional Educators* (New York: Teachers College Press, 1993); Alan Tom, *Teaching as a Moral Craft* (White Plains, NY: Longman, 1984); Henry A. Giroux and Michele Schmidt, "Closing the Achievement Gap: A Metaphor for Children Left Behind," *Journal for Educational Change* 5, no. 3 (2004): 213–28; Walt Haney, "The Myth of the Texas Miracle in Education," *Education Policy Analysis Archives* 8, no. 41 (2000).

32. For example, Richard Dufour and Robert Eaker, *Professional Learning Communities at Work: Best Practices for Enhancing Student Achievement* (Bloomington, IN: National Education Services, 1998); Sharon D. Kruse, Karen S. Louis, and Anthony S. Bryk, "An Emerging Framework for Analyzing School-Based Professional Community," in *Professionalism and Community: Perspectives on Reforming Urban Schools*, ed. K. S. Louis, S. D. Kruse, and Associates (Thousand Oaks, CA: Corwin Press, 1995), 23–44; McLaughlin and Talbert, *Professional Communities*; and Fred Newmann and Gary Wehlage, *Successful School Restructuring* (Madison, WI: Center on Organization and Restructuring of Schools, 1995); Judith Warren Little, "The Persistence of Privacy: Autonomy and Initiative in Teachers' Professional Relations," *Teachers College Record* 91, no. 4 (1990): 509–36; Campbell, "Challenges in Fostering Ethical Knowledge."

33. Waller, *The Sociology of Teaching*, 10).

34. Sarason, *The Predictable Failure*.

35. Amanda Datnow, Lea Hubbard, and Hugh Mehan, *Extending Educational Reform: From One School to Many* (London: Routledge Falmer, 2002).

36. Darling-Hammond and Bransford, *Preparing Teachers for a Changing World*; Linda Darling-Hammond, Brigid Barron, P. David Pearson, Alan H. Schoenfeld, Elizabeth K. Stage, Timothy D. Zimmerman, Gina N. Cervetti, and Jennifer L. Tilson, *Powerful Learning: What We Know about Teaching for Understanding* (San Francisco: Jossey-Bass, 2008).

37. Andy Hargreaves, "Progressivism and Pupil Autonomy," *Sociological Review* 25 (1977): 585–621; Andy Hargreaves, "The Significance of Classroom Coping Strategies," in *Sociological Interpretations of Schooling and Classrooms: A Reappraisal*, ed. Len Barton and Roland Meighan (Driffield, England: Nafferton Books, 1978); and D. H. Hargreaves, "The Occupational Culture of Teaching," in *Teaching Strategies*, ed. Peter Woods (London: Croom Helm, 1980).

38. James Hoetker and William P. Ahlbrand Jr., "The Persistence of Recitation," *American Educational Research Journal* 6, no. 2 (1969): 145–67; Ian Westbury, "Conventional Classrooms, 'Open' Classrooms, and the Technology of Teaching," *Journal of Curriculum Studies* 5, no. 2 (1973): 99–121; Martyn Hammersley, "The Organization of Pupil Participation," *Sociological Review* 22, no. 3 (1974): 355–68; Galton, Simon and Croll, *Inside the Primary Classroom*.

39. Mary Metz, "Real School: A Universal Drama Amid Disparate Evidence," in *Education Politics for the New Century: The Twentieth Anniversary Yearbook of the Politics of Education Association*, ed. Douglas Mitchell and Margaret Gnesta (Philadelphia: Falmer Press, 1991); David Tyack and William Tobin, "The 'Grammar' of Schooling: Why Has it Been So Hard to Change?" *American Educational Research Journal* 31, no. 3 (1994): 453–80; Doyle and Ponder, "The Practicality Ethic"; Andy Hargreaves and Noreen Jacka, "Induction or Seduction?" *Peabody Journal of Education* 70, no. 3 (1995): 41–63; Colin Lacey, *The Socialization of Teachers* (London: Methuen, 1977); Paul G. Schempp, Andrew C. Sparkes, and Thomas J. Templin, "The Micropolitics of Teacher Induction," *American Educational Research Journal* 30, no. 3 (1993): 447–72; Seymour Sarason, *The Creation of Settings and the Future Societies* (San Francisco: Jossey-Bass, 1972); Lortie, *Schoolteacher*.

40. Jean Anyon, "Social Class and the Hidden Curriculum of Work," *Journal of Education* 162, no. 1 (1980): 67–92; Lisa Delpit, *Other People's Children* (New York: New Press, 1995); Gloria Ladson-Billings, "Toward a Theory of Culturally Relevant Pedagogy," *American Educational Research Journal* 32, no. 3 (1995): 465–91.

41. Andy Hargreaves and Dean Fink, *Sustainable Leadership* (San Francisco: Jossey-Bass, 2006); Robert Eaker, Richard Dufour, and Rebecca Burnette, *Getting Started: Reculturing Schools to Become Professional Learning Communities* (Bloomington, IN: National Education Service, 2002). Restructuring of the education workforce is currently occurring in the UK with teacher union support from the Department for Education and Skills.

42. Datnow, Hubbard, and Mehan, *Extending Educational Reform*; Richard Elmore, "Hard Questions about Practice," *Educational Leadership* 59, no. 8 (2002): 22–25; Michael Fullan, *Leadership and Sustainability: System Thinkers in Action* (Thousand Oaks, CA: Corwin Press, 2005); Hargreaves and Fink, *Sustainable Leadership*.

43. D. H. Hargreaves, "The Occupational Culture of Teaching," in Woods, *Teaching Strategies*; Andy Hargreaves, "Time and Teachers' Work: An Analysis of the Intensification Thesis," *Teachers College Record* 94, no. 1 (1992): 87–107; A. Hargreaves, *Changing Teachers*.

44. David J. Flinders, "Teachers' Isolation and the New Reforms," *Journal of Curriculum and Supervision* 4, no. 1 (1988): 17–29; Little, "The Persistence of Privacy"; Lortie, *Schoolteacher*; Robin McTaggart, "Bureaucratic Rationality and the Self-Educating Profession: The Problem of Teacher Privatism," *Journal of Curriculum Studies* 21, no. 4 (1989): 345–61; Susan M. Johnson, *Teachers at Work* (New York: Basic Books, 1990); J. Nias, Geoff Southworth, and Robin Yeomans, *Staff Relationships in the Primary School* (London: Cassells, 1989); Andy Hargreaves and Robert MacMillan, "The Balkanization of Secondary School Teaching," in *The Subjects in Question: Departmental Organization and the High School*, ed. Leslie Santee Siskin and J. W. Little (New York: Teachers College Press, 1995), 141–71; A. Hargreaves, *Changing Teachers.*

45. Reba Page, "Teachers' Perceptions of Students: A Link Between Classrooms, School Cultures, and The Social Order," *Anthropology and Education Quarterly* 18, no. 1 (1987): 77–99; Patricia Ashton and Rodman Webb, *Making a Difference: Teachers' Sense of Efficacy* (New York: Longman, 1986); Susan Rosenholtz, *Teachers' Workplace: The Social Organization of Schools* (New York: Longman, 1989); McLaughlin and Talbert, "What Matters Most"; McLaughlin and Talbert, *Professional Communities;*Stephen Anderson and Wendy Togneri, *Beyond Islands of Excellence: What Districts Can Do to Improve Instruction and Achievement in All Schools* (Washington, DC: Learning First Alliance, 2002).

46. Little, "The Persistence of Privacy"; Nias, *Primary Teachers Talking;* Jorge Avila de Lima, "Forgetting about Friendship: Using Conflict in Teacher Communities as a Lever for School Change," *Journal of Educational Change* 2, no. 2 (2001): 97–122; Gill Helsby, *Changing Teachers' Work: The Reform of Secondary Schooling* (Milton Keynes, England: Open University Press, 1999); Bryk and Schneider, *Trust in Schools;* Ronald Heifetz and Martin Linsky, *Leadership on the Line: Staying Alive Through the Dangers of Leading* (Boston, MA: Harvard 2002; Fullan, *Leading in a Culture of Change* (San Francisco: Jossey-Bass, 2001); Terrence E. Deal and Kent Peterson, *The Leadership Paradox* (San Francisco: Jossey-Bass, 1995); Kenneth Leithwood and Doris Jantzi, "Transformational School Leadership Effects," *School Effectiveness and School Improvement* 10, no. 4 (1999): 451–79; Thomas J. Sergiovanni, *Building Community Schools* (San Francisco: Jossey-Bass, 1994); Frank Crowther, Stephen Kaagan, Margaret Ferguson, and Leonne Hann, *Developing Teacher Leaders: How Teacher Leadership Enhances School Success* (Thousand Oaks, CA: Corwin Press, 2002); James Spillane, Rich Halverson, and John Diamond, "Investigating School Leadership Practice: A Distributed Practice," *Educational Researcher* 30, no. 3 (2001): 23–28.

47. Anderson and Togneri, *Beyond Islands of Excellence;* Fullan, *Leadership and Sustainability*; "Research into Teacher Effectiveness: A Model of Teacher Effectiveness," report by Hay/McBer to the Department for Education and Employment, London, Englan, accessed September 7, 2008, from http://www.teachernet.gov.uk/_doc/1487/haymacber.doc; A. Hargreaves, "Revisiting Voice"; Andy Hargreaves and Dean Fink, "The Seven Principles of Sustainable Leadership," *Educational Leadership* 61, no. 7 (2004): 8–13; Elmore, "Hard Questions about Practice."

48. M. Huberman and Matthew Miles, *Innovation Up Close* (New York: Plenum, 1984); Ron Wideman, "How Secondary School Teachers Change Their Classrooms Practices" (Ph.D. diss., University of Toronto, 1991); Michael Fullan, *The New Meaning of Educational Change*, 3rd ed. (New York: Teachers College Press, 2001); Oakes et al, *Becoming Good American Schools.*

49. Cochran-Smith and Lytle, "Relationships of Knowledge and Practice"; Shirley M. Hord, *Evaluating Educational Innovation* (London: Croom Helm, 1987); Louis and Kruse, *Pro-*

fessionalism and Community; McLaughlin and Talbert, *Professional Communities*; Meier, *In Schools We Trust*; Jay Paredes Scribner, Karen Sunday Cockrell, Dan H. Cockrell, and Jerry W. Valentine, "Creating Professional Communities in Schools Through Organizational Learning: An Evaluation of a School Improvement Process," *Educational Administration Quarterly* 35, no. 1 (1999): 130–60.

50. Milbrey Wallin McLaughlin and Dana Mitra, *The Cycle of Inquiry as the Engine of School Reform: Lessons from the Bay Area School Reform Collaborative* (Stanford, CA: Center for Research on the Context of Teaching, 2003); K. S. Louis, *Organizing for School Change* (London: Taylor and Francis, 2006).

51. Jenny Lewis and Brian J. Caldwell, "Evidence-Based Leadership," *The Educational Forum* 69, no. 2 (2005): 192–202.

52. McLaughlin and Mitra, *The Cycle of Inquiry*; Wilfred Carr and Stephen Kemmis, *Becoming Critical: Education, Knowledge, and Action Research* (London: Falmer Press, 1985); Office for Standards in Education, Children's Services, and Skills (OFSTED), *Inspecting New Developments in the Secondary Curriculum 11–16 with Guidance of Self-Evaluation* (London: OFSTED, 2001); Eaker, Dufour, and Burnette, *Getting Started.*

53. Fullan, *Leadership and Sustainability*; D. H. Hargreaves, *Education Epidemic*; David Hopkins, *School Improvement for Real* (London: Routledge Falmer, 2001); McLaughlin and Mitra, *The Cycle of Inquiry*; National College for School Leadership (NCSL), *Making the Difference: Successful Leadership in Challenging Circumstances—A Practical Guide to What School Leaders Can Do to Improve and Energise Their Schools* (Nottingham, England: NCSL, 2003); Wiel Veugelers and Mary John O'Hair, *Network Learning for Education Change* (Buckingham: Open University Press, 2005); A. Lieberman and Diane R. Wood, "The National Writing Project," *Educational Leadership* 59, no. 6 (2002): 40–43; Donna E. Muncey and Patrick J. McQuillan, *Reform and Resistance in Schools and Classrooms: An Ethnographic View of the Coalition of Essential Schools* (New Haven, CT: Yale University Press, 1996).

54. Marvin Wideen and Ivy Pye, *The Struggle for Change: The Story of One School* (London: Falmer Press 1994).

55. Michael Fullan and Suzanne Stiegelbauer, *The New Meaning of Educational Change* (New York: Teachers College Press, 1991); Peter Marris, *Loss and Change* (London: Routledge, 1974); Heifetz and Linsky, *Leadership on the Line*; Meier, *In Schools We Trust*; Bryk and Schneider, *Trust in Schools.*

56. Andrew Gitlin and Frank Margonis, "The Political Aspects of Reform," *The American Journal of Education* 103, no. 4 (1995): 377–405; Andy Hargreaves and Michal Fullan, *What's Worth Fighting for Beyond Your School?* (New York: Teachers College Press, 1998); McLaughlin and Mitra, *The Cycle of Inquiry.*

57. Campbell, "Challenges in Fostering Ethical Knowledge."

58. Sarason, *The Predictable Failure*; A. Hargreaves, L. Earl, and M. Schmidt, "Four Perspectives on Classroom Assessment," *American Educational Research Journal* 39, no. 1 (2002): 69–100; Richard J. Stiggins, *Student-Centered Classroom Assessment* (Upper Saddle River, NJ: Merrill Prentice Hall, 1996); Donald A. Schön, *The Reflective Practitioner: How Professionals Think in Action* (New York: Basic Books, 1983); Anderson and Togneri, *Beyond Islands of Excellence*; A. Hargreaves, *Teaching in the Knowledge Society.*

59. McLaughlin and Talbert, *Professional Communities*; Michael Baker and Martha Foote, "Changing Spaces: Urban School Interrelationships and the Impact of Standards-Based

Reform," *Educational Administrative Quarterly* 42, no. 1 (2006): 90–123; Datnow, Hubbard, and Mehan, *Extending Educational Reform.*

60. A. Hargreaves, *Teaching in the Knowledge Society;* Richard Elmore and Deanna Burney, "Investing in Teacher Learning: Staff Development and Instructional Improvement," in *Teaching as the Learning Profession: Handbook of Policy and Practice,* ed. Linda Darling-Hammond and Gary Sykes (San Francisco: Jossey-Bass, 1999), 236–91; Fullan, *Leading in a Culture of Change;* Datnow, Hubbard, and Mehan, *Extending Educational Reform;* Lorna Earl, Benjamin Levin, Kenneth Leithwood, Michael Fullan, and Nancy Watson, *Watching and Learning,* vol. 3 (London: Department for Education and Skills, 2003).

61. Datnow, Hubbard, and Mehan, *Extending Educational Reform;* Earl et al., *Watching and Learning;* Kathleen K. Manzo, "Social Studies Losing Out to Reading and Math," *Education Week* 24, no. 27 (2004): 1–16.

CHAPTER 5. NONPROFIT ORGANIZATIONS AND THE PROMOTION OF EVIDENCE-BASED PRACTICE

1. Brian Rowan, "The Ecology of School Improvement: Notes on the School Improvement Industry in the United States," *Journal of Educational Change* 3 (2002): 283–314 (quote 284).

2. We drew on several literatures to shape and support our analysis. The first concerns the characteristics and behaviors of nonprofit organizations; the second concerns emerging trends and issues in the nonprofit sector. These literatures consist largely of descriptive, nonanalytical, and promotional works. We looked beyond these works to empirically and theoretically based reviews and syntheses and to a relatively small number of reports of original empirical research. In addition to these literatures, we looked to the literature on intermediary organizations—many of which are nonprofits—and the factors associated with their effectiveness working in education and other areas of human service provision. The literature on intermediaries provided additional insight into issues that might shape the work of nonprofits in promoting evidence-based practice in schools. To supplement these literatures, we identified several examples of nonprofit organizations working with schools that illustrate different aspects of our analysis. Some examples come from published reports; others are drawn from our own observations and experiences working at the state and local levels. Because of the varied nature of our "evidence," our findings and conclusions are necessarily speculative and provisional. They may best be considered propositions for discussion, study, and future research.

3. Robert E. Slavin, "The PET and the Pendulum: Faddism in Education and How to Stop It," *Phi Delta Kappan* 70, no. 10 (1989): 752–58.

4. Sam Stringfield, Steven M. Ross, and Lana Smith, *Bold Plans for School Restructuring: The New American Schools Designs* (Mahwah, NJ: Erlbaum, 1996).

5. U.S. Department of Education, "*No Child Left Behind*: Subpart 1—Reading First SEC. 1201," accessed August 30, 2004, from http://www.ed.gov/ESEA02/pg4.html#sec1208; Paul Shaker and Elizabeth E. Heilman, "The New Common Sense of Education: Advocacy Research versus Academic Authority," *Teachers College Record* 106, no. 7 (2004): 1444–70.

6. Chris Argyris and Donald A. Schon, *Organizational Learning II: Theory, Method, and Practice* (Reading, MA: Addison-Wesley, 1996).

7. Robert L. Crowson and William Boyd, "Coordinated Services for Children: Designing Arks for Storms and Seas Unknown," *American Journal of Education* 10, no. 2 (1993): 140–79; Claire E. Smrekar and Hanne B. Mawhinney, "Integrated Services: Challenges in Linking Schools, Families, and Communities," in *Handbook of Research on Educational Administration*, eds. J. Murphy and K. S. Louis (San Francisco: Jossey-Bass, 1999), 443–61.

8. Kanter and Summers, "Doing Well"; Lester M. Salamon, "The Changing Partnership Between the Voluntary Sector and the Welfare State," in *The Future of the Nonprofit Sector: Challenges, Changes, and Policy Considerations*, eds. Virginia A. Hodgkinson, Richard W. Lyman, and Associates (San Francisco: Jossey-Bass, 1989), 41–60; Dennis R. Young, "Beyond Tax Exemption: A Focus on Organizational Performance versus Legal Status," in Hodgkinson et al., *The Future of the Nonprofit Sector*, 183–99.

9. Burton A. Weisbrod, "The Complexities of Income Generation for Nonprofits," in Hodgkinson et al., *The Future of the Nonprofit Sector*, 103–22; James Douglas, "Political Theories of Nonprofit Organization," in Powell, *The Nonprofit Sector*, 43–54; Steinberg, "Nonprofit Organizations and the Market"; Thomas Silk, "The Legal Framework of the Nonprofit Sector in the United States," in Herman, *The Jossey-Bass Handbook*, 65–82.

10. Jeffrey Pfeffer and Gerald R. Salancik, *The External Control of Organizations* (New York: Harper and Row, 1978); Ferris and Grady, "Fading Distinctions"; Powell and Friedkin, "Organizational Change."

11. Weisbrod, "The Complexities of Income Generation,"171; Reid Lifset, "Cash Cows or Sacred Cows: The Politics of the Commercialization Movement," in Hodgkinson et al., *The Future of the Nonprofit Sector*, 140–67; Susan Rose-Ackerman, "Ideals Versus Dollars: Donors, Charity Managers, and Government Grants," *Journal of Political Economy* 95, no. 4 (1987): 810–23; Walter W. Powell and Rebecca Friedkin, "Organizational Change in Nonprofit Organizations," in Powell, *The Nonprofit Sector*.

12. Tuckman, "Competition, Commercialization"; Powell and Friedkin, "Organizational Change"; Hall, "Historical Perspectives"; Paul N. Ylvisaker, "Foundations and Nonprofit Organizations," in Powell, *The Nonprofit Sector*, 360–79; Burton A. Weisbrod, "The Nonprofit Mission and its Financing," *Journal of Policy Analysis and Management* 17, no. 2 (1998): 165–74.

13. James M. Ferris and Elizabeth Graddy, "Fading Distinctions Among the Nonprofit, Government, and For-Profit Sectors," in Hodgkinson et al., *The Future of the Nonprofit Sector*, 123–39; Powell and Friedkin, "Organizational Change."

14. Paul C. Light, *Making Nonprofits Work: A Report on the Tides of Nonprofit Management Reform* (Washington, DC: Brookings Institution Press, 2000), 7; Kirsten A. Grønberg and Curtis Child, "Illinois Nonprofits: A Profile of Charities and Advocacy Organizations" (Chicago: Donors Forum of Chicago, December 2003); Lester M. Salamon, *Partners in Public Service: Government-Nonprofit Relations in the Modern Welfare State* (Baltimore: Johns Hopkins University Press, 1995).

15. Light, *Making Nonprofits Work*; Salamon, *Partners in Public Service*; Salamon, "The Nonprofit Sector at a Crossroads."

16. Light, *Making Nonprofits Work*; Salamon, "The Nonprofit Sector at a Crossroads."

17. Salamon, "The Nonprofit Sector at a Crossroads"; Grønberg and Child, "Illinois Nonprofits"; Ferris and Grady, "Fading Distinctions"; Henry Hansmann, "The Two Nonprofit Sectors: Free for Service versus Donative Organizations," in Hodgkinson et al., *The Future of the Nonprofit Sector*, 91–102; Edward Skloot, "Enterprise and Commerce in Non-

profit Organizations," in Powell, *The Nonprofit Sector,* 360–79; Burton A. Weisbrod, "The Future of the Nonprofit Sector: Its Entwining with Private Enterprise and Government," *Journal of Policy Analysis and Management* 16, no. 4 (1997): 541–55; Salamon, *The Resilient Sector;* Tuckman, "Competition, Commercialization."

18. Douglas, "Political Theories"; Powell and Friedkin, "Organizational Change"; Light, *Making Nonprofits Work.*

19. Weisbrod, "The Future of the Nonprofit Sector"; Light, *Making Nonprofits Work;* Joseph Galaskiewicz and Wolfgang Bielefeld, *Nonprofit Organizations in an Age of Uncertainty: A Study of Organizational Change* (New York: Aldine de Gruyter, 1998); Ferris and Grady, "Fading Distinctions."

20. Kanter, "The Measurement of Organizational Effectiveness"; James A. Wooten, "The Emergence of Nonprofit Legal Education in New York: A Case Study of the Economic Theory of Nonprofit Organizations" (PONPO Working Paper No. 154, New Haven, CT: Yale University, Institution for Social and Policy Studies, Program on Non-Profit Organizations, May 1990); Paul C. Light, *Pathways to Nonprofit Excellence* (Washington, DC: Brookings Institution Press, 2002); and Paul C. Light, Elizabeth T. Hubbard, and Barbara Kibbe, "The Capacity Building Challenge" (New York: The Foundation Center, Improving Philanthropy Project, April 2004).

21. Douglas, "Political Theories"; Ferris and Grady, "Fading Distinctions"; Weisbrod, "The Nonprofit Mission"; Rosabeth M. Kanter and David V. Summers, "Doing Well While Doing Good: Dilemmas of Performance Measurement in Nonprofit Organizations and the Need For a Multiple-Constituency Approach," in Powell, *The Nonprofit Sector,* 154–66; Rosabeth M. Kanter, "The Measurement of Organizational Effectiveness, Productivity, Performance, and Success: Issues and Dilemmas in Service and Non-Profit Organizations" (PONPO Working Paper No. 8, New Haven, CT: Yale University, Institution for Social and Policy Studies, Program on Non-Profit Organizations, 1979).

22. Michael Useem, "Corporate Philanthropy," in Powell, *The Nonprofit Sector,* 340–59.

23. Useem, "Corporate Philanthropy."

24. Douglas, "Political Theories"; Powell and Friedkin, "Organizational Change"; Salamon, "Partners in Public Service"; Howard P. Tuckman, "Competition, Commercialization, and the Evolution of Nonprofit Organizational Structures," *Journal of Policy Analysis and Management* 17, no. 2 (1998): 175–94.

25. Kanter and Summers, "Doing Well"; Powell and Friedkin, "Organizational Change"; Young, "Beyond Tax Exemption"; Lifset, "Cash Cows or Sacred Cows"; Dennis R. Young, "Commercialization in Nonprofit Social Service Associations: Its Character, Significance, and Rationale," *Journal of Policy Analysis and Management* 17, no. 2 (1998): 278–97.

26. Kanter and Summers, "Doing Well"; Mark S. Granovetter, "The Strength of Loose Ties," *American Journal of Sociology* 78, no. 5 (1973): 1360–80.

27. Lester M. Salamon, "The Nonprofit Sector at a Crossroads: The Case of America," *Voluntas: International Journal of Voluntary and Nonprofit Organizations* 10, no. 1 (1999): 5–23; Skloot, "Enterprise and Commerce."

28. Lester M. Salamon, "The Nonprofit Sector and the Evolution of the American Welfare State," in Herman, *The Jossey-Bass Handbook,* 83–99; Tuckman, "Competition, Commercialization"; Powell and Friedkin, "Organizational Change."

29. Hansmann, "The Two Nonprofit Sectors"; and Lester M. Salamon, *The Resilient Sector: The State of Nonprofit America* (Washington, DC: Brookings Institution Press, 2003).

30. Richard Steinberg, "Nonprofit Organizations and the Market," in Powell, *The Nonprofit Sector*, 118–38.
31. Rowan, "The Ecology of School Improvement"; Salamon, "The Nonprofit Sector"; Salamon, *The Resilient Sector*; Tuckman, "Competition, Commercialization."
32. Kronley and Handley, "Reforming Relationships."
33. Ibid.
34. Galaskiewicz and Bielefeld, *Nonprofit Organizations in an Age of Uncertainty*.
35. Tom B. Corcoran, Clair Gerry, and Gail Passantino, "Professional Development in Kentucky: Needs and Objectives" (Lexington, KY: Partnership for Kentucky Schools, 2001).

CHAPTER 6: K–12 EDUCATION AND THE ROLE OF FOR-PROFIT PROVIDERS

1. Andy Hargreaves, *Teaching in the Knowledge Society* (Berkshire, England: McGraw-Hill, 2003).
2. Phyllis Blumenfeld, Elliot Soloway, Ron Marx, Joseph Krajcik, Mark Guzdial, and Anne-Marie Palincsar, "Motivating Project-Based Learning: Sustaining the Doing, Supporting the Learning," *Educational Psychologist* 26, nos. 3 & 4 (1991): 369–98; James P. Spillane and Nancy E. Jennings, "Aligned Instructional Policy and Ambitious Pedagogy: Exploring Instructional Reform from the Classroom Perspective," *Teachers College Record* 98, no. 3 (1997): 449–81.
3. The New London Group (Courtney Cazden, Bill Cope, Mary Kalantzis et al.), "A Pedagogy of Multiliteracies: Designing Social Futures," *Harvard Educational Review* 66, no.1 (1996): 60–92; Bill Cope and Mary Kalantzis, eds, *Multiliteracies: Literacy Learning and the Design of Social Futures* (London: Routledge, 2000).
4. Dan C. Lortie, *Schoolteacher* (Chicago: University of Chicago Press, 1975); Karl E. Weick, "Educational Organizations as Loosely Coupled Systems," *Administrative Science Quarterly* 21, no. 1 (1976): 1–19.
5. Richard R. Nelson, "On the Uneven Evolution of Human Know-How," *Research Policy* 32, no. 6 (2003): 909–922; Richard R. Nelson and Katherine Nelson, "Technology, Institutions, and Innovation systems," *Research Policy* 31, no. 2 (2002): 265–72; Nathan Rosenberg, "Science, Invention and Economic Growth," *The Economic Journal* 84, no. 333 (1974): 90–108.
6. National Research Council, *How People Learn: Brain, Mind, Experience, and School*, Exp. ed. (Washington, DC: National Academies Press, 2000), available at http://www.nap.edu/html/howpeople1/; Richard Murnane and Richard Nelson, "Production and Innovation When Techniques are Tacit: The Case of Education," *Journal of Economic Behavior and Organization* 5, no. 3-4 (1984): 353–73; Richard R. Nelson, "On the Uneven Evolution of Human Know-How."
7. *DIAGNOSER: Fact-Based Instruction*, accessed November 1, 2008, from http://depts.washington.edu/huntlab/diagnoser/facet.html (accessed November 1, 2008).
8. R. Nelson, "On the Uneven Evolution of Human Know-How."
9. David E. Rumelhart and Donald A. Norman, "Accretion, Tuning, and Restructuring: Three Modes of Learning," in *Semantic Factors in Cognition*, ed. John R. Cotton and Roberta L. Klatzky (Hillsdale, NJ: Erlbaum, 1978); Earl B. Hunt and Jim Minstrell, "A Cognitive Approach to the Teaching of Physics," in *Classroom Lessons: Integrating Cognitive Theory and Classroom Practice*, ed. Kate McGilly (Cambridge, MA: MIT Press/Bradford

Books, 1996), 51–74; Jim Minstrell, "Facets of Students Knowledge and Relevant Instruction," in *Proceedings of an International Workshop—Research in Physics Learning: Theoretical Issues and Empirical Studies*, ed. Reinders Duit, Fred Goldberg, and Hans Niedderer
(Kiel, Germany: The Institute for Science Education, 1982), 110–28; Earl Hunt and Jim
Minstrell, "The DIAGNOSER Project: Assessment in the Service of Learning," in *Proceedings of the 30th Conference of the International Association for Educational Assessment* (Philadelphia, PA: Educational Testing Service, June 2004).

10. For example, http://tappedin.org/tappedin/ accessed November 1, 2008; Jean Lave and
Etienne Wenger, *Situated Learning: Legitimate Peripheral Participation* (Cambridge, England: University of Cambridge Press, 1991).

11. Bonnie Nardi, ed., *Context and Consciousness: Activity Theory and Human-Computer Interaction* (Cambridge, MA: MIT Press, 1996).

12. Clayton Christenson, *The Innovator's Dilemma: When New Technologies Cause Great Firms
to Fail* (Boston, MA: Harvard Business School Press, 1997); Clayton Christensen, Curtis
Johnson, and Michael Horn, *Disrupting Class: How Disruptive Innovation Will Change the
Way the World Learns* (Boston, MA: Harvard Business School Press, 2008).

13. Guilbert C. Hentschke, "Characteristics of Growth in the Education Industry: Illustra-
tions from U.S. Education Businesses," in *New Arenas of Education Politics: The Impact of
International Organizations and Markets on Educational Policymaking*, ed. Kathrin Leuze,
Kerstin Martens, and Alessandra Rusconi (London: Palgrave Macmillan, 2007).

14. Despite this fact, growing privatization of the education industry is likely to accelerate
the emerging role of the types of for-profit education firms discussed in this chapter. See
Guilbert Hentschke and Priscilla Wohlstetter, "K–12 Education in a Broader Privatization Context," *Educational Policy* 21, no.1 (2007): 297–307.

15. Drawn from Ed Source 2006, p. 9, accessed November 1, 2008, from http://www.
edsource.org/; Susanna Loeb, Anthony Bryk, and Eric Hanushek, "Getting Down to
Facts: School Finance and Governance in California" (Institute for Research on Education Policy and Practice, Stanford University, March 2007).

16. Matt Stein, *Making Sense of the Data: Overview of the K–12 Data Management and Analysis Market* (Boston, MA: Eduventures, 2003), 19; *The Eduventures 100: Leading Businesses
Transforming the Education Economy* (Boston, MA: Eduventures.com, 2003).

17. Stein, *Making Sense of the Data*, 38.

18. State adoption of a text greatly increases demand, and postponing an adoption decision
is tantamount to a decision not to adopt. *Education Quarterly Investment Report, March
2001* (Boston, MA: Eduventures, 2001), available at http://www.interversity.org/lists/
arn-l/archives/May2000/msg00771.html.

19. For an extensive treatment on the role of investment capital and innovation and the
resulting "destructive" as well as creative forces they unleash, see Richard Foster and
Sarah Kaplan, *Creative Destruction: From Built-to-Last to Built-to-Perform* (London: Financial Times/Prentice Hall, 2001).

20. *Education Quarterly Investment Report, March 2001*.

21. See Foster and Kaplan, *Creative Destruction*.

22. Hentschke, "Characteristics of Growth in the Education Industry."

23. Louis M. Gomez, Barry Fishman, and Roy Pea, "The CoVis Project: Building a Large-
Scale Science Education Testbed," *Interactive Learning Environments* 6, no. 1–2 (1998):
59–92.

24. Bill Bavin and John McLaughlin, "A Proposal to Create a Perpetual Venture Fund for Comprehensive School Improvement Solutions" (Alexandria, VA, 2003).

25. These organizations tend to be lead by unusually entrepreneurial educators. See Jeffrey Fromm, Guilbert Hentschke, and Todd Kern, "Education Leader as Educational Entrepreneur: Managing the Educational Mission within and across the Economic Sectors," in *Handbook of Educational Leadership and Management,* ed. Brent Davies and John West-Burnham (London: Pearson Education, 2003), 291–303.

26. Institute of Education Sciences, What Works Clearinghouse, accessed November 1, 2008, from http://ies.ed.gov/ncee/wwc/.

CHAPTER 7: INSTRUCTIONAL RESEARCH AND THE IMPROVEMENT OF PRACTICE

1. See Roschelle et al., "Scaling up SimCalc"; Roschelle et al., *Extending the SimCalc Approach to Grade 8 Mathematics*; and Jeremy Roschelle, Deborah Tatar, Nicole Shechtman, Stephen Hegedus, Bill Hopkins, Jennifer Knudsen, and Antoinette Stroter, *Can A Technology-Enhanced Curriculum Improve Student Learning of Important Mathematics? Overview of Findings from the Seventh-Grade Year 1 Study* (No. 1) (Menlo Park, CA: SRI International, 2007).

2. See Fritz Mosher and Michael Smith, "Education from the Perspective of Federal Policymakers and Foundation Grant Makers," in this volume.

3. For an extended discussion of the relationships between theories, models, and the phenomena being modeled, see Alan H. Schoenfeld, "Toward a Theory of Teaching-in-Context," *Issues in Education* 4, no. 1 (1998): 1–94. For a related discussion of *quality* in educational research, see Dennis C. Phillips, *A Quixotic Quest? Philosophical Issues in Assessing the Quality of Education Research,* paper presented at the annual meeting of the American Educational Research Association, San Diego, CA, April 2004.

4. For different approaches to research, see Donald E. Stokes, *Pasteur's Quadrant: Basic Science and Technical Innovation* (Washington, DC: Brookings Institute, 1997).

5. I should issue an important caveat at this point. The main focus on this chapter is on the ability of schools to help all students learn academic subject matter. While this is a major goal of contemporary schooling—and one that needs work!—it is hardly a school's only function, nor is it uncontroversial. As Patricia Albjerg Graham noted when she reviewed a draft of this chapter, "Education in America . . . has been quite effective, not at making everyone knowledgeable in academic subjects at a high level, but rather at what it has tried to do over the last century: assimilate immigrant children to make them loyal and efficient participants in the society; facilitate social, psychological and emotional adjustment of children by making the school routine less rigid and more encompassing of their personalities; and provide access to educational experiences for groups of children previously denied them (disabled, non-English speaking, low income, and children of color)." This paper does not address those issues, or the philosophical issues they raise—questions pertaining to the purposes of schooling. That is partly a matter of space, partly a matter of the current political context, and partly a matter of the author's limitations.

6. Arthur Powell, *The Uncertain Profession: Harvard and the Search for Educational Authority* (Cambridge, MA: Harvard University Press, 1980); Ellen C. Lagemann, *An Elusive Science: The Troubling History of Educational Research* (Chicago: University of Chicago Press, 2000).

7. Jeremy Kilpatrick, "Variables and Methodologies in Research on Problem Solving," in *Mathematical Problem Solving: Papers from a Research Workshop*, ed. Larry Hatfield (Columbus, OH: ERIC, 1978); and Hidenori Fujita, "How Craft Knowledge of Teaching Is Generated and Disseminated in Japan: Collaborative Culture, Organizational Learning, and Their Institutional Foundations," in this volume, provides a similar story from Japan.

8. John Flavell, "Metacognitive Aspects of Problem Solving," in *The Nature of Intelligence*, ed. Lauren B. Resnick (Hillsdale, NJ: Erlbaum, 1976), 231–36.

9. For example, K. Anders Ericsson and Herbert A. Simon, "Verbal Reports as Data," *Psychological Review* 87, no. 3 (1980): 215–51.

10. David P. Ausubel, "The Use of Advance Organizers in the Learning and Retention of Meaningful Verbal Material," *Journal of Educational Psychology* 51 (1960): 267–72.

11. See Benjamin S. Bloom, Max D. Englehart, Edward J. Furst, Walker H. Hill, and David R. Krathwohl, *Taxonomy of Educational Objectives: The Classification of Educational Goals, Handbook I: Cognitive Domain* (New York: Longman, 1956).

12. Howard Gardner, *The Mind's New Science* (New York: Basic Books, 1987).

13. Ann L. Brown, "Metacognition, Executive Control, Self-Regulation, and Other More Mysterious Mechanisms," in *Metacognition, Motivation, and Understanding*, ed. Franz Weinert and Rainer Kluwe (Hillsdale, NJ: Erlbaum,1987), 65–116; Flavell, "Metacognitive Aspects"; Alan H. Schoenfeld, *Mathematical Problem Solving* (Orlando, FL: Academic Press, 1985).

14. Schoenfeld, *Mathematical Problem Solving*; see also Cognition and Technology Group at Vanderbilt, "The Jasper Series as an Example of Anchored Instruction: Theory, Program Description, and Assessment Data," *Educational Psychologist* 27, no. 3 (1992): 291–315.

15. For detail, see Alan H. Schoenfeld, "Learning to Think Mathematically: Problem Solving, Metacognition, and Sense-Making in Mathematics," in *Handbook for Research on Mathematics Teaching and Learning*, ed. Douglas A. Grouws (New York: MacMillan, 1992), 334–70.

16. *Curriculum and Evaluation Standards for School Mathematics* (Reston, VA: National Council of Teachers of Mathematics, 1989).

17. Alan H. Schoenfeld, "Making Mathematics Work for All Children: Issues of Standards, Testing, and Equity," *Educational Researcher* 31, no. 1 (2002): 13–25; and Philip Uri Treisman, *What Is Known about Effective Ways for Students to Make the Transition from Arithmetic to Algebra?* presentation at the conference of the Mathematical Sciences Research Institute, Berkeley, CA, May 2008.

18. Sharon L. Senk and Denisse R. Thompson, eds., *Standards-Based School Mathematics Curricula: What Are They? What Do Students Learn?* (Mahwah, NJ: Erlbaum, 2003).

19. See Patricia A. Alexander and Philip H. Winne, eds., *Handbook of Educational Psychology*, 2nd ed. (Mahwah, NJ: Erlbaum, 2006); and John D. Bransford, Ann L. Brown, and Rodney R. Cocking, eds., *How People Learn: Brain, Mind, Experience, and School* (Washington, DC: National Academies Press, 1999).

20. See Schoenfeld, "Teaching-in-Context"; Bransford et al., "Learning Theories and Education."

21. *Recommendations Regarding Research Priorities: An Advisory Report to the National Educational Research Policy and Priorities Board* (New York: National Academy of Education, 1999); and Alan H. Schoenfeld, "Looking Toward the 21st Century: Challenges of Educational Theory and Practice," *Educational Researcher* 28, no. 7 (1999): 4–14; Stokes, *Pasteur's Quadrant*.

22. *Strategic Plan 2002–2007* (Washington, DC: U.S. Department of Education, 2002), 51.
23. As of June 27, 2004, video of the conference could still be accessed at http://www.excel-gov.org/displayContent.asp?NewsItemID=4543&Keyword=prppcEvidence; *Rigorous Evidence: The Key to Progress in Education? Lessons from Medicine, Welfare, and Other Fields. Proceedings of a Forum with the Honorable Rod Paige, U.S. Secretary of Education* (Washington, DC: Council for Excellence in Government, 2002).
24. For example, Carl Kaestle, "The Awful Reputation of Education Research," *Educational Researcher* 22, no. 1 (1993): 23–31.
25. Discussed in greater depth in Hugh Burkhardt and Alan H. Schoenfeld, "Improving Educational Research: Toward a More Useful, More Influential, and Better Funded Enterprise," *Educational Researcher* 32, no. 9 (2003): 3–14.
26. Note that more established fields manage to handle their disputes in ways such that the foundations of the field are not challenged. Physics and medicine change, but not in ways that bring the robustness of the fields into doubt. Indeed, one physicist told me that battles are buried when physicists go to Congress to seek funding for big projects.
27. Richard J. Shavelson and Lisa Towne, eds., *Scientific Research in Education* (Washington, DC: National Academy Press, 2003).
28. Alan H. Schoenfeld, "Research Methods in (Mathematics) Education," in *Handbook of International Research in Mathematics Education*, ed. Lyn D. English (Mahwah, NJ: Erlbaum, 2002), 466–67.
29. Burkhardt and Schoenfeld, "Improving Educational Research," 8.
30. For exceptions, see K. Anders Ericsson, Neil Charness, Robert R. Hoffman, and Paul J. Feltovich, eds., *The Cambridge Handbook of Expertise and Expert Performance* (New York: Cambridge University Press, 2006); and Ericsson, ed., *The Measurement and Development of Professional Expertise*.
31. Judith L. Green, Gregory Camilli, and Patricia B. Elmore, *Handbook of Complementary Methods in Education Research* (Washington, DC: American Educational Research Association and Lawrence Erlbaum Associates, 2006).
32. David F. Larabee, "The Peculiar Problems of Preparing Educational Researchers," *Educational Researcher* 32, no. 3 (2003): 13–22.
33. Having said this, I should also note that such disconnects may be more common than is generally acknowledged. Research is an arcane exercise, and most beginning graduate students know very little about it. That was the case for me as I began doing mathematics research in graduate school; that was the case for my wife, who said after obtaining her Ph.D. in French that had she known that the Ph.D. was about literature rather than about the language, she might have majored in English.
34. Phillips, "A Quixotic Quest?" 20.
35. Ibid., 8.
36. For a discussion of alternatives, see Alan H. Schoenfeld, "The Core, the Canon, and the Development of Research Skills: Issues in the Preparation of Education Researchers," in *Issues in Education Research: Problems and Possibilities*, ed. Ellen C. Lagemann and Lee S. Shulman (San Francisco: Jossey-Bass, 1999), 166–202.
37. For a description of the Science of Learning Centers program and links to each of the six funded centers, see the National Science Foundation's website at http://www.nsf.gov/funding/pgm_summ.jsp?pims_id=5567.

38. For example, David C. Berliner, "Educational Research: The Hardest Science of All," *Educational Researcher* 31, no. 8 (2003): 18–20; D. F. Labaree, "Educational Researchers: Living with a Lesser Form of Knowledge," *Educational Researcher* 27, no. 8 (1998): 4–12; D. C. Phillips, "A Quixotic Quest?"

39. Geraldine Clifford and James W. Guthrie, *Ed School* (Chicago: University of Chicago Press, 1988); Lagemann, *An Elusive Science*; and Powell, *The Uncertain Profession;* Lagemann and Shulman, *Issues in Education Research*; Shavelson and Towne, *Scientific Research in Education*; Ralph Tyler, "The Field of Educational Research," in *The Training and Nurture of Educational Researchers*, ed. Egon G. Guba and Stanley M. Elam (Bloomington, IN: Phi Delta Kappa, 1965), 1–12.

40. Burkhardt and Schoenfeld, "Improving Educational Research," 3.

41. Bransford, Brown, and Cocking, *How People Learn;* John D. Bransford and Marcia K. Johnson, "Contextual Prerequisites for Understanding: Some Investigations of Comprehension and Recall," *Journal of Verbal Learning and Verbal Behavior* 4, no. 2 (1972): 717–26.

42. For example, J. D. Bransford, "Preparing People for Rapidly Changing Environments," *Journal of Engineering Education* 96, no. 1 (2007): 1–3; Daniel L. Schwartz and John D. Bransford, "A Time for Telling," *Cognition and Instruction* 16, no. 4 (1998): 475–522; Daniel L. Schwartz and Taylor Martin, "Inventing to Prepare for Future Learning: The Hidden Efficiency of Encouraging Original Student Production in Statistics Instruction," *Cognition and Instruction* 22, no. 2 (2004): 129–84.

43. For example, John Seeley Brown and Richard R. Burton, "Diagnostic Models for Procedural Bugs in Basic Mathematical Skills," *Cognitive Science* 2 (1978): 155–92; and Pamela Grossman, Alan Schoenfeld, and Carol Lee, "Teaching Subject Matter," in Darling-Hammond and Bransford, *Preparing Teachers for a Changing World*, 201–31.

44. See "Theme Issue: Scientific Research in Education," *Educational Researcher* 32, no. 1 (2003), especially Paul Cobb, Jere Confrey, Andrea diSessa, Richard Lehrer, and Leona Schauble, "Design Experiments in Educational Research," 9–13.

45. See Burkhardt and Schoenfeld, "Improving Educational Research." For worked-out examples of the full process, see Alan H. Schoenfeld, "Method," in *Second Handbook of Research on Mathematics Teaching and Learning*, ed. Frank K. Lester (New York: MacMillan, 2007); for discussions of experimental methods, see *Using Statistics Effectively in Mathematics Education Research* (Washington, DC: American Statistical Association, 2007); and *Educational Researcher* 37, no. 1 (2008), especially Finbarr Sloan, "Through the Looking Glass: Experiments, Quasi-Experiments, and the Medical Model," 41–46.

46. See Cobb et al., "Design Experiments."

47. Roschelle et al., "Scaling up SimCalc"; Roschelle et al., *Extending the SimCalc Approach*; and Roschelle et al., *Technology-Enhanced Curriculum;* Jeremy D. Finn and Charles M. Achilles, "Tennessee's Class Size Study: Findings, Implications, Misconceptions," *Educational Evaluation and Policy Analysis* 21, no. 2, (1999): 97–109.

48. The What Works Clearinghouse (WWC) is intended by the Institute of Educational Sciences to provide a high-quality vetting mechanism of this type—a "Good Housekeeping Seal of Approval" for educational interventions. It is a federally funded effort to determine the adequacy of research studies and, in effect, "certify" educational and other interventions as having been rigorously validated. See http://www.w-w-c.org.49.

For example, the Shell Centre at the University of Nottingham in England and the Freudenthal Institute at the University of Utrecht in the Netherlands.

50. "High Performance Learning Communities," accessed August 9, 2008, from http://www.lrdc.pitt.edu/hplc/hplc.html.

51. Lauren B. Resnick, personal communication, April 13, 2004.

52. Strategic Education Research Partnership, "Boston Field Site," accessed August 9, 2008, from http://www.serpinstitute.org/content/page.php?cat=4&content_id=17; Strategic Education Research Partnership, "San Francisco Field Site," accessed August 9, 2008, from http://www.serpinstitute.org/content/page.php?cat=4&content_id=20.

53. Anthony Bryk, personal communication, March 24, 2005.

54. U.S. House Committee on Science, "Unlocking Our Future: Toward a New National Science Policy: A Report to Congress by the House Committee on Science" (Washington, DC: House Committee on Science, 1998), 46.

55. *Smithsonian* (June 1999): 14–15.

56. Lortie, *Schoolteacher;* however, see Andy Hargreaves and Corrie Stone-Johnson, "Evidence-Informed Change and the Practice of Teaching," and Fujita, "How Craft Knowledge of Teaching is Developed in Japan," both in this volume.

57. For a description of how such contexts hamstring teachers, see Hilda Borko, Margaret Eisenhart, Catherine A. Brown, Robert G. Underhill, Doug Jones, and Patricia C. Agard, "Learning to Teach Hard Mathematics: Do Novice Teachers and Their Instructors Give Up Too Easily?" *Journal for Research in Mathematics Education* 23, no. 3 (1992): 194–222. Note also the impact of the "high stakes" tests mandated by the No Child Left Behind Act in terms of coercing teachers to "teach to the test," whether or not the test is very good or aligned with the curriculum.

58. For details and for other examples, see Alan H. Schoenfeld, "Working with Schools: The Story of a Mathematics Education Collaboration," *American Mathematical Monthly* (March 2009).

59. Catherine E. Snow, M. Susan Burns, and Peg Griffin, eds., *Preventing Reading Difficulties in Young Children* (Washington, DC: National Academies Press, 1998); and M. Susan Burns, Peg Griffin, and Catherine E. Snow, eds., *Starting Out Right* (Washington, DC: National Academies Press, 1999).

60. Shavelson and Towne, *Scientific Research in Education.*

61. I was the "senior content adviser" for WWC's mathematics curriculum studies from its inception in early 2003. Some of the events described below led me to resign in early 2005. This is also described in detail in Alan H. Schoenfeld, "What Doesn't Work: The Challenge and Failure of the What Works Clearinghouse to Conduct Meaningful Reviews of Studies of Mathematics Curricula," *Educational Researcher* 35, no. 2 (2006): 13–21.

62. What Works Clearinghouse, accessed April 1, 2006, from http://www.w-w-c.org.

63. Schoenfeld, "What Doesn't Work."

64. Jim Ridgway, Rita Crust, Hugh Burkhardt, Sandra Wilcox, Linda Fisher, and David Foster, *The MARS Report on the 2000 Tests* (San Jose, CA: Mathematics Assessment Collaborative, 2000); Schoenfeld, "What Doesn't Work"; Schoenfeld, "Method."

65. National Academy of Education, *Recommendations Regarding Research Priorities.*

66. Schoenfeld, "Working with Schools."

67. Unfortunately, such funding is in jeopardy because of a general diminution of research-related funding in NSF's Division of Education and Human Resources.

CHAPTER 8. HOW CRAFT KNOWLEDGE OF TEACHING IS GENERATED AND DISSEMINATED IN JAPAN

1. OECD Programme for International Student Assessment (PISA) accessed August 27, 2008, from http://www.pisa.oecd.org/pages/0,2987,en_32252351_32235731_1_1_1_1 _1,00.html; International Association for the Evaluation of Educational Achievement (IEA) Trends in International Mathematics and Science Study (TIMSS), accessed August 27, 2008, from http://timss.bc.edu/index.html#.

2. Organization for Economic Co-operation and Development, *Education at a Glance: OECD Indicators* (Paris: OECD, 2005).

3. "Formal Education," Ministry of Education, Culture, Sports, Science, and Technology, accessed August 27, 2008, from http://www.mext.go.jp/english/org/f_formal_16.htm.

4. MEXT 2004 Teacher Survey Statistics Report, Ministry of Education, Culture, Sports, Science and Technology, Heisei 16nendo GakkouKyoinTokeiChosa, accessed August 27, 2008, from http://www.mext.go.jp/b_menu/toukei/001/002/2004/index.htm.

5. National Commission on Teaching and America's Future, *No Dream Denied: A Pledge to America's Children*, accessed August 31, 2008, from http://www.nctaf.org/documents/ no-dream-denied_full-report.pdf.

6. Harold W. Stevenson and James W. Stigler, *The Learning Gap* (New York: Summit, 1992). See also Hidenori Fujita, "KyoikuKaikaku to Kiki-ni-Hinsuru Nihon no Kyoiku [Education Reform and Japan's Education at Risk]," in *GakkoKyoiku Kenkyu* [*Research Journal of School Education*] 18 (Tokyo: KyoikuKaihatsu Kenkyusho, 2003), 8–23; Hidenori Fujita, *GimuKyoiku o Toinaosu* [*Reappraisal of Compulsory Education*] (Tokyo: Chikuma Shobou, 2005).

7. MEXT 2004 Teacher Survey Statistics Report.

8. Hidenori Fujita, "The Qualifications of the Teaching Force in Japan," in *A Comparative Study of Teacher Preparation and Qualifications in Six Nations*, ed. Richard M. Ingersoll (Consortium for Policy Research in Education; Philadelphia, PA: University of Pennsylvania , 2007), 41–54.

9. A. Hargreaves, *Changing Teachers*; Andy Hargreaves, "Time and Teachers' Work: An Analysis of the Intensification Thesis (Teachers' Work Load Problem)," *Teachers College Record* 94, no. 1 (1992): 87–108; Hidenori Fujita, *Kyoiku-Kaikaku* [*Education Reform*] (Tokyo: Iwanami Shoten, 1997); Margaret Wilkin and Derek Sankey, *Collaboration and Transition in Initial Teacher Training* (London: Kogan Page, 1994); Gordon A. Donaldson and David R. Sanderson, *Working Together in Schools: A Guide for Educators* (Thousand Oaks, CA: Corwin Press, 1996); Geoff Troman, "Models of the Good Teachers: Defining and Redefining Teacher Quality," in *Contemporary Issues in Teaching and Learning*, ed. Peter Woods (Buckingham, England: Open University Press, 1996); Gill Nicholls, *Collaborative Change in Education* (London: Kogan Page, 1997); H. Fujita, "Kyosei-Kuhkan toshiteno Gakkou [School as a Symbiotic Learning Space]," in *Manabiau Kyodoutai* [*Learning Community*], ed. Y. Saeki, H. Fujita and M. Sato (Tokyo: Tokyo-Daigaku Shuppankai 1996), 1–51; H. Fujita, "Towareru Kyoiku no Koukyosei to Kyoshi no Yakuwari [Issues on the Public Nature of Education and Roles of Teacher]," in *Kyoshi no Genzai, Kyoshoku no*

Mirai [*The Present of Teachers and the Future of Teaching Prpfession*], ed. S. Yufu (Tokyo: Kyoiku Shuppan 1999), 180–204; Imazu Koujirou, "Gakkou no KyodouBunka: Nihon to Oubei no Hikaku [Collaborative Culture of School: A Comparison of Japan and the West]," in H. Fujita and K. Shimizu, eds., *HendouShakai no-nakano Kyoiku, Chishiki, Kenryoku* [*Education, Knowledge and Power in Changing Society*] (Tokyo: Shinyo-sha 2000), 300–321.

10. Catherine Lewis and Ineko Tsuchida, "Planned Educational Change in Japan: The Shift to Student-Centered Elementary Science," *Journal of Educational Policy* 12 (1997): 313–31; Clea Fernandez, "Learning from Japanese Approaches to Professional Development: The Case of Lesson Study," *Journal of Teacher Education* 53 (2002): 393; Catherine Lewis, "Does Lesson Study Have a Future in the United States?" *Nagoya Journal of Education and Human Development* 1 (January 2002): 1–23; James W. Stigler and James Hiebert, *The Teaching Gap: Best Ideas from the World's Teachers for Improving Education in the Classroom* (New York: Simon & Schuster, 1999).

11. Stevenson and Stigler, *The Learning Gap*, 177.

12. Chris Argyris and Donald A. Schon, *Organizational Learning* (Reading, MA: Addison-Wesley, 1978); and Chris Argyris and Donald A. Schon, *Organizational Learning II* (Reading, MA: Addison-Wesley, 1996).

CHAPTER 9: TOWARD A DEEPER UNDERSTANDING OF THE EDUCATIONAL ELEPHANT

1. See, for example, Bransford, Brown, and Cocking, *How People Learn;* Suzanne Donovan and John Bransford, eds., *How Students Learn: History, Mathematics, and Science in the Classroom* (Washington, DC: National Academies Press, 2005); Richard A. Duschl, Heidi A. Schweingruber and Andrew W. Shouse, eds., *Taking Science to School: Learning and Teaching Science in Grades K–8* (Washington, DC: National Academies Press, 2007).

2. The importance of theories of action is explained in Janet A. Weiss, "Theoretical Foundations of Policy Intervention," in *Public Management Reform and Innovation*, ed. H. George Frederickson and Jocelyn M. Johnston (Tuscaloosa: University of Alabama Press, 1999), 37–69.

3. See Sharon L. Nichols and David C. Berliner, *Collateral Damage: How High-Stakes Testing Corrupts America's Schools* (Cambridge, MA: Harvard University Press, 2007) for an extensive treatment.

4. Paul Tough, "A Teachable Moment," *New York Times Magazine*, August 14, 2008.

5. See Atul Gawande, Better: A Surgeon's Notes on Performance (New York: Metropolitan Books, 2007), for a discussion of a performance culture in medicine.

6. James S. Coleman, Ernest Q. Campbell, Carol J. Hobson, James McPartland, Alexander M. Mood, Frederic D. Weinfeld, and Robert L. York, *Equality of Educational Opportunity* (Washington, DC: Government Printing Office, 1966).

7. Stephen Raudenbush, "Advancing Educational Policy by Advancing Research in Education," *American Educational Research Journal* 45, no. 1 (2008): 206–230.

8. Sandra M. Nutley, Isabel Walter, and Huw T. O. Davies, *Using Evidence: How Research Can Inform Public Services* (Bristol, England: Policy Press, 2007). See Andy Hargreaves and Corrie Stone-Johnson, "Evidence-Informed Change and the Practice of Teaching," in this volume.

9. Bill Penuel, personal communication, September 5, 2008.

10. See LeAnn Sawyers, Patricia Scharer, and Lisa Walker, "Designing a Web-Based Professional Development Support System for School-Based Literacy Coaches," in *Proceedings of Society for Information Technology and Teacher Education International Conference*, ed. Caroline Crawford et al. (Chesapeake, VA: AACE, 2006), 2671–78.

11. A review of this literature identifies differences in language, time horizon, responsiveness to constituencies, written versus oral communication, concern with validity and rigor, and lack of understanding about one another's work environments. See Carol H. Weiss, Erin Murphy-Graham, Anthony Petrosino, and Allison Gandhi, "The Fairy Godmother and Her Warts: Making the Dream of Evidence-Based Policy Come True," *American Journal of Evaluation* 29, no. 1 (2008): 29–47.

12. Anthony S. Bryk and Louis M. Gomez, *Reshaping Schools Toward Evidence-Based Cultures: Learning Through Design*, paper presented at the annual meeting of the American Educational Research Association, Chicago, IL, 2007.

13. National Research Council, *How People Learn: Brain, Mind, Experience, and School* (Expanded Edition). (Washington, DC: National Academy Press, 2000), available at http://www.nap.edu/html/howpeople1/.

14. Ibid.

15. David K. Cohen, Stephen W. Raudenbush, and Deborah B. Ball, "Resources, Instruction, and Research," *Educational Evaluation and Policy Analysis* 25, no. 2 (2003): 119–42.

16. Ibid.

17. See, for example, Schwartz, Bransford, and Sears, "Efficiency and Innovation in Transfer"; John D. Bransford and Daniel L. Schwartz, "Rethinking Transfer: A Simple Proposal with Multiple Implications," *Review of Research in Education* 24 (1999): 61–100; Partners in Learning, *School Leader Development: Building 21st Century Schools* (Redmond, WA: Microsoft Corporation, 2005), CD-ROM; and Partners in Learning, *School Leader Development: Assessing 21st Century Learning* (Redmond, WA: Microsoft Corporation, 2006), CD-ROM.

18. Michael J. Feuer, Lisa Towne, and Richard J. Shavelson, "Scientific Culture and Educational Research," *Educational Researcher* 31, no. 8 (2002): 4–14, 9.

19. Blue Ribbon Commission on Testing and Accountability, "Report to the North Carolina State Board of Education," January 2008.

20. Fred M. Newmann and Gary G. Wehlage, *Successful School Restructuring: A Report to the Public and Educators* (Washington, DC: American Federation of Teachers, 1995).

21. Anthony S. Bryk and Barbara L. Schneider, *Trust in Schools* (New York: Russell Sage Foundation, 2002).

22. James G. March and Herbert A. Simon, *Organizations* (New York: Wiley, 1958).

23. The ostensive (the "what") and the performative (the "how") roles that of organizational routines can play in supporting change is explained in Martha S. Feldman and Brian T. Pentland, "Reconceptualizing Organizational Routines as a Source of Flexibility and Change," *Administrative Science Quarterly* 48, no. 1 (2003): 94–121.

24. Geoffrey C. Bowker and Susan L. Star, *Sorting Things Out: Classification and Its Consequences* (Cambridge, MA: MIT Press, 1999), 297.

25. Margaret S. Smith, Victoria Bill, and Elizabeth Hughes, "Thinking through a Lesson: Successfully Implementing Higher Order Tasks," *Mathematics Teaching in Middle School* 14, no. 3 (2008): 132–39.

26. Feuer, Towne, and Shavelson, "Scientific Culture and Educational Research."

27. Julian E. Orr, "Ethnography and Organizational Learning: In Pursuit of Learning at Work," in *Organizational Learning and Technological Change,* ed. Sebastiano Bagnara, Cristina Zucchermaglio, and Susan Stucky (New York: Springer Verlag, 1993).

28. Laura Stokes, "Taking on the Real Struggles of Teaching: A Study of the National Writing Project as an Infrastructure for Building Practitioner Knowledge," paper presented to MacArthur Foundation Network on Teaching and Learning, January 2005.

29. See www.patientslikeme.com.

30. Lortie, *Schoolteacher.*

About the Contributors

John D. Bransford is Shauna C. Larson University Professor of Education and Psychology at the University of Washington in Seattle. Bransford is also coprincipal investigator and codirector of the LIFE Center, a National Science Foundation Science of Learning Center that studies learning in informal and formal environments. Previously, Bransford was Centennial Professor of Psychology and Education and codirector of the Learning Technology Center at Vanderbilt University. He received the Sutherland Prize for Research at Vanderbilt, has been elected to the National Academy of Education, and was awarded the 2001 Edward L. Thorndike Award. He served as cochair of several National Academy of Science committees that authored *How Students Learn: History, Mathematics, and Science in the Classroom* (2005), *How People Learn: Brain, Mind, Experience and School* (1999, 2000), and *How People Learn, Bridging Research and Practice* (1999). He also coedited a National Academy of Education volume (with Linda Darling-Hammond) on *Preparing Teachers for a Changing World* (2005).

Cynthia E. Coburn is assistant professor in policy, organization, measurement, and evaluation at the Graduate School of Education, University of California at Berkeley. Her research uses the tools of organizational sociology to understand the relationship between instructional policy and teachers' classroom practices in urban schools. She has studied these issues in the context of state and national reading policy, attempts to scale-up innovative school reform programs, and districtwide professional development initiatives. Coburn was a core member of the MacArthur Network on Teaching and Learning and, in this capacity, codirected a study of innovative attempts to rethink the relationship between research and practice for school improvement. She received a BA in philosophy from Oberlin College and an MA in sociology and PhD in education from Stanford University.

Thomas B. Corcoran is codirector of the Consortium for Policy Research in Education at Teacher's College, Columbia University. His interests include strategies for improving instruction, the use of research findings and clinical expertise to inform instructional policy and practice, the effectiveness of different approaches to professional development, knowledge management systems for schools, and the impact of changes in work environments on the productivity of teachers and students. Corcoran is currently a principal investigator on four projects: a

Hewlett-funded project to promote continuous improvement of instruction and improve the quality and use of formative assessment tools; the evaluation of IN-STEP, a project to improve science teaching in Thailand; a study of instructional coaching in science and mathematics in nine Texas school districts; and a study of the Children's First inquiry process in New York City. He was a member of the National Research Council's K–8 Science Learning Study. He is a visiting professor of education policy at the Woodrow Wilson School of International and Public Affairs at Princeton University.

Hidenori Fujita is professor at the International Christian University (ICU) in comparative education. He received his PhD from Stanford University in 1978. Before moving to ICU, he had been professor at the University of Tokyo for seventeen years and served as dean of the Graduate School of Education there from 2000 to 2003. He is a member of the Science Council of Japan and was chief researcher of the Japan Society for the Promotion of Science (2004–07), president of the Japanese Association of Educational Sociology (2000-03), and a member of the National Commission on Education Reform (2000) and the Central Council for Education (2005). His major publications (in Japanese) include *Child, School and Society: Irony of an Affluent Society* (1991); *Education Reform* (1997; Chinese trans. 2001); *Culture and Society: Distinction, Structuration and Reproduction* (1993); *Sociology of Education* (1998); *Civic Society and Education* (2000)); *Family and Gender* (2003); *Reappraisal of Compulsory Education* (2005); and *Destinations of Education Reform* (2006).

Louis M. Gomez is the Helen S. Fasion Chair in Urban Education at the University of Pittsburgh in the Leaning Science and Policy Program within the School of Education. He is also senior scientist at the Learning Research and Development Center. Previously, he was Aon Professor of Learning Sciences and Professor of Computer Science at Northwestern University. Gomez's primary interest is in working with school communities to create social arrangements and curriculum that support school improvement. Along with his colleagues, he has been dedicated to collaborative research and development with urban schools to bring state-of-the-art instruction and support for community formation to traditionally underserved schools. He received a BA in psychology from the State University of New York at Stony Brook and a PhD in cognitive psychology from the University of California at Berkeley.

Andy Hargreaves is the Thomas More Brennan Chair in Education at Boston College. His research deals with teachers and leaders and their experiences of educational change. His most recent books are *Teaching In the Knowledge Society* (1983); *Sustainable Leadership,* with Dean Fink (2006); *Change Wars,* with Michael

Fullan (edited 2008); and *The Fourth Way*, with Dennis Shirley (2009). His current research is on organizations that perform above expectations in education, health, business, and sport.

Guilbert C. Hentschke is the Richard T. Cooper and Mary Catherine Cooper Chair in Public School Administration at the University of Southern California's Rossier School of Education. His most recent book is *New Players, Different Game: Understanding the Rise of For-profit Colleges and Universities*. Current board directorships include the National Center on Education and the Economy and WestEd Regional Educational Laboratory. Prior to USC Hentschke served at the University of Rochester, Columbia University, the Chicago Public Schools, and the East Side Union High School District. His undergraduate degree is from Princeton University and his graduate degrees are from Stanford University.

Meredith I. Honig is assistant professor of educational leadership and policy studies at the University of Washington, Seattle. Her research and teaching focus on policy implementation, decisionmaking, and organization change in urban educational systems. She is particularly interested in how public policymaking bureaucracies such as school district central offices innovate and collaborate to improve opportunities for all youth to learn. She examines these challenges using a variety of cases including school-community partnerships, new small autonomous schools initiatives, and initiatives to reinvent urban school district central offices to support districtwide teaching and learning improvement. Evidence-based decisionmaking has been a major focus of these projects—particularly how policymakers incorporate local or practitioner knowledge into their decisionmaking. Her research has appeared in various publications including *Educational Evaluation and Policy Analysis*, *Educational Researcher*, and *Educational Administration Quarterly*.

Diana Lam is currently vice president for global education and community outreach for Christel House International. Most recently, she was the deputy chancellor for teaching and learning at the New York City Department of Education, where she was responsible for joint implementation of Children First reforms, a multiyear effort aimed at dramatically improving New York City Public Schools. She has served as superintendent in various school districts. In San Antonio, Texas, Lam was the first female superintendent, and there she won national acclaim for her accomplishments, which included a dramatic increase in student achievement. In the communities where she has served as superintendent, she has envisioned the changes required, put in place the structures, and built relationships that allow educators and families to work together to reach new levels of achievement.

Susan M. Kardos is an independent researcher and a research affiliate at the Project on the Next Generation of Teachers at the Harvard Graduate School of Education. Kardos studies education policy, new teacher support and retention, workplace culture and school organization, and leadership and school improvement. Recent publications include *On Their Own and Presumed Expert: New Teachers' Experience with their Colleagues* (2007) and *Finders and Keepers: Helping New Teachers Survive and Thrive in Our Schools* (2004). Kardos is also the director of strategy and education planning at the AVI CHAI Foundation in New York City.

Frederic A. "Fritz" Mosher is a senior consultant to the Consortium for Policy Research in Education (CPRE) based at Teachers College, Columbia, and a member of the MacArthur Research Network on Teaching and Learning. He has been an adviser to the Spencer Foundation, a RAND Corporation adjunct staff member, an adviser to the assistant secretary for research and improvement in the U.S. Department of Education, and a consultant to Achieve, Inc. In 1998 he retired from Carnegie Corporation of New York after thirty-six years as a program specialist and policy analyst. In recent years Mosher has focused on what it might take for the public education system to learn how to enable all students to reach high standards of achievement. He is a cognitive/social psychologist by training, with a PhD from Harvard University.

Alan H. Schoenfeld is the Elizabeth and Edward Conner Professor of Education and affiliated professor of mathematics at the University of California at Berkeley. He is a fellow of the American Association for the Advancement of Science and of the American Educational Research Association and a laureate of the education honor society Kappa Delta Pi. He has served as president of the American Educational Research Association and as the vice president of the National Academy of Education. In addition to his basic research on problem-solving, teaching, and issues of diversity in mathematics education, Schoenfeld has long been concerned with finding productive mechanisms for systemic change and for deepening the connections between educational research and practice.

Robert B. Schwartz has, since 1996, been a faculty member at Harvard Graduate School of Education, where he currently serves as academic dean and Bloomberg Professor of Practice. From 1997 to 2002 he also served as president of Achieve, Inc., a national nonprofit established by governors and corporate leaders to help states strengthen academic performance. Schwartz previously served in a variety of roles in education and government, including high school teacher in California and principal in Oregon; education adviser to Boston mayor Kevin White and Massachusetts governor Michael Dukakis; executive director of The Boston Compact; and education program director at The Pew Charitable Trusts. He currently cochairs The Aspen Institute's Education Program and serves on the boards of The Education Trust, The Noyce Foundation, and The Rennie Center for Education Research and Policy.

Corrie Stone-Johnson is a doctoral candidate at Boston College. Her research focuses on the impact of mandated reform on teachers' careers and how teachers' generations influence their work and engagement with reform.

Marshall S. Smith is currently the education program director at the William and Flora Hewlett Foundation. He served in the government for fourteen years, including a stint in the National Institute of Education as head of the reading and mathematics program and as associate director for policy and planning. He also served in the Carter and Clinton administrations in high-level policy positions, including acting deputy secretary and undersecretary of the Department of Education under President Clinton. In between times in government, he was an associate professor at the Harvard Graduate School of Education; a professor at the University of Wisconsin and director of the Wisconsin Center for Education Research; and a professor and dean of education at Stanford University.

Mark A. Smylie is professor of education at the University of Illinois at Chicago. He received his PhD from Vanderbilt University and his BA and MEd degrees from Duke University. Smylie's research concerns school organization and organizational change, administrative and teacher leadership, teacher and teacher workforce development, and urban school improvement. He has served as secretary-treasurer of the National Society for the Study of Education and as a director of the Consortium on Chicago School Research at the University of Chicago. He was recently a residential fellow at the Spencer Foundation.

Mary Kay Stein holds a joint appointment at the University of Pittsburgh as professor of learning policy and senior scientist at the Learning Research and Development Center. Her research has focused on classroom-based teaching and learning, with the aim of understanding the nature of effective instructional practices in mathematics, and the school and district contexts of teacher learning and professional development. Most notably, she studied the connections between district policy and classroom practice in New York City's Community School District No. 2 under Anthony Alvarado as well as the districtwide instructional reforms in the San Diego City Schools initiated under Alan Bersin and Anthony Alvarado, which resulted in a number of widely read articles and a book, *Reform as Learning: School Reform, Organizational Culture, and Community Politics in San Diego* (2006). Currently she is investigating how the teacher learning demands of different curricula (*Everyday Mathematics* versus *Investigations*) influences teacher learning in large-scale reforms in two urban districts. Stein has served on several national panels, including the National Academy of Education's Panel on Strengthening the Capacity of Research to Impact Policy and Practice, the National Institute for Science Education's Professional Development Project, and NCTM's Standards Impact Research Group. She is the founding director of the Learning Policy Center at the University of Pittsburgh.

Deborah J. Stipek is the James Quillen Dean and Professor of Education at Stanford University. Her doctorate from Yale University is in developmental psychology. Her scholarship concerns instructional effects on children's achievement motivation, early childhood, and elementary education. She served for five years on the Children, Youth, and Families board of the National Academy of Sciences and chaired the National Academy of Sciences Committee on Increasing High School Students' Engagement and Motivation to Learn. Stipek served ten of her twenty-three years at UCLA as director of the Corinne Seeds University Elementary School and the Urban Education Studies Center. She joined the Stanford School of Education as dean and professor of education in January 2001. She is a member of the National Academy of Education.

Nancy J. Vye is senior research scientist in the LIFE Center (Learning in Informal and Formal Learning Environments) at COE–University of Washington. Prior to joining the University of Washington, she was codirector, along with John Bransford, of the Learning Technology Center at Vanderbilt University. She has extensive experience in learning technology research and design in K–16 settings and has worked in private-sector healthcare training and development. She received her doctorate in cognitive psychology from Vanderbilt University.

Janet A. Weiss is vice provost and dean of the graduate school at the University of Michigan. She is a professor in the Stephen M. Ross School of Business and the Gerald R. Ford School of Public Policy at Michigan. Her research is focused on public management and public policy, with a special interest in the effective governance of education.

Index